EMPLOYMENT DISCRIMINATION LAW

FROM THEORY TO PRACTICE SERIES

Rachel Croskery-Roberts, Series Editor

EMPLOYMENT DISCRIMINATION LAW

RACHEL CROSKERY-ROBERTS

Professor of Law
University of California, Irvine School of Law

MARGARET CURTISS HANNON

Clinical Assistant Professor of Law
University of Michigan Law School

Wolters Kluwer

Law & Business

Published by Wolters Kluwer Law & Business in New York.

Wolters Kluwer Law & Business serves customers worldwide with CCH, Aspen Publishers, and Kluwer Law International products. (www.wolterskluwerlb.com)

To contact Customer Service, e-mail customer.service@wolterskluwer.com, call 1-800-234-1660, fax 1-800-901-9075, or mail correspondence to:

Wolters Kluwer Law & Business
Attn: Order Department
PO Box 990
Frederick, MD 21705

Printed in the United States of America.

1 2 3 4 5 6 7 8 9 0

ISBN 978-0-7355-8989-6

Library of Congress Cataloging-in-Publication Data

Croskery-Roberts, Rachel, 1971- author.
   Employment discrimination law / Rachel Croskery-Roberts, Professor of Law, University of California, Irvine School of Law, Margaret Curtiss Hannon, Clinical Assistant Professor of Law, Legal Practice Program, University of Michigan Law School.
      p. cm.
   Includes bibliographical references and index.
   ISBN 978-0-7355-8989-6 (alk. paper) -- ISBN 0-7355-8989-5 (alk. paper)
1. Discrimination in employment--Law and legislation--United States. I. Hannon, Margaret Curtiss, author. II. Title.
   KF3464.C76 2013
   344.7301'3--dc23
                              2013034946

About Wolters Kluwer Law & Business

Wolters Kluwer Law & Business is a leading global provider of intelligent information and digital solutions for legal and business professionals in key specialty areas, and respected educational resources for professors and law students. Wolters Kluwer Law & Business connects legal and business professionals as well as those in the education market with timely, specialized authoritative content and information-enabled solutions to support success through productivity, accuracy and mobility.

Serving customers worldwide, Wolters Kluwer Law & Business products include those under the Aspen Publishers, CCH, Kluwer Law International, Loislaw, ftwilliam.com and MediRegs family of products.

CCH products have been a trusted resource since 1913, and are highly regarded resources for legal, securities, antitrust and trade regulation, government contracting, banking, pension, payroll, employment and labor, and healthcare reimbursement and compliance professionals.

Aspen Publishers products provide essential information to attorneys, business professionals and law students. Written by preeminent authorities, the product line offers analytical and practical information in a range of specialty practice areas from securities law and intellectual property to mergers and acquisitions and pension/benefits. Aspen's trusted legal education resources provide professors and students with high-quality, up-to-date and effective resources for successful instruction and study in all areas of the law.

Kluwer Law International products provide the global business community with reliable international legal information in English. Legal practitioners, corporate counsel and business executives around the world rely on Kluwer Law journals, looseleafs, books, and electronic products for comprehensive information in many areas of international legal practice.

Loislaw is a comprehensive online legal research product providing legal content to law firm practitioners of various specializations. Loislaw provides attorneys with the ability to quickly and efficiently find the necessary legal information they need, when and where they need it, by facilitating access to primary law as well as state-specific law, records, forms and treatises.

ftwilliam.com offers employee benefits professionals the highest quality plan documents (retirement, welfare and non-qualified) and government forms (5500/PBGC, 1099 and IRS) software at highly competitive prices.

MediRegs products provide integrated health care compliance content and software solutions for professionals in healthcare, higher education and life sciences, including professionals in accounting, law and consulting.

Wolters Kluwer Law & Business, a division of Wolters Kluwer, is headquartered in New York. Wolters Kluwer is a market-leading global information services company focused on professionals.

SUMMARY OF CONTENTS

CONTENTS

PREFACE

Law schools are increasingly recognizing that a student's legal education is incomplete if it does not provide the student with a solid foundation in some of the key practical skills and ethical issues facing new lawyers. Unfortunately, the traditional law school education has placed too little emphasis on teaching the practical skills needed by every new associate entering the workforce. Thus, schools are beginning to add more clinical and practical experience into the law school curriculum.

This book is part of a new series of practice area-specific books targeted at both law students and new practitioners. It is designed to be responsive to the increasing demand for skills training in American law schools (a demand coming from numerous sources, including the students themselves, the external legal market, and the American Bar Association). Your professor may choose to use this book by itself in a practicum or seminar, though the book is also useful as a supplemental text for those professors seeking to add a practical component to the traditional casebook classroom experience.

Regardless of the field in which you may end up practicing, you must master a wide range of skills to be an effective lawyer. The traditional casebook method of teaching law does a good job of teaching legal theory and challenging students to think critically about complex legal questions. A casebook, however, cannot teach a student the difficult and multifaceted expectations facing a new attorney. This book is designed to complement the casebook method by introducing students to legal issues in concrete ways: drafting relevant documents, researching using practice area-specific source materials, and advising clients.

In short, this book is designed to be a bridge into practice for students planning to work in a particular field or for new associates just learning the ropes in that given field. This book will provide: (1) a basic overview of the types of laws and legal concepts any new lawyer practicing employment discrimination must know; (2) an introduction to the key research strategies and sources for researching employment discrimination issues; (3) general drafting principles important to lawyers in any field as well as a specific overview of drafting issues arising for a young lawyer practicing employment discrimination law; and (4) an introduction to client counseling and preventative lawyering.

Throughout the book or on the book's website, you will find sample documents as well as targeted exercises designed to help you build a solid foundation for practicing employment discrimination law. You will also find useful drafting checklists that both students and attorneys can use when drafting and negotiating documents and agreements.

Given the book's length, we have not attempted to cover every possible statute and regulation governing employment discrimination, nor do we think such an all-inclusive tome would be either necessary or even helpful to a student just beginning to understand the wide variety of laws governing the employment relationship or the skills required to become a great employment lawyer. Rather, this text will provide a roadmap for dealing with some of the most common issues in employment discrimination law, and introduce necessary skills training in researching and drafting to allow students and new attorneys to feel confident when approaching new situations. Although litigation topics certainly come up throughout, the book consciously avoids extensive coverage of litigation documents (pleadings, motions, etc.), as students already receive significant exposure to basic litigation skills through the first year legal writing course and through work in clinics.

The book is broken into several major parts, representing key skills required of any student or practitioner approaching an issue in employment discrimination law. Part I provides a broad introduction to (and overview of) employment discrimination laws, from traditional prohibitions on discrimination on the basis of race, gender, and national origin, to more cutting edge topics like discrimination through the use of genetic testing. Both federal and state laws governing the employment relationship are covered.

Then, having received an overview of basic employment discrimination laws and principles in Part I, students can begin to think about how to provide advice in both written and oral form. Part II attempts to identify the many ways in which attorneys are expected to provide advice and to prepare students to meet the expectations of clients and assigning attorneys in completing assignments. Part II also addresses the process of researching employment discrimination issues.

In Part III, we begin to put all the skills that you have been developing into practice. First, Part III addresses the transactional component of an employment discrimination lawyer's practice. We provide an introduction to general drafting principles key to good legal drafting in any area of law. We also address basic terminology used in drafting agreements. Part III includes chapters addressing selected drafting and client counseling/strategy issues. You will be expected to work through common areas of client concern, including sexual harassment and discrimination policies, genetic and drug testing policies, mandatory arbitration clauses, and the like.

The material in Part III is crucial, as it addresses a key aspect of modern law practice: litigation is not the only way (not even the primary way) to solve problems. Lawyers are not simply warriors in a fierce battle against other lawyers. The most valuable lawyers are able to counsel clients in ways to avoid litigation in the first place. Therefore, the exercises in Part III primarily focus on preventative lawyering through client counseling and drafting techniques to avoid litigation.

The material in this book is cumulative. What you learn in Part I, for example, you should apply to the exercises in later parts in the book. When you have completed the readings and exercises in this book, you should find that you are more than prepared to enter practice confidently, assured that you have a solid foundation in the key areas necessary to be an effective employment discrimination lawyer. The checklists and charts provided should continue to be useful as you enter practice.

One Important Note About Using This Book

Traditional casebooks reproduce excerpts from cases for students to read. Casebook authors have edited down cases to focus on one or more specific issues. While this makes the cases easier for students to digest (and for professors to teach), it deprives students of an opportunity to practice one of the most important skills attorneys must develop: critically reading cases and determining what portions are relevant or helpful for a given analysis. This book does not reproduce cases. Rather, it provides citations to cases and expects you to retrieve those cases using a fee-based or free Internet source. Some cases will be quite long, and it will be your job to begin to develop an ability to quickly identify the relevant material in long cases and to read that material in more depth.

ACKNOWLEDGMENTS

Rachel Croskery-Roberts

This project began more than five years ago when I decided to teach a course on business drafting skills for employment lawyers. I went searching for a text that would address the key transactional skills an employment lawyer needs to know and also convey the richness and complexity of employment discrimination law. No such text existed. I am deeply grateful to one of my national colleagues, Mary Beth Beazley, for suggesting that the solution was to create the text myself. I am also so happy that the people at Wolters Kluwer Law & Business recognized what this project represented—a revolutionary and sophisticated way to teach doctrine and key lawyering skills together. And when my former student and now colleague Margaret Curtiss Hannon agreed to co-author this book with me, I became the luckiest person on earth.

I want to thank the many people who have supported me throughout the process of writing this book. I am certain I will forget someone, however, so I apologize in anticipation of doing just that. If you helped me and don't see your name here, please make sure you contact me to make me feel suitably (and appropriately) guilty. Thanks to my colleagues at Michigan Law School who saw this as a worthy project but weren't afraid to ask me the tough questions to make the text better. In particular, thanks to Ted Becker, Phil Frost, Nick Rine, Sam Gross, Angela Onwuachi-Willig, and Tim Pinto for allowing me to bounce ideas off them. You may not even remember your feedback, but I do. You're all amazing. Thanks also to the incredible support I received from my faculty assistants at Michigan: Kathi Ganz and Helen Ryan. Finally, thanks to the student research assistants at Michigan who helped in early stages of the book, including Charlie Maule, Caitlin Kozan, Stefan Atkinson, Caroline Wenzke Hudson, Matthew Crowe, Ben Odell, Isabel Daniels, Kendal Kloostra, Becca Klein, Dario Borghesan, Greg York, and Carrie Bierman.

I am now at the University of California, Irvine School of Law, and my colleagues there have simply amazed me with their willingness to share ideas, critique work, and push me to do more (and better). Thanks especially to my colleagues in the Lawyering Skills program, including Grace Tonner, Henry Weinstein, Trilby Robinson-Dorn, and Ezra Ross. Thanks also to Catherine Fisk, who helped me to think through precisely what a text like this one should do. Thanks to my research assistants, Dan Schieffer and Sarah Vehian, and my superhero faculty assistants, Marisela Galindo and Ana Duong. Finally, I would be completely remiss if I didn't thank our amazing dean, Erwin Chemerinsky. His support of cutting-edge scholarship and the improvement of legal education made this author's job so much easier.

I also want to thank the brave UCI Law students who served as guinea pigs of sorts, taking my course in the spring of 2013 using an unfinished manuscript of this book. Their insights made the book and the way in which I teach the class infinitely better. Thanks to Shaleen Shanbhag, Hagop Boyaci, Dan Schieffer, Sabyl Landrum, Erna Mamikonyan, Cinthia Flores, Lisa Petak, Melissa Katow, Jin Chong, Renee Amador, and Sahar Naseery.

Finally, thanks to my amazing family. Without an unreasonable amount of understanding on the part of my husband and children, this book would never have been completed. Thanks, Dave, Micah, and Daniel! You are my world.

Margaret Curtiss Hannon

I owe a huge debt of gratitude to Rachel Croskery-Roberts. I was lucky enough to be a student in Rachel's first legal research and writing course, and later, to be one of her teaching assistants. At that time, I never could have imagined that I would become one of Rachel's colleagues, and then, her co-author. Rachel's teaching, advice, and guidance have been irreplaceable, and I'm so grateful for the opportunity to continue working with her.

I won't repeat what Rachel has so eloquently said above about the unique coverage and role of this textbook. Instead, I wanted to add a brief note about the experience of writing it. When I started working on this project, I was a relatively new legal research and writing professor. My work on this book brought together my practice and teaching experience, which in turn helped me to become a better teacher. I hope that this book enables other faculty to do the same.

I'd like to thank the many individuals who helped me throughout the process of writing this book. Thank you so very much to my former colleagues at Northwestern University School of Law. I'd particularly like to thank Pegeen G. Bassett and Heidi Frostestad Kuehl, two of Northwestern's fantastic librarians. Both Pegeen and Heidi provided valuable advice regarding the research portions of the book. In addition, Sue Provenzano, Susie Spies Roth, and Brian Silbernagel provided thoughtful feedback about the structure, coverage, and substance of the book. Thank you to my awesome teaching and research assistants for their help: Jennifer Aronoff, Erica Embree, Jeanne John, and Yosef Schwartz. I'd also like to thank my new colleagues at Michigan Law School, as well as the many members of the national legal-writing community who have provided their advice and assistance.

Last but not least, thank you to my wonderful family and friends for their support throughout this process. A special thank you goes to my husband, Dave, and son, Henry. I couldn't have done this without your love and patience. Thank you also to Pippin, Penny, and Maizie—working on the book wouldn't have been the same without a cat lying across my keyboard or begging for food and a dog (usually) patiently waiting for some attention.

EMPLOYMENT DISCRIMINATION LAW

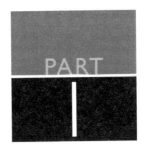

PART

I

AN INTRODUCTION TO EMPLOYMENT DISCRIMINATION LAW

One of the most important (and difficult) skills a lawyer can develop is the ability to spot legal issues in a client's problem. While sophisticated corporate clients may well know some of the specific laws implicated by a given employment issue or conflict arising in the workplace, many clients will not present their problems to you in easy-to-research packages.

In a perfect world, you might have a client come to you and ask the following question:

QUESTION **(FROM IN-HOUSE ATTORNEY FOR LARGE CORPORATE CLIENT):**

As you know, we are a large corporation incorporated in Delaware and doing business in New York. Because we employ more than 500 employees, we are subject to all major federal employment laws. We would like to fire one of our branch managers, and we know we may have some issues with age discrimination and gender discrimination. The employee is 45 years old, and the Age Discrimination in Employment Act applies to employees over the age of 40. Moreover, the employee is female, and we have no other female branch managers. We are fairly certain that might implicate the anti-discrimination provisions of Title VII as well as applicable state and local anti-discrimination statutes. However, we have kept good records of the employee's past performance, and we have followed all standard procedures in warning her prior to termination. We would like you to make sure we have not violated the Age Discrimination in Employment Act or Title VII, and we have put together a file with all of the employee's records to help with your research.

Of course, we all know we don't live in a perfect world. Here's the more likely type of question you'll receive from a client:

QUESTION   **(FROM HUMAN RESOURCES MANAGER OR IN-HOUSE ATTORNEY AT CLIENT COMPANY):**

We just fired a female branch manager from our company yesterday and gave her an hour to clean out her desk. Her supervisor contacted me to say that, as the employee was cleaning out her desk, she muttered something about how she knew the company just wanted to push out all the women, minorities, and "old fogies" to make room for all the "corporate warriors straight out of business school." She had been having performance issues, but we're worried she may sue. Should we be worried?

As the attorney, you will be responsible for identifying what legal issues arise from the factual scenario presented by a client. Unfortunately, countless laws touch the employment relationship, so this is not an easy task. This section explores many of the employment laws governing the employment relationship. While not exhaustive, this overview should provide a strong foundation for understanding what legal issues might arise when working as an employment lawyer representing either employers or employees. The overview does not cover every nuance to the laws listed. Rather, it is designed to help you more easily spot issues in a client's situation and determine where further analysis and research are necessary. You will perform more nuanced and detailed research, analysis, and drafting using these laws in later portions of the book.

Part I is divided into several chapters. Chapter 1 provides an overview of some core employment law concepts. Several important issues are discussed, including (1) the traditional at-will employment rule; (2) the difference between an independent contractor and an employee (and a brief summary of the practical implications of that difference); (3) the definition of "employer" and "employee" under various statutory regimes; and (4) the importance of administrative agencies in employment law.[1] Chapter 2 briefly discusses the role of the Constitution

---

[1] Although these concepts are not all directly related to employment discrimination law, they are threshold questions that lawyers must analyze in employment discrimination cases. For that reason, we have included a brief overview of these concepts.

in employment discrimination law. Chapter 3 sets out a summary of many of the statutory protections for employees, including anti-discrimination laws, and laws requiring accommodation of disabilities, religious beliefs, pregnancy, and illness suffered by the employee or the employee's family members. Finally, Chapter 4 discusses some typical common law claims raised in employment discrimination lawsuits.

CORE EMPLOYMENT LAW CONCEPTS

I. TRADITIONAL DOCTRINE OF AT-WILL EMPLOYMENT

In most states, the default presumption is that employment for an indefinite term is at-will. The basic concept of "at-will" employment is simple. If an employee is "at-will," the employer may terminate that employee at any time and for any reason whatsoever (or even for no reason at all). Some courts have clarified that if an employee is an at-will employee, the employer does not even have to show that it acted in good faith when discharging an employee. *See, e.g., Trakis v. Manhattanville Coll.*, 859 N.Y.S.2d 453, 455 (App. Div. 2008).

The presumption of at-will employment is grounded in the common law, though some states have codified the presumption. For example, California Labor Code section 2922 provides that "[a]n employment, having no specified term, may be terminated at the will of either party on notice to the other. Employment for a specified term means an employment for a period greater than one month." Cal. Lab. Code § 2922 (West 2012).

Most states provide that the presumption of at-will employment is rebuttable, although states have widely varying standards for doing so. In Michigan, for example, a party can only overcome the presumption by showing "a contract provision for a definite term of employment or one that forbids discharge absent just cause." *Lytle v. Malady*, 579 N.W.2d 906, 911 (Mich. 1998). According to the court in *Lytle*, "[c]ourts have recognized the following three ways by which a plaintiff can prove such contractual terms: (1) proof of 'a contractual provision for a definite term of employment or a provision forbidding discharge absent just cause;' (2) an express agreement, either written or oral, regarding job security that is clear and unequivocal; or (3) a contractual provision, implied at law, where an employer's policies and procedures instill a 'legitimate expectation' of job security in the employee." *Id.* (internal citations omitted). An oral statement may rebut the presumption if it is "clear" and "unequivocal." *Rowe v. Montgomery Ward & Co.*, 473 N.W.2d 268, 275 (Mich. 1991).

In contrast, California courts arguably take a less stringent approach to rebutting the presumption. The presumption of at-will employment "may be overcome by evidence regarding the personnel policies or practices of the employer, the employee's longevity of service, actions or communications by the employer reflecting assurances of continued employment, and the practices of the industry in which the employee is engaged." *Alexander v. Nextel Commc'n, Inc.*, 61 Cal. Rptr. 2d 293, 296 (Ct. App. 1997).

Various courts have developed limited exceptions to the at-will employment rule. For example, in *Sabine Pilot Service, Inc. v. Hauck*, the Texas Supreme Court recognized an exception to the employment-at-will doctrine for an employee discharged "for the sole reason that the employee refused to perform an illegal act." 687 S.W.2d 733, 735 (Tex. 1985); *Winters v. Houston Chronicle Publ'g Co.*, 795 S.W.2d 723, 724 (Tex. 1990). Discharge for an otherwise illegal reason (like discrimination) is also prohibited, even in the employment at-will context. For this reason, employment discrimination law is a crucial tool allowing at-will employees to enforce their rights.

QUESTIONS AND EXERCISES

1)   At-will employment provides employers with much flexibility in hiring and firing. Why would an employer ever wish to alter the at-will employment relationship?

2)   Do you prefer the standards for rebutting the presumption of at-will employment imposed by courts in Michigan or those in California? Why?

   a)   What standard is easier for courts to apply, and why?

   b)   What standard provides better predictability for employers? Employees?

   c)   What policy interests do you think courts are trying to balance when addressing a challenge to the presumption of at-will employment?

   d)   Can you craft a standard that better balances competing policy interests?

3)   You are an employer, and you want to make it very clear that employment is at-will. Should you rely on the fact that the default presumption is at-will employment, or should you articulate the at-will employment standard to new or prospective employees? If the latter, at what time(s) and in what manner?

4)   The Texas Supreme Court recently revisited *Sabine Pilot* in *Safeshred, Inc. v. Martinez*, 365 S.W.3d 655 (Tex. 2012). In *Safeshred*, the court addressed two key questions. First, the court addressed whether a *Sabine Pilot* claim sounds

in tort or contract. Second, the court addressed whether punitive damages are available for a violation and, if so, what the standards are for determining punitive damages. Assume you are a new attorney at a large law firm representing major corporations. Read *Safeshred*, and come prepared to explain to an assigning attorney what information your corporate clients need to know about how (or if) *Safeshred* changes the legal landscape for Texas employers.

II. THE LEGAL EFFECT OF CLASSIFICATION AS AN EMPLOYEE RATHER THAN AN INDEPENDENT CONTRACTOR

One of the most important threshold questions an employment lawyer must ask is whether the individual wishing to bring a discrimination claim is an employee or an independent contractor. Under most federal and many state discrimination statutes, only an "employee" can bring a claim. However, determining whether an individual is an employee or an independent contractor is not always easy to do. For example, Title VII provides a definition of "employee" that offers little guidance. Under Title VII, an "employee" is "an individual employed by an employer." 42 U.S.C. § 2000e(f).[2]

There are two basic tests that courts have historically used to determine whether an employee is an independent contractor: the "control" test and the "economic realities" test. The control test derives from the vicarious liability doctrine of traditional agency law[3] and asks whether the "hiring party" has a "right to control the manner and means" by which a "hired party" completes tasks. *Nat. Mut. Ins. Co. v. Darden*, 503 U.S. 318, 323 (1992) (addressing whether an individual was an employee or an independent contractor under the Employee Retirement Income Security Act). In general, the factors relevant to this question include:

(1) The skill required[;]
(2) The source of the instrumentalities and tools[;]
(3) The location of the work[;]
(4) The duration of the relationship between the parties[;]
(5) Whether the hiring party has the right to assign additional projects to the hired party[;]
(6) The extent of the hired party's discretion over when and how long to work[;]

---

[2] The same circular definition appears in many other employment-related statutes, including the Americans with Disabilities Act (ADA), the Age Discrimination in Employment Act (ADEA), and the Employee Retirement Income Security Act (ERISA). *See* 42 U.S.C. § 12111(4) (the ADA) (defining an employee as "an individual employed by an employer"); 29 U.S.C. § 630(f) (the ADEA) (defining an employee as "an individual employed by any employer," though exempting political officials and their staff); 29 U.S.C. § 1002-(6) (ERISA) (defining an employee as "any individual employed by an employer").
[3] Under that doctrine, when determining whether an employer would be vicariously liable for torts committed by its employees, courts asked whether the employer was exercising a degree of control over the employee when that employee committed the tort.

(7) The method of payment;
(8) The hired party's role in hiring and paying assistants;
(9) Whether the work is part of the regular business of the hired party;
(10) Whether the hiring party is in business;
(11) The provision of employee benefits; and
(12) The tax treatment of the hired party.

Id. at 323-24 (citing *Cmty. for Creative Non-Violence v. Reid*, 490 U.S. 730, 751-52 (1989)). The test is a totality of the circumstances test: "Since the common-law test contains 'no shorthand formula or magic phrase that can be applied to find the answer, . . . all of the incidents of the relationship must be assessed and weighed with no one factor being decisive.'" *Id.* at 324 (quoting *NLRB v. United Ins. Co. of America*, 390 U.S. 254, 258 (1968)).

■ **PRACTICE NOTE:** Some statutes and regulatory schemes prescribe the test to be used. For example, the Treasury Regulations of the Internal Revenue Service state that "the relationship of employer and employee exists when the person for whom services are performed has the right to control and direct the individual who performs the services, not only as to the result to be accomplished by the work but also as to the details and means by which that result is accomplished. That is, an employee is subject to the will and control of the employer not only as to what shall be done but how it shall be done. In this connection, it is not necessary that the employer actually direct or control the manner in which the services are performed; it is sufficient if he has the right to do so. The right to discharge is also an important factor indicating that the person possessing that right is an employer. Other factors characteristic of an employer, but not necessarily present in every case, are the furnishing of tools and the furnishing of a place to work to the individual who performs the services. In general, if an individual is subject to the control or direction of another merely as to the result to be accomplished by the work and not as to the means and methods for accomplishing the result, he is not an employee." 26 C.F.R. § 31.3401(c)–1(b).[4]

Some have criticized the control test as being too formalistic to deal with the multifaceted and complex relationships between individuals and those who

---

[4] The IRS used to have a 21-point test to determine whether an individual was an employee for tax purposes. Responding to complaints regarding the complexity of that test, the IRS recently simplified its test (which is basically a derivative of the common law control test) by breaking down the factors related to "control" into three areas. Under the new test, the IRS expects hiring parties to evaluate their level of control in three areas: behavioral, financial, and type of relationship. Behavioral control is analyzed by examining the type and degree of instruction given to hired individuals and the hiring party's evaluation systems and training. http://www.irs.gov/Businesses/Small-Businesses-&-Self-Employed/Behavioral-Control (last accessed December 29, 2012). Financial control involves "whether or not the business has the right to control the economic aspects of the worker's job." http://www.irs.gov/Businesses/Small-Businesses-&-Self-Employed/Financial-Control (last accessed December 29, 2012). The factors related to the type of relationship attempt to discern "how the worker and business perceive their relationship to each other." http://www.irs.gov/Businesses/Small-Businesses-&-Self-Employed/Type-of-Relationship (last accessed December 29, 2012).

hire them. Another test, the "economic realities" test, arguably responds to some of the concerns regarding the perceived inflexibility of the control test by focusing on the economic realities of a given work relationship. It is often used in the context of claims under the Fair Labor Standards Act (FLSA), the National Labor Relations Act (NLRA), and the Family Medical Leave Act. *See, e.g., Dole v. Elliott Travel & Tours, Inc.*, 942 F.2d 962, 965 (6th Cir. 1991) (noting that "[t]he remedial purposes of the FLSA require the courts to define 'employer' more broadly than the term would be interpreted in traditional common law applications" and applying an economic realities test). Although there are multiple formulations of the economic realities test, most courts focus heavily on the economic dependence of the hired individual on the hiring party. In *Martin v. Selker Bros., Inc.*, 949 F.2d 1286, 1293 (3d Cir. 1991), the court noted that the economic realities test requires both a determination of "the circumstances of the whole activity" and a determination of "whether, as a matter of economic reality, the individuals are dependent upon the business to which they render service." *Id.* (internal citations and quotations omitted). Analyzing "the circumstances of the whole activity" requires a determination of the following:

(1) The degree of the alleged employer's right to control the manner in which the work is to be performed;

(2) The alleged employee's opportunity for profit or loss depending upon his managerial skill;

(3) The alleged employee's investment in equipment or materials required for his task, or his employment of helpers;

(4) Whether the service rendered requires a special skill;

(5) The degree of permanence of the working relationship; and

(6) Whether the service rendered is an integral part of the alleged employer's business.

Id. (citations omitted). An opinion in the Second Circuit recently highlighted the intended flexibility of the economic realities test. *See Barfield v. New York City Health & Hosp. Corp.*, 537 F.3d 132, 142 (2d Cir. 2008). Noting that "employment for FLSA purposes [i]s a flexible concept to be determined on a case-by-case basis," the court declined to identify one set of inflexible factors to be used in all cases. *Id.* Rather, the court found that the relevant factors might change "based on the factual challenges posed by particular cases." *Id.*

Some courts have turned to a hybrid test, particularly in Title VII cases. The hybrid test attempts to combine the two tests discussed above. However, the focus of the hybrid test is whether the hiring party has the "right to control the 'means and manner' " of the hired individual's performance. *Oestman v. Nat'l Farmer's Union Ins. Co.*, 958 F.2d 303, 305 (10th Cir. 1992) (citations omitted). According to the Tenth Circuit in *Oestman*,

Other factors considered by courts applying the hybrid test are:

(1) the kind of occupation, with reference to whether the work usually is done under the direction of a supervisor or is done by a specialist without supervision;

(2) the skill required in the particular occupation;

(3) whether the "employer" or the individual in question furnishes the equipment used and the place of work;

(4) the length of time during which the individual has worked;

(5) the method of payment, whether by time or by the job;

(6) the manner in which the work relationship is terminated; i.e., by one or both parties, with or without notice and explanation;

(7) whether annual leave is afforded;

(8) whether the work is an integral part of the business of the "employer";

(9) whether the worker accumulates retirement benefits;

(10) whether the "employer" pays social security taxes; and

(11) the intention of the parties.

Id. (citation omitted). Circuit courts addressing claims under statutes with circular definitions like the one analyzed by the court in *Darden* have divided over the question of whether the appropriate test is the common law control test or the hybrid test. For example, in analyzing claims under the ADEA, many circuits have applied the common law control test discussed in *Darden. See Shah v. Deaconess Hosp.*, 355 F.3d 496, 499 (6th Cir. 2004); *Barnhart v. N.Y. Life Ins. Co.*, 141 F.3d 1310, 1313 (9th Cir. 1998); *Speen v. Crown Clothing Corp.*, 102 F.3d 625, 631 (1st Cir. 1996); *Frankel v. Bally, Inc.*, 987 F.2d 86, 90 (2d Cir. 1993). In contrast, other circuits have concluded that the hybrid test is more appropriate. *See, e.g., Mangram v. Gen. Motors Corp.*, 108 F.3d 61, 62-63 (4th Cir. 1997); *Oestman v. Nat'l Farmers Union Ins. Co.*, 958 F.2d 303, 305 (10th Cir. 1992); *Fields v. Hallsville Indep. Sch. Dist.*, 906 F.2d 1017, 1019 (5th Cir. 1990) (per curiam).

▨ **PRACTICE NOTE:** Because tests vary from circuit to circuit and state to state, it is crucial to determine the specific independent contractor test used in a given jurisdiction. Furthermore, as demonstrated above, a different test may be applied depending upon the particular statute under which a plaintiff is suing.

QUESTIONS AND EXERCISES

1) Numerous Circuits have concluded that the "hybrid" test used by many courts in Title VII cases is functionally indistinguishable from the common law "control" test set out in *Darden. See, e.g., Lambertsen v. Utah Dep't of Corr.*, 79 F.3d 1024, 1028 (10th Cir. 1996); *Folkerson v. Circus Circus Enters.*, No. 93-17158, 1995 WL 608432 (9th Cir. 1995); *Wilde v. Cnty. of Kandiyohi*, 15 F.3d 103, 106 (8th Cir. 1994); *Frankel v. Bally*, 987 F.2d 86, 90 (2d Cir. 1993). Do you agree? Why or why not? Why do you think some courts continue to apply a hybrid test?

2) There is a doctrinal difference between the control test and the economic realities test. With the control test, the fundamental inquiry is simply one

regarding who has control over the way in which an individual performs a job. With the economic realities test, the ultimate question is one of economic dependence. Do the tests set out in the illustrative cases above actually get at that fundamental doctrinal difference? Can you think of hypotheticals where there would actually be a *functional* difference in the outcome of the analysis when using each of the three tests? Can you think of a better test than the ones currently used by courts?

3) Your client is a major corporation that has recently laid off its entire information technology department. Your client believes it is cheaper and more efficient to use contractors instead of employees. Your client has informed you that it is currently classifying these contractors as independent contractors rather than employees. After some questioning, you have discovered the following facts about the contractors:

☐ The employer laid off a staff of five full-time IT professionals. Those professionals worked 8 a.m. to 5 p.m., though the two professionals doing systems administration were expected to be on call 24/7 in case of emergencies. All five IT professionals had their own cubicles at the office, and they were expected to be in the office from 8 a.m. to 5 p.m. Off-hours emergencies could be handled remotely.

☐ The employer has hired five contractors who are only paid for the hours they work.

☐ The contractors provide their own tools and equipment, though they can use equipment at the company if necessary.

☐ The contractors set their own hours for the most part, though they have each been assigned a five-hour period of time during the week when they have to be in the company's office and available for in-person help. During that time, they are provided an office at the company with a computer and all necessary supplies.

☐ The contractors are on call 24/7, though the company allows contractors to take up to two hours to respond in case contractors are currently on jobs for other clients.

☐ The contractors are paid an hourly fee of $100. They are paid automatically through direct deposit to their checking account like all employees at the company.

☐ The contractors are not reimbursed for expenses, except that they are reimbursed for mileage on the days when they have to travel to the office for in-person office hours.

☐ The contractors do not have an employment contract per se, but they do have a work agreement to provide services for two years. The contract renews automatically for two year terms if both parties are happy with the working relationship.

☐ The contractors do not report to anyone at the company, except that the vice-president of operations for the company directs the contractors' work assignments during the five hour period of time during the week when they have to be in the company's office.

a) Determine whether the contractors would be considered independent contractors under each of the competing tests: (a) the economic realities test; (b) the control test; and (c) the hybrid test. If you feel you need additional information from the employer to answer the question, provide a list of the additional facts you need.

b) If you determine that the company has misclassified the IT professionals as independent contractors under one or more of the tests, identify what the employer could change about the professionals' work requirements to properly classify them as independent contractors.

III. WHO IS AN EMPLOYER?

Not all employers are covered by federal and state employment laws, and the definition of "employer" varies by statute. The most common exemption to the definition of a covered "employer" involves one for smaller employers. Thus, the term "employer" may be defined under statute to only include entities with a certain number of employees. For example, a business is not subject to suit under Title VII unless it employs at least fifteen employees,[5] while the Age Discrimination in Employment Act (ADEA) defines an "employer" as one employing at least twenty employees.[6] State non-discrimination statutes often have lower thresholds for finding a business is an "employer," so employees of smaller companies may be forced to file suit under state statutes rather than federal statutes.

Still other statutes limit coverage to employers with a minimum amount in annual sales. For example, the Fair Labor Standards Act (FLSA) defines "employer" without reference to the number of employees. However, the minimum wage and maximum hours provisions of the FLSA only apply to an "[e]nterprise engaged in commerce or in the production of goods for commerce," which means the enterprise must (1) have "employees engaged in commerce or in the production of goods for commerce"; and (2) have at least $500,000 in "annual gross volume of sales made or business done." 29 U.S.C. § 203(s)(1)(A)(i-ii).

QUESTIONS AND EXERCISES

1) What rationale(s) can you think of that might justify an exemption of small employers from liability under employment discrimination laws?

2) What are the potential arguments against such an exemption?

---

[5] 42 U.S.C. § 2000e(b) (defining "employer" under Title VII as "a person engaged in an industry affecting commerce who has fifteen or more employees").
[6] 29 U.S.C. § 630(b) (defining "employer" under the ADEA as "a person engaged in an industry affecting commerce who has twenty or more employees").

3) Assuming that an exemption for small employers makes sense, what is the best way to implement the exemption: (1) a minimum-number-of-employees test; (2) a minimum-annual-sales test; or (3) some other test? What are the potential drawbacks (or benefits) of the types of tests currently used?

Still other types of employers may be specifically exempted in the text of various statutes. For example, the ADEA explicitly states that the term employer "does not include the United States, or a corporation wholly owned by the Government of the United States." 29 U.S.C. § 630(b).[7] Likewise, Title VII states that the term employer "does not include . . . the United States, a corporation wholly owned by the Government of the United States, an Indian Tribe . . . any department or agency of the District of Columbia subject by statute to procedures of the competitive service . . . or a bona fide private membership club (other than a labor organization) [that is tax exempt]." 42 U.S.C. § 2000e (b). Other employment discrimination statutes provide similar exclusions, so it is necessary to carefully read the language of the statute to determine relevant coverage.

IV. EXEMPT EMPLOYEES

As discussed earlier, only "employees" are covered by various state and federal employment discrimination laws. However, determining that an individual is an "employee" does not end the inquiry. Some statutes explicitly exempt certain employees from coverage, so it is important to read the definition sections and exclusions carefully.

Some statutes provide only limited exemptions. For example, the ADEA only applies to employees who are 40 years of age or older. 29 U.S.C. § 631. In contrast, one of the most exhaustive lists of exemptions appears in the FLSA. 29 U.S.C. §§ 201-19. Some types of employees are excluded from both the minimum wage and maximum hour requirements of the FLSA, including (but not limited to) "any employee employed in a bona fide executive, administrative, or professional capacity"; outside salespeople; "any employee employed by an establishment which is an amusement or recreational establishment, organized camp, or religious or non-profit educational conference center"; employees involved in certain fishing and agricultural activities; and babysitters and other types of caregivers. 29 U.S.C. § 213(a). Even more employees are protected by the minimum wage provisions of the FLSA but not the overtime provisions. Some employees in this category include "any individual employed as an outside buyer of poultry, eggs, cream, or milk, in their raw or natural state"; certain individuals employed as "a seaman"; certain salespeople and delivery drivers; live-in household

---

[7] Importantly, though, another section, § 633a, deals with age discrimination by federal government employers. Furthermore, specific prohibitions against age discrimination also apply to employment agencies, 29 U.S.C. §§ 623(b), 630(c), and labor organizations, 29 U.S.C. §§ 623(c), 630(d), (e). Always make sure to review the whole statute to ensure that you understand the scope of coverage.

helpers; and others. *Id.* Still other occupations are exempt from the child labor provisions in the FLSA. *Id.*

Another example of a statute with multiple exemptions and limitations is the Employee Polygraph Protection Act (EPPA). Under the EPPA, it is illegal to "discharge, discipline, discriminate against in any manner, or deny employment or promotion to, or threaten to take any such action against" an employee or prospective employee who refuses to take a lie detector test or opposes the use of such tests. 29 U.S.C. § 2002. However, several types of employees are exempt from the protections of the EPPA. The most significant exemption involves the inapplicability of the Act to governmental employers. 29 U.S.C. § 2006(a). Specific exemptions also exist for employees employed in the area of national security and defense. Limited exemptions exist to allow employers to polygraph employees where the employee is subject to an "ongoing investigation involving economic loss or injury to the employer's business." 29 U.S.C. § 2006(d).

Finally, some statutes may simply attempt to define who qualifies as an "employee" more narrowly rather than providing a broad definition of employee with a separate lengthy section of exemptions. For example, the Family Medical Leave Act (FMLA) limits protection to "eligible" employees. Under the FMLA,

> The term "eligible employee" means an employee who has been employed—(i) for at least 12 months by the employer with respect to whom leave is requested . . . and (ii) for at least 1,250 hours of service with such employer during the previous 12-month period.
>
> . . .
>
> The term "eligible employee" does not include-- (i) any Federal officer or employee covered under subchapter V of chapter 63 of Title 5; or (ii) any employee of an employer who is employed at a worksite at which such employer employs less than 50 employees if the total number of employees employed by that employer within 75 miles of that worksite is less than 50.

29 U.S.C. § 2611(2).

■ **PRACTICE NOTE:** An employer may seek to limit its liability by imposing a contract on those it hires that states that the individuals hired are independent contractors. Or an employee may sign an employment contract acknowledging that the employee falls within one or more exemptions under various statutory schemes. For example, an employer may have employees sign a contract acknowledging that they are not entitled to the protection of the minimum wage and maximum hours provisions of the Fair Labor Standards Act because the employees are employed in a "bona fide executive, administrative, or professional capacity." However, in most (but not all) cases, employment rights cannot be waived by contract.[8] Therefore, such agreements will not normally preclude a court from performing its own analysis as to whether a given individual is a covered employee under a particular statute.

QUESTIONS AND EXERCISES

1) Retrieve a copy of the list of exemptions in the FLSA (found at 29 U.S.C. § 213). Using that list, answer the following questions:

    a) Computer programmers are exempt from some provisions of the FLSA in certain circumstances. What provisions, and under what circumstances?

    b) You own a small family farm. Can you require your 13-year-old son to work on the farm? If so, do you have to pay him minimum wage? Why or why not? Would your answer change if your son was using dangerous farm equipment?

---

[8] Some rights can, in fact, be waived, if the waiver is "knowing and voluntary." *See, e.g.*, 29 U.S.C. § 626(f) (allowing "knowing and voluntary" waiver of rights under the Age Discrimination in Employment Act (ADEA)). For example, the ADEA explicitly provides that:

> (1) An individual may not waive any right or claim under this chapter unless the waiver is knowing and voluntary . . . [A] waiver may not be considered knowing and voluntary unless at a minimum—
>   (A) the waiver is part of an agreement between the individual and the employer that is written in a manner calculated to be understood by such individual, or by the average individual eligible to participate;
>   (B) the waiver specifically refers to rights or claims arising under this chapter;
>   (C) the individual does not waive rights or claims that may arise after the date the waiver is executed;
>   (D) the individual waives rights or claims only in exchange for consideration in addition to anything of value to which the individual already is entitled;
>   (E) the individual is advised in writing to consult with an attorney prior to executing the agreement;
>   (F) (i) the individual is given a period of at least 21 days within which to consider the agreement; or
>   (ii) if a waiver is requested in connection with an exit incentive or other employment termination program offered to a group or class of employees, the individual is given a period of at least 45 days within which to consider the agreement;
>   (G) the agreement provides that for a period of at least 7 days following the execution of such agreement, the individual may revoke the agreement, and the agreement shall not become effective or enforceable until the revocation period has expired;
>   (H) if a waiver is requested in connection with an exit incentive or other employment termination program offered to a group or class of employees, the employer (at the commencement of the period specified in subparagraph (F)) informs the individual in writing in a manner calculated to be understood by the average individual eligible to participate, as to—
>   (i) any class, unit, or group of individuals covered by such program, any eligibility factors for such program, and any time limits applicable to such program; and
>   (ii) the job titles and ages of all individuals eligible or selected for the program, and the ages of all individuals in the same job classification or organizational unit who are not eligible or selected for the program.

Id.

c) You have been hired to work at the Green City Gazette as a newspaper editor. Green City has a population of 55,000 and is located over an hour away from any major metropolitan area. Are you covered by the FLSA?

2) An employee at your client's insurance company is suspected of taking kickbacks from outside vendors. Can you require the employee to take a polygraph test? If so, what must you do in order to comply with the EPPA? (Review 29 U.S.C. § 2006(d)).

V. THE PUBLIC VS. PRIVATE EMPLOYER DISTINCTION

Some employment discrimination laws apply equally to public (government) employers and private employers, while others only apply to one type of employer or the other. For example, with few exceptions, a plaintiff may bring a Title VII claim against either a public or a private employer. In contrast, a claim under 42 U.S.C. § 1983 only imposes liability on state or local government officials whose actions "under color of" state law deprive any person within the United States of "any rights, privileges, or immunities secured by the Constitution and laws." 42 U.S.C. § 1983.

Therefore, one of the first questions to ask when beginning research on a case or issue is whether the employer is public or private and how that affects the availability of certain claims.

VI. THE IMPORTANCE OF AGENCIES TO EMPLOYMENT DISCRIMINATION LAW

Agencies play a pivotal role in enforcing many employment discrimination laws. Understanding administrative law, therefore, is a key component to being an effective employment attorney in the United States. A complete primer in administrative law is, of course, well beyond the scope of this book. This short section simply introduces some of the key ways in which agencies are involved in the process of making and enforcing employment discrimination laws.

At the federal level, the two entities most involved in employment discrimination regulation and enforcement are the Equal Employment Opportunity Commission (EEOC) and the Department of Labor (DOL). The EEOC is responsible for issuing regulations, providing guidance, and enforcing a number of federal laws, including:

- Title VII;
- The Pregnancy Discrimination Act (appears as an amendment to Title VII);
- The Equal Pay Act (part of the Fair Labor Standards Act);
- The Age Discrimination in Employment Act;

- Title I of the Americans with Disabilities Act (and the ADA Amendments Act of 2008);
- Sections 102 and 103 of the Civil Rights Act of 1991;
- Sections 501 and 505 of the Rehabilitation Act of 1973; and
- The Genetic Information Nondiscrimination Act (Effective November 21, 2009).

In addition to issuing regulations, memoranda of understanding, and handling administrative charges of discrimination, the EEOC assists federal agencies with equal employment opportunity (EEO) complaint adjudication, monitors the affirmative action programs of federal agencies, and creates compliance assistance materials for the federal sector. Additional information about researching agency guidance can be found in the research chapters of this book.

Various divisions of the DOL enforce other laws related to employment law and employment discrimination. The Wage and Hour Division of the DOL enforces the following laws:[9]

- The Fair Labor Standards Act;
- The Family and Medical Leave Act;
- The Immigration and Nationality Act of 1990;
- The Davis-Bacon Act (requires "payment of prevailing wage rates and fringe benefits" for those working on "federally-financed or assisted construction");
- The Service Contract Act (requires "payment of prevailing wage rates and fringe benefits" for those working on "contracts to provide services to the federal government");
- The Contract Work Hours and Safety Standards Act ("sets overtime standards for most federal service contracts, federally funded construction projects, and federal supply contracts over $100,000"); and
- The Walsh-Healey Public Contracts Act ("requires payment of minimum wage rates and overtime pay on federal contracts to manufacture or provide goods to the federal government").

The DOL also has other divisions responsible for enforcing laws related to employment. For example, the Occupational Safety and Health Administration helps investigate and enforce claims under the OSH Act. The Office of Federal Contract Compliance Programs enforces both Executive Order 11246 and Section 503 of the Rehabilitation Act. *See* http://www.dol.gov/OFCCP/reg-library.htm (last accessed January 12, 2013). Executive Order 11246 outlaws discrimination by federal contractors on the basis of race, color, religion, sex, or national origin. Section 503 outlaws disability discrimination by federal contractors.

---

[9] Quoted material in this list is taken from http://www.dol.gov/dol/topic/wages/ (last accessed January 12, 2013).

Divisions within the Department of Justice also enforce and provide guidance on the following laws (this list is illustrative, not exhaustive, and focuses on laws with relevance to employment discrimination lawyers):

- Anti-discrimination provisions of the Immigration and Nationality Act (enforced by the Office of Special Counsel for Immigration-Related Unfair Employment Practices, http://www.justice.gov/crt/about/osc/ (last accessed January 12, 2013));
- Title VI of the Civil Rights Act of 1964 (enforced by the Civil Rights Division of the Department of Justice), which outlaws discrimination on the basis of race, color, or national origin in programs receiving financial assistance from the federal government; and
- Section 504 of the Rehabilitation Act (enforced by the Civil Rights Division of the Department of Justice), which outlaws discrimination on the basis of a disability in programs and activities receiving financial assistance from the federal government.

Other federal agencies and offices are responsible for enforcement of still other laws related to employment discrimination. For example, the Merit Systems Protection Board enforces the Civil Service Reform Act of 1978, a law that outlaws discrimination against federal employees or job applicants. Information about the Merit Systems Protection Board can be found at http://www.mspb.gov/About/about.htm (last accessed January 12, 2013). Another example is the National Labor Relations Board, which enforces the National Labor Relations Act.

■ **PRACTICE NOTE:** Not all employment laws are enforced by an agency. Section 1981 claims, for example, are only enforced in court. Guidance on § 1981, therefore, can only be found in court cases.

Federal agencies provide guidance in several forms. First, agencies may produce regulations to help interpret statutes, and those regulations are then codified in the Code of Federal Regulations. Courts will give great deference to an agency's interpretation of a statute it has been tasked with enforcing. The Supreme Court articulated this concept of administrative deference in the landmark case of *Chevron, U.S.A., Inc. v. Natural Resources Defense Council, Inc.*, 467 U.S. 837 (1984). The court noted as follows:

> [w]hen a court reviews an agency's construction of the statute which it administers, it is confronted with two questions. First, always, is the question whether Congress has directly spoken to the precise question at issue. If the intent of Congress is clear, that is the end of the matter; for the court, as well as the agency, must give effect to the unambiguously expressed intent of Congress. If, however, the court determines Congress has not directly addressed the precise question at issue, the court does not simply impose its own construction on the statute, as would be necessary in the absence of an administrative interpretation. Rather, if the statute is silent or ambiguous with respect to the specific issue, the question for the court is whether the agency's answer is based on a permissible construction of the statute.

Chevron, 467 U.S. at 842-43.

The court further noted that some delegations of authority to agencies may be explicit, while others may be implicit. In a case in which "Congress has explicitly left a gap for the agency to fill, there is an express delegation of authority to the agency to elucidate a specific provision of the statute by regulation. Such legislative regulations are given controlling weight unless they are arbitrary, capricious, or manifestly contrary to the statute." *Id.* at 843-44 (internal citations omitted). In contrast, where "the legislative delegation to an agency on a particular question is implicit rather than explicit . . . a court may not substitute its own construction of a statutory provision for a reasonable interpretation made by the administrator of an agency . . . [C]onsiderable weight should be accorded to an executive department's construction of a statutory scheme it is entrusted to administer." *Id.*[10]

QUESTION

It is relatively clear that an explicit delegation to an agency deserves deference. Why is such deference appropriate where Congress has not explicitly delegated authority to the federal agency? Are there reasons why a federal agency would be in a better position than a court to interpret a statute's meaning?

VII. EXHAUSTION OF ADMINISTRATIVE REMEDIES

Most employment discrimination laws require a complainant to file an administrative charge with the agency charged with enforcing the law prior to filing suit. For example, an individual who wants to file a lawsuit based on nearly any law enforced by the EEOC must file a charge of discrimination with the EEOC prior to filing a discrimination lawsuit in federal court. (The only exception is the Equal Pay Act, which allows a complainant to bring a lawsuit in federal court without first filing an administrative charge.) A complaining party has only a limited amount of time after the alleged discrimination to file a charge with the EEOC. Once an individual files a charge of discrimination with the EEOC,[11] investigators may choose to do several things. First, the EEOC may ask both parties to try to settle the dispute through mediation. If the charge of discrimination is resolved through mediation, then that is the end of the process.[12] Second, the EEOC may decide the charge of discrimination has little or no chance of succeeding. If so, it may decline to offer mediation or conduct an investigation and dismiss the charge outright. Third, the EEOC may conduct a complete investigation. If the EEOC finds a violation, it will take one of three actions:

---

[10] A full discussion of the *Chevron* doctrine, erosions to *Chevron*, and critiques of *Chevron* deference is beyond the scope of this book.
[11] The EEOC has many field offices around the country, so it is relatively simple to find a local office for filing.
[12] In certain circumstances, the EEOC may choose not to suggest mediation, the parties may not agree to mediation, or mediation may not resolve the dispute.

- Work with the employer to reach a voluntary settlement;
- Refer the case to the EEOC's legal staff for a determination of whether the EEOC will file a lawsuit on your behalf; or
- Give the complaining party a "Notice of Right to Sue."[13]

If the EEOC concludes that no violation occurred, the agency will simply issue a Notice of Right to Sue. At this point, the complaining party has "exhausted" administrative remedies and can file suit in court.

■ PRACTICE NOTE: The EEOC also enforces discrimination laws on behalf of federal employees and job applicants. However, the complaint process is different. An overview of that complaint process can be found on the EEOC's website at http://www.eeoc.gov/federal/fed_employees/complaint_overview.cfm (last accessed January 12, 2013).

■ PRACTICE NOTE: Every employment discrimination law has a different exhaustion requirement. For example, a plaintiff cannot file in federal court under Title VII without first receiving a Notice of Right to Sue Letter. However, other laws contain more lenient requirements. Here are just a couple of examples:

☐ *The EPA*: The EPA does not contain an exhaustion requirement. In other words, plaintiffs do not have to file an administrative charge or receive a Notice of Right to Sue prior to bringing a claim under the Act. (There is, however, a statute of limitations. Plaintiffs must file within two years of the alleged discrimination, or three years if the discrimination was "willful.")[14]

☐ *The ADEA*: Although an aggrieved individual must file a charge with the EEOC within 180 days of the alleged discrimination,[15] the individual can file a lawsuit 60 days after filing a charge with the EEOC (even without receipt of a Notice of Right to Sue).

---

[13] http://www.eeoc.gov/employees/charge.cfm (last accessed January 12, 2013).
[14] 29 U.S.C. § 255(a).
[15] 29 U.S.C. § 626(d)(1) provides:

No civil action may be commenced by an individual under this section until 60 days after a charge alleging unlawful discrimination has been filed with the Equal Employment Opportunity Commission. Such a charge shall be filed: (A) within 180 days after the alleged unlawful practice occurred; or (B) in a case to which section 633(b) of this title applies [the section applying to federal government employees], within 300 days after the alleged unlawful practice occurred, or within 30 days after receipt by the individual of notice of termination of proceedings under State law, whichever is earlier.

A NOTE ON DUAL FILING

Many plaintiffs want to bring multiple discrimination claims, including claims under federal, state, and local laws. State and local governments often have their own agencies responsible for enforcing state and local anti-discrimination laws, respectively. To solve the potential problem of competing exhaustion requirements at the federal and state levels, the EEOC has work sharing agreements with many state and local anti-discrimination agencies. The EEOC calls these parallel agencies Fair Employment Practices Agencies (FEPAs). If you file a claim of discrimination with a state or local FEPA that has a work sharing agreement with the EEOC, the charge will also be filed with the EEOC if the FEPA determines that federal anti-discrimination laws are also implicated (called "dual filing"). Likewise, filing with the EEOC will satisfy the exhaustion requirements of a state agency that coordinates with the EEOC. Each EEOC field office maintains a list of FEPAs who have work sharing agreements with the EEOC. Essentially, the office in which you initially file will do the investigation and simply report the results to the other agency. There are limited provisions for review by one agency of an unsatisfactory result from the other.

QUESTION

What do you imagine are the practical benefits and potential drawbacks of such a worksharing agreement to an aggrieved individual? To the agencies?

VIII. PREEMPTION AND EXCLUSIVITY OF REMEDIES

In some situations, a federal law may preempt the application of a state or local law. Or courts may conclude that one federal law provides the exclusive remedy for a plaintiff, precluding suit under another federal statute or constitutional provision. This section briefly summarizes some of the most common situations in which preemption arises and where courts may find that one statute or another provides plaintiffs with an exclusive remedy for harm suffered.

A. PREEMPTION OF STATE LAW BY FEDERAL LAW – AN EXAMPLE

Some federal statutes explicitly provide that their provisions preempt state law. For example, the Employee Retirement Income Security Act (ERISA)[16] explicitly

---

[16] ERISA is codified at 29 U.S.C. § 1144 (also referred to as ERISA § 514).

provides that it "shall supersede any and all State laws" inasmuch as they "relate to any employee benefit plan" as described under ERISA.[17] According to the terms of ERISA, "State law includes all laws, decisions, rules, regulations, or other State action having the effect of law, of any State."[18] Furthermore, a "State" includes "a State, any political subdivisions thereof, or any agency or instrumentality of either, which purports to regulate, directly or indirectly, the terms and conditions of employee benefit plans [covered under ERISA]."[19] ERISA preemption is a complex area of the law,[20] but one in which lawyers should be familiar when practicing employment law.[21]

B. PREEMPTION AND EXCLUSIVE REMEDIES – EXAMPLES OF RELATIONSHIPS BETWEEN TWO FEDERAL LAWS

In some areas of employment discrimination law, courts may conclude that one federal law so comprehensively covers a subject that claims under another federal law are precluded. For example, almost every court addressing the issue has concluded that the ADEA preempts claims under 42 U.S.C. § 1983. Section 1983 protects United States citizens from "the deprivation of any rights, privileges, or immunities secured by the Constitution and laws." *Id.* However, according to the United States Supreme Court, "[w]hen the remedial devices provided in a particular Act are sufficiently comprehensive, they may suffice to demonstrate congressional intent to preclude the remedy of suits under § 1983." *Middlesex Cnty. Sewerage Auth. v. Nat'l Sea Clammers Ass'n*, 453 U.S. 1, 20 (1981) ("*Sea Clammers*").

The Ninth Circuit recently addressed the question of whether a claim under § 1983 was preempted by the ADEA. *Ahlmeyer v. Nevada Sys. of Higher Ed.*, 555 F.3d 1051 (9th Cir. 2009). In *Ahlmeyer*, the court noted that "Congress passed the Age Discrimination in Employment Act . . . to promote the employment of older persons and prohibit arbitrary discrimination by employers based on age. Congress crafted a detailed administrative scheme with complex enforcement mechanisms to accomplish these goals." *Ahlmeyer*, 555 F.3d at 1053-54

---

[17] ERISA § 514(a). As with most laws, this broad statement is subject to exceptions. ERISA § 514(b).
[18] ERISA § 514(c)(1).
[19] ERISA § 514(c)(2).
[20] Examples of the types of complexities arising in ERISA law abound. What does it mean to "relate to" an employee benefit plan? Does the plan at issue qualify under ERISA as an employee benefit plan? Are there statutory exceptions to preemption? For example, ERISA provides that nothing in its terms "shall be construed to alter, amend, modify, invalidate, impair, or supersede any law of the United States." ERISA § 514(d). Likewise, in a section of ERISA known as the "savings clause," ERISA provides that its terms shall not "be construed to exempt or relieve any person from any law of any State which regulates insurance, banking, or securities." ERISA § 514(b)(2)(A). On the other hand, the "deemer clause" then provides that no employee benefit plan "shall be deemed to be an insurance company or other insurer, bank, trust company, or investment company or to be engaged in the business of insurance or banking for purposes of any law of any State purporting to regulate insurance companies, insurance contracts, banks, trust companies, or investment companies." ERISA § 514(b)(2)(B). The "savings" and "deemer" clauses have been the subject of much interpretation and litigation. Finally, one other example of an exception to the provisions of ERISA is that it does "not apply to any generally applicable criminal law of a State." ERISA § 514(b)(4).
[21] In many large firms, the Employment and Labor Law practice group is separate from the Employee Benefits group. Nevertheless, employment law attorneys should be familiar enough with the basics of employee benefits law to at least recognize key issues and know when to bring in experts in that field.

(internal citations omitted). The court concluded that the comprehensive nature of the ADEA demonstrated that Congress intended to preclude an age discrimination claim under § 1983. *Id.* at 1060-61.[22]

In contrast, courts have concluded that Title VII is not the exclusive remedy for employment discrimination claims and does not preclude suit against state actors under § 1983. *See, e.g., Keller v. Prince George's Cnty.*, 827 F.2d 952 (4th Cir. 1987) (addressing question based on the legislative history of the original Civil Rights Act of 1967); *Johnson v. City of Ft. Lauderdale*, 148 F.3d 1228 (11th Cir. 1998) (concluding same after passage of the Civil Rights Act of 1991).

C. STATE LAW AS THE EXCLUSIVE REMEDY FOR DISCRIMINATION – AN EXAMPLE

Another hotly contested issue is the relationship between workers' compensation statutes and discrimination claims. Almost every state workers' compensation statute provides that it is the exclusive remedy for workplace injuries. One tactic routinely taken by employers is to raise these exclusive remedies provisions as an affirmative defense in employment discrimination cases. For example, in a sexual harassment lawsuit, an employee might assert numerous tort claims in addition to statutory sexual harassment claims. Thus, the employee may attempt to bring claims for wrongful termination in violation of public policy, invasion of privacy, intentional or negligent infliction of emotional distress, assault and battery, and others. Depending upon the courts' interpretation of the language of the workers' compensation law in the state in which you practice and the specific claims brought by an employee, a court may or may not find some of the claims barred by the exclusive remedies provisions of the state workers' compensation law.

D. EXPLICIT STATEMENT THAT A GIVEN LAW DOES NOT PREEMPT MORE FAVORABLE LAWS

Finally, some federal statutes may explicitly provide that more favorable state law provisions are not preempted by federal law. For example, the Fair Labor Standards Act (FLSA) provides that:

> No provision of this chapter or of any order thereunder shall excuse noncompliance with any Federal or State law or municipal ordinance establishing a minimum wage higher than the minimum wage established under this chapter or a maximum work week lower than the maximum workweek established under this chapter, and no provision of this chapter relating to the employment of child labor shall justify noncompliance with

---

[22] The Seventh Circuit has held otherwise. *Levin v. Madigan*, 692 F.3d 607 (7th Cir. 2012), creating a split among the circuits. Because *Levin* is the only circuit to find that the ADEA does not preempt a claim under § 1983, the United States Supreme Court granted certiorari in *Levin* on March 18, 2013. *Levin v. Madigan*, 692 F.3d 607 (7th Cir.), *cert. granted sub nom. Madigan v. Levin*, 132 S. Ct. __ (2013). Oral arguments are set for October 7, 2013. When the Supreme Court decides the issue, we will add an update to the companion website for this book.

any Federal or State law or municipal ordinance establishing a higher standard than the standard established under this chapter. No provision of this chapter shall justify any employer in reducing a wage paid by him which is in excess of the applicable minimum wage under this chapter, or justify any employer in increasing hours of employment maintained by him which are shorter than the maximum hours applicable under this chapter.

29 U.S.C. § 218(a) (discussing the FLSA's relation to other laws).

QUESTIONS AND EXERCISES

1) In *Zombro v. Baltimore City Police Department*, 868 F.2d 1364 (4th Cir. 1989), *cert. denied*, 493 U.S. 850 (1989), the Fourth Circuit concluded that the ADEA preempts a claim brought under § 1983. The Ninth Circuit has agreed, relying heavily on the majority reasoning in *Zombro*. *Ahlmeyer*, 555 F.3d at 1056-58. In fact, until very recently, every circuit to address the issue agreed that the ADEA preempts section 1983 claims.[23] Swimming against the tide, the Seventh Circuit recently concluded that the ADEA does not, in fact, preempt a claim under § 1983. *Levin v. Madigan*, 692 F.3d 607 (7th Cir. 2012). Read the opinions in *Zombro* and *Levin*. What reasoning is more persuasive? Why?

2) As mentioned earlier, the United States Supreme Court granted certiorari on March 18, 2013 to resolve the circuit split created by the Seventh Circuit's decision in *Levin*. Your professor will assign you a side. Using only the relevant statutory language and the opinions in *Zombro*, *Ahlmeyer*, and *Levin*, prepare for an oral argument on the issue of whether the ADEA preempts section 1983 claims. Your professor will provide guidance on the amount of time you will have to present your arguments.[24]

3) In *Zombro*, Judge Murnaghan concurred in part and dissented in part. 868 F.2d at 1372. He specifically disagreed with the majority on the preemption issue. Review Judge Murnaghan's dissent in *Zombro* and the court's opinion in *Levin*. Using these materials, craft a dissent to the opinion in *Ahlmeyer*.

4) In *Ahlmeyer*, the court recognized that "[i]f the ADEA is the exclusive remedy for age discrimination in the workplace, then plaintiffs are left without a federal forum for age discrimination claims against state actors." *Ahlmeyer*, 555 F.3d at 1060. Is this an argument that Congress did not pass a "sufficiently comprehensive legislative scheme to address violations of a given right?" *Id.* The court in *Ahlmeyer* concluded that it was not. Is the reasoning of the court in *Ahlmeyer* on this issue persuasive? Why or why not?

---

[23] District courts in circuits that have yet to decide the issue have reached varied conclusions. For an example of a district court opinion declining to find the ADEA preempts a claim under § 1983, see *Mummelthie v. City of Mason City*, 873 F. Supp. 1293 (N.D. Iowa 1995), *aff'd*, 78 F.3d 589 (8th Cir. 1996).

[24] Actual oral arguments in the case are set for October 7, 2013. In lieu of the above exercise, your professor may ask you to listen to the oral arguments and to assess the relative merits of the arguments on both sides.

5) Some courts have concluded that section 501 of the Rehabilitation Act is the exclusive remedy for alleged disability discrimination against a federal employee by a federal employer. Other courts have found that employees may also bring a cause of action against a federal employer under section 504 of the Rehabilitation Act. Review the relevant statutory language as well as the discussion of this issue in *Rivera v. Heyman*, 157 F.3d 101 (2d Cir. 1998). Are you persuaded by the reasoning in *Rivera*? What are your best arguments against the position in *Rivera*?

IX. TYPES OF EMPLOYMENT DISCRIMINATION LAW CLAIMS

Employment discrimination cases may be brought by individuals or, in certain circumstances, by a class of individuals. The alleged discrimination may be intentional or unintentional. In the context of Title VII, for example, the United States Supreme Court recently noted that "Title VII prohibits both intentional discrimination (known as 'disparate treatment') as well as, in some cases, practices that are not intended to discriminate but in fact have a disproportionately adverse effect on minorities (known as 'disparate impact')." *Ricci v. DeStefano*, 129 S. Ct. 2658, 2672 (2009). This section briefly describes the range of claims available to individual plaintiffs or classes of plaintiffs alleging discrimination in the workplace.

A. INDIVIDUAL DISPARATE TREATMENT CLAIMS

The typical employment discrimination case involves a claim by an individual that an employer engaged in intentional discrimination. In fact, the text of the original Civil Rights Act of 1964 only outlawed intentional discrimination. The provisions of Title VII regarding intentional discrimination state that it is unlawful to do the following:

(1) to fail or refuse to hire or to discharge any individual, or otherwise to discriminate against any individual with respect to his compensation, terms, conditions, or privileges of employment, because of such individual's race, color, religion, sex, or national origin; or

(2) to limit, segregate, or classify his employees or applicants for employment in any way which would deprive or tend to deprive any individual of employment opportunities or otherwise adversely affect his status as an employee, because of such individual's race, color, religion, sex, or national origin.

42 U.S.C. § 2002e-2(a)(1-2). In rare situations, employees or prospective employees have direct evidence of such discrimination.[25] However, the vast majority

---

[25] Even overtly discriminatory policies or actions may be permissible in the case of discrimination based on sex, religion, or national origin if the court determines that sex, religion, or national origin is a "bona fide occupational qualification" (BFOQ) for the job. Race and color, however, are never BFOQs.

of employment discrimination cases do not involve direct evidence. Where a plaintiff seeks to prove discrimination using circumstantial evidence, courts use a three-part burden shifting proof structure initially established by the Supreme Court in *McDonnell Douglas Corp. v. Green*, 411 U.S. 792 (1973). Under the *McDonnell Douglas* test, the employee must initially establish a prima facie case for disparate treatment. If the plaintiff is able to establish the minimal burden at the prima facie case stage, the burden then shifts to the employer to produce a legitimate nondiscriminatory reason for the adverse action. If the employer meets its production burden, the burden shifts back to the employee to demonstrate that the employer's proffered reason is merely a pretext for discrimination.

■ **PRACTICE NOTE:** A plaintiff alleging intentional discrimination does not have to show that the employer acted in bad faith or with malice.

■ **PRACTICE NOTE:** Even direct evidence of intentional discrimination may not be enough to establish disparate treatment if the court determines that the only evidence of discrimination involves "stray remarks." *See, e.g., Jackson v. Cal-Western Packaging Corp.*, 602 F.2d 374, 380 (5th Cir. 2010); *Sun v. Bd. Of Trustees of Univ. of Ill.*, 473 F.3d 799, 813 (7th Cir. 2007) (internal citations omitted) ("[S]tray remarks that are neither proximate nor related to the employment decision are insufficient to defeat summary judgment. . . . At the same time, though, the statements of a person who lacks the final decision-making authority may be probative of intentional discrimination if that individual exercised a significant degree of influence over the contested decision.") In *Jackson*, the Fifth Circuit noted that "comments are evidence of discrimination only if they are 1) related to the protected class of persons of which the plaintiff is a member; 2) proximate in time to the complained-of adverse employment decision; 3) made by an individual with authority over the employment decision at issue; and 4) related to the employment decision at issue. Comments that do not meet these criteria are considered 'stray remarks,' and standing alone, are insufficient to defeat summary judgment." *Id.* (internal quotations and citations omitted).

QUESTION

Read *Jackson* as well as *Reeves v. Sanderson Plumbing Products, Inc.*, 530 U.S. 133 (2000). Should the "stray remarks" doctrine survive *Reeves*? Why or why not?

A NOTE ON "MIXED MOTIVE" CASES

In *Price Waterhouse v. Hopkins*, 490 U.S. 228 (1989), the Supreme Court concluded in a plurality opinion that "Title VII meant to condemn even those decisions based on a mixture of legitimate and illegitimate considerations." 490 U.S. at 240 (opinion authored by Justice Brennan, with three other justices joining, and two more concurring in the judgment). The court also concluded, however, that "once a plaintiff in a Title VII case shows that gender played a motivating part in an employment decision, the defendant may avoid a finding of liability ... by proving that it would have made the same decision even if it had not allowed [the plaintiff's protected status] to play such a role." *Id.* at 240-41. The latter part of the court's conclusion was superseded by statute with the enactment of the Civil Rights Act of 1991. Title VII now explicitly provides that "an unlawful employment practice is established when the complaining party demonstrates that race, color, religion, sex, or national origin was a motivating factor for any employment practice, even though other factors also motivated the practice." 42 U.S.C. § 2000e-2(m). In 2003, the Supreme Court issued another landmark ruling in a mixed motive case, concluding that a plaintiff need not provide direct evidence of discrimination in such a case. *Desert Palace, Inc. v. Costa*, 539 U.S. 90 (2003).

Importantly, however, the Supreme Court has recently declined to permit a mixed motive instruction in age discrimination claims filed under the ADEA. *Gross v. FBL Financial Svcs., Inc.*, 557 U.S. 167 (2009). On March 13, 2012, Senator Harkin introduced Senate Bill 2189, a bipartisan bill entitled the *Protecting Older Workers Against Discrimination Act*. The Act would effectively overturn *Gross* in the same way the Civil Rights Act of 1991 overturned *Price Waterhouse*. As of the publication of this book, the most recent activity on the bill was on March 13, 2012, when the bill was referred to the Senate Committee on Health, Education, Labor, and Pensions.

B. SYSTEMIC DISPARATE TREATMENT CLAIMS

Where there is systemic (class-wide) disparate treatment, a plaintiff may claim that the employer engaged in a "pattern or practice" of discrimination. The Supreme Court addressed the availability of such a claim in *International Brotherhood of Teamsters v. United States*, 431 U.S. 324 (1977). The EEOC can bring a claim that an employer engaged in a "pattern or practice" of discrimination in violation of Title VII if the EEOC "has reasonable cause to believe that [1] any person or group of persons is engaged in a pattern or practice of" discrimination ... and ... [2] the pattern or practice is of such a nature and is intended to deny the full exercise of the rights" under Title VII. 42 U.S.C. § 2000e-6(a) (granting the attorney general the right to bring such suits); 42 U.S.C. § 2000e-6(c) (transferring the attorney general's functions under Title VII to the EEOC "two years after March 24, 1972"). The court may also certify a class of private plaintiffs in a pattern and practice case. *See, e.g., EEOC v. Joe's Stone Crab, Inc.*, 220 F.3d 1263, 1274-75 (11th Cir. 2000).

In a pattern or practice case, the initial burden at the liability stage is simply to establish a prima facie case that the employer had a discriminatory policy. The plaintiff need not show that a specific individual or individuals suffered discrimination as a result of that policy. However, the plaintiff must "prove more than the mere occurrence of isolated or 'accidental' or sporadic discriminatory acts." *Teamsters*, 431 U.S. at 336. Rather, the plaintiff must "establish by a preponderance of the evidence that . . . discrimination was the company's standard operating procedure[,] the regular rather than the unusual practice." *Id.* In demonstrating that an employer's discriminatory practice was its standard operating procedure, statistical evidence is often used. *Joe's Stone Crab*, 220 F.3d at 1287 (citing *Lujan v. Franklin Cnty. Bd. of Educ.*, 766 F.2d 917, 929 (6th Cir.1985)); *Teamsters*, 431 U.S. at 335 n.15. More than one circuit has concluded that "[a] plaintiff may establish a pattern or practice claim "through a combination of strong statistical evidence of disparate impact coupled with anecdotal evidence of the employer's intent to treat the protected class unequally." *Id.* (quoting *Mozee v. Am. Commercial Marine Serv. Co.*, 940 F.2d 1036, 1051 (7th Cir. 1991)).

If the plaintiff succeeds, "[t]he burden then shifts to the employer to defeat the prima facie showing of a pattern or practice by demonstrating that the [plaintiff's] proof is either inaccurate or insignificant." *Id.* at 360-61. Typically, "the question of individual relief" only arises after "it has been proved that the employer has followed an employment policy of unlawful discrimination." *Id.* at 361-62. At the remedial stage,

> [t]he proof of the pattern or practice supports an inference that any particular employment decision, during the period in which the discriminatory policy was in force, was made in pursuit of that policy. [Therefore, the plaintiff] . . . need only show that an alleged individual discriminatee unsuccessfully applied for a job and therefore was a potential victim of the proved discrimination . . . the burden then rests on the employer to demonstrate that the individual applicant was denied an employment opportunity for lawful reasons.

Id. (internal citations omitted).

■ **PRACTICE NOTE:** A defendant's burden in rebutting the prima facie case in an individual disparate treatment case is merely a production burden. In systemic disparate treatment cases, some circuits have explicitly held defendants to a higher burden. For example, in *Cox v. American Cast Iron Pipe Co.*, 784 F.2d 1546 (11th Cir. 1986), the Eleventh Circuit stated that "once a pattern and practice of discrimination is established, a rebuttable presumption that [the] plaintiff was discriminated against because of her sex and is entitled to recovery obtains. The employer may overcome this presumption only with clear and convincing evidence that job decisions made when the discriminatory policy was in force were not made in pursuit of that policy." 784 F.2d at 1559; *see also Castaneda v. Pickard*, 648 F.2d 989 (5th Cir. 1981).

C. DISPARATE IMPACT CLAIMS

The disparate impact theory of liability was initially recognized by the United States Supreme Court in *Griggs v. Duke Power Co.*, 401 U.S. 424 (1971). In *Griggs*, the court recognized that a plaintiff alleging discrimination under Title VII need not prove intentional discrimination. Rather, the plaintiff can demonstrate that an otherwise facially neutral employment practice has a disparate impact on those in a particular protected class.[26] The Supreme Court recently summarized the disparate impact theory of liability as it existed post-*Griggs*:

> The *Griggs* Court stated that the "touchstone" for disparate-impact liability is the lack of "business necessity": "If an employment practice which operates to exclude [minorities] cannot be shown to be related to job performance, the practice is prohibited." *Griggs*, 401 U.S. at 432 (employer's burden to demonstrate that practice has "a manifest relationship to the employment in question"); *Albemarle Paper Co. v. Moody*, 422 U.S. 405, 426 (1975). Under those precedents, if an employer met its burden by showing that its practice was job-related, the plaintiff was required to show a legitimate alternative that would have resulted in less discrimination. 422 U.S. at 425 (allowing complaining party to show "that other tests or selection devices, without a similarly undesirable racial effect, would also serve the employer's legitimate interest").

Ricci v. DeStefano, 129 S. Ct. 2658, 2672-73 (2009).

After *Griggs*, the Supreme Court attempted to refine the relevant shifting burdens for disparate impact cases.[27] Responding to the *Wards Cove* decision (a decision perceived as being too favorable to defendant employers), Congress codified the disparate impact theory in the Civil Rights Act of 1991 and articulated the burden-shifting proof structure as follows:

Burden of Proof in Disparate Impact Cases

(A) An unlawful employment practice based on disparate impact is established under this subchapter only if—**(i)** a complaining party demonstrates that a respondent uses a particular employment practice that causes a disparate impact on the basis of race, color, religion, sex, or national origin and the respondent fails to demonstrate that the challenged practice is job related for the position in question and consistent with business necessity; or **(ii)** the complaining party makes the demonstration described in subparagraph (C) with respect to an alternative employment

---

[26] The court in *Griggs* addressed whether (even in the absence of an intent to discriminate on the part of an employer) Title VII prohibited the employer "from requiring a high school education or passing of a standardized general intelligence test as a condition of employment in or transfer to jobs when (a) neither standard is shown to be significantly related to successful job performance, (b) both requirements operate to disqualify Negroes at a substantially higher rate than white applicants, and (c) the jobs in question formerly had been filled only by white employees as part of a longstanding practice of giving preference to whites." *Smith v. City of Jackson*, 544 U.S. 228, 234 (2005) (citing *Griggs*, 401 U.S. at 425-26). The Supreme Court concluded that "good intent or absence of discriminatory intent does not redeem employment procedures or testing mechanisms that operate as 'built-in headwinds' for minority groups and are unrelated to measuring job capability." *Griggs*, 401 U.S. at 432.

[27] *See, e.g., Wards Cove Packing Co. v. Antonio*, 409 U.S. 642 (1990); *Albemarle Paper Co. v. Moody*, 422 U.S. 405 (1975).

practice and the respondent refuses to adopt such alternative employment practice.

(B) (i) With respect to demonstrating that a particular employment practice causes a disparate impact as described in subparagraph (A)(i), the complaining party shall demonstrate that each particular challenged employment practice causes a disparate impact, except that if the complaining party can demonstrate to the court that the elements of a respondent's decisionmaking process are not capable of separation for analysis, the decisionmaking process may be analyzed as one employment practice.

(ii) If the respondent demonstrates that a specific employment practice does not cause the disparate impact, the respondent shall not be required to demonstrate that such practice is required by business necessity.

(C) The demonstration referred to by subparagraph (A)(ii) shall be in accordance with the law as it existed on June 4, 1989, with respect to the concept of "alternative employment practice".

(2) A demonstration that an employment practice is required by business necessity may not be used as a defense against a claim of intentional discrimination under this subchapter.

42 U.S.C. § 2000e-2(k). After the codification of the disparate impact theory of liability, the shifting burdens operate as follows:

a plaintiff establishes a prima facie violation by showing that an employer uses "a particular employment practice that causes a disparate impact on the basis of race, color, religion, sex, or national origin."42 U.S.C. § 2000e-2(k)(1)(A)(i). An employer may defend against liability by demonstrating that the practice is "job related for the position in question and consistent with business necessity." *Id.* Even if the employer meets that burden, however, a plaintiff may still succeed by showing that the employer refuses to adopt an available alternative employment practice that has less disparate impact and serves the employer's legitimate needs. §§ 2000e-2(k)(1)(A)(ii) and (C).

Ricci, 129 S. Ct. at 2673. Disparate impact cases often boil down to thorny questions of causation and to warring statistical analyses of relevant data.[28]

---

[28] The following more detailed explanation of the relevant burdens in a Title VII disparate impact case demonstrates the key role of statistical analysis in such a case:

[A] plaintiff . . . must establish three elements: *first,* that there is a significant statistical disparity between the proportion of women in the available labor pool and the proportion of women hired; *second,* that there is a specific, facially-neutral, employment practice which is the alleged cause of the disparity; and *finally,* . . . that a causal nexus exists between the specific employment practice identified and the statistical disparity shown . . . . As the Supreme Court explained in *Watson,* 'the plaintiff must offer statistical evidence of a kind and degree sufficient to show that *the practice in question* has *caused* the exclusion of applicants for jobs or promotions because of their membership in a protected group.' [*Watson v. Ft. Worth Bank & Trust,* 487 U.S. 977, 994 (1988)] (emphasis added) . . . The burden of production then shifts to the defendant to establish that the challenged employment

QUESTION

In recent years, the Supreme Court has also addressed issues surrounding the parties' respective burdens in disparate impact cases arising under the Age Discrimination in Employment Act (ADEA). In *Meacham v. Knolls Atomic Power Laboratory*, 554 U.S. 84 (2008), for example, a group of government contractors sued under the ADEA after they were terminated during the course of an involuntary reduction in force (referred to by many employment lawyers as a "RIF"). *Id.* at 88. Although 30 of the 31 individuals terminated in the RIF were at least 40 years old, the defendant in *Meacham* claimed that it terminated the employees based upon "reasonable factors other than age" (RFOA). *Id.*[29] The court defined the issue in the case as "whether an employer facing a disparate-impact claim and planning to defend on the basis of RFOA must not only *produce* evidence raising the defense, but also *persuade* the factfinder of its merit. We hold that the employer must do both." *Id.* at 87 (emphasis added). Read the portion of the courts' decisions in *Meacham* and in *Smith v. City of Jackson*, 544 U.S. 228, 234 (2005) dealing with the differences between disparate impact liability under Title VII and the ADEA. Prepare a short presentation (to be given orally) regarding how the differences between the two statutes would affect an employer's burdens under each statute. Prepare as if you will be giving the presentation to a group of human resource professionals employed by your corporate clients at an educational lunch talk. Expect questions. You may be asked to turn in the notes you use in giving your presentation, though you may use whatever format for your notes that you find most useful (flash cards, an outline, a short paragraph, a bullet list of key points and likely questions, etc.).

---

practice serves a legitimate, non-discriminatory business objective. . . . However, even if the defendant satisfies this burden, a plaintiff may still prevail by proving that an alternative, non-discriminatory practice would have served the defendant's stated objective equally as well.

EEOC v. Joe's Stone Crab, Inc., 220 F.3d 1263, 1274-75 (11th Cir. 2000) (most internal citations omitted).

[29] The language regarding RFOA appears in a provision separate from the one setting out the general prohibition on age discrimination. Notwithstanding the general prohibition in the ADEA, section 623(f)(1) provides that "It shall not be unlawful for an employer, employment agency, or labor organization [] to take any action otherwise prohibited . . . where age is a bona fide occupational qualification reasonably necessary to the normal operation of the particular business, or where the differentiation is based on reasonable factors other than age." *Id.*

A NOTE ON INTERSECTIONAL CLAIMS

One of the most interesting areas of employment discrimination involves the availability of intersectional claims. The EEOC has plainly stated that "Title VII prohibits discrimination not just because of one protected trait (e.g., race), but also because of the intersection of two or more protected bases (e.g., race and sex). For example, Title VII prohibits discrimination against African American women even if the employer does not discriminate against White women or African American men. Likewise, Title VII protects Asian American women from discrimination based on stereotypes and assumptions about them 'even in the absence of discrimination against Asian American men or White women.' The law also prohibits individuals from being subjected to discrimination because of the intersection of their race and a trait covered by another EEO statute – e.g., race and disability, or race and age." EEOC Compliance Manual, Section 15(IV) (C) (internal citations and quotations omitted) (available at http://www.eeoc.gov/policy/docs/race-color.html#IVC (last accessed May 29, 2011)).

THE CONSTITUTION IN EMPLOYMENT DISCRIMINATION LAW

Most prohibitions against employment discrimination appear in federal and state statutes. However, the United States Constitution provides some protection against employment discrimination when that discrimination is perpetrated by a government entity. The main source of Constitutional law related to employment discrimination is the Fourteenth Amendment, which states in relevant part that a state may not "deprive any person of life, liberty, or property, without due process of law; nor deny to any person within its jurisdiction the equal protection of the laws." U.S. Const. Amend. XIV. When analyzing whether the Fourteenth Amendment has been violated, however, courts use a different level of scrutiny depending upon the protected class. For example, decisions based on race that might otherwise violate the equal protection clause of the Fourteenth Amendment are subject to strict scrutiny. On the other hand, decisions based on disability, sex, age, and other classifications will only violate the Fourteenth Amendment if the government lacked a rational basis for its actions.

Other constitutional provisions occasionally apply in the employment context. For example, a body of law has developed regarding employee free speech rights under the First Amendment. Under the United States Constitution, only public employees are protected. Likewise, in almost all states, private employees lack a constitutional right to free speech. In those states, private employees who believe they have been terminated or discriminated against because of something they said must rely on state whistleblower protection statutes. An exception is Connecticut, a state that has extended constitutional free speech protections to private employees by statute. Conn. Gen. Stat. § 31-51q. Under this statute, employees may not be disciplined or discharged for exercising rights guaranteed by the First Amendment or the Connecticut constitution if the speech "does not substantially or materially interfere with the employee's bona fide job performance or the working relationship between the employee and the employer." *Id.* Employees who prove an employer violated this statute may be entitled to damages, including punitive damages and reasonable attorney's fees. *Id.* However, should a court decide that a plaintiff-employee brought a lawsuit under this statute "without substantial justification," the court can award attorney's fees and costs to the defendant-employer. Although the statute applies to public and private employers and is not limited to freedom of speech in the public arena, "[t]he statute applies only to expressions regarding public concerns that are motivated by an employee's desire to speak out as a citizen." *Campbell v. Windham Cmty. Mem. Hosp.*, 389 F. Supp. 2d 370, 381-82 (D. Conn. 2005) (internal citations and quotations omitted).

Federal statutes, like Section 1983 of the Civil Rights Act of 1871, have been enacted to facilitate suits alleging violations of constitutional rights. Some of these key statutes are introduced in the next chapter.

CHAPTER 3

STATUTES GOVERNING EMPLOYMENT DISCRIMINATION ISSUES

Often employment discrimination laws are codified in federal or state codes. Local ordinances may also prohibit employment discrimination and retaliation. Many employment discrimination courses focus heavily on discrimination, retaliation, and sexual harassment in violation of Title VII. Title VII is indeed a key statute in this area. However, prohibitions of various types of employment discrimination arise in a much wider range of federal and state statutes. This section will provide a broad overview of the key statutes with which you should be familiar as well as a summary of many lesser-known statutes. Of course, given the short length of this text, this list is not meant to be exhaustive.

I. FEDERAL STATUTES

A. TITLE VII

Title VII of the Civil Rights Act of 1964 is the main source of federal law on job discrimination. It forbids employment discrimination against job applicants and existing employees on the basis of "race, color, religion, sex, or national origin" by employers with respect to "compensation, terms, conditions, or privileges of employment." 42 U.S.C. § 2000e-2(a)(1) (2012). The Supreme Court has held that Title VII's prohibitions also include sexual harassment and the creation of a "hostile or abusive work environment." *Meritor Sav. Bank, FSB v. Vinson*, 477 U.S. 57, 66 (1986) (holding hostile environment sexual harassment is a form of sex discrimination under Title VII and describing the application of a similar principle to cases involving race, religion, and national origin). One important exception permits distinctions based on religion, sex, or national origin where it is a "bona fide occupational qualification" reasonably necessary to perform the job. 42 U.S.C. § 2000e-2(e)(1). In addition, § 2000e-2(a) has been limited to its express terms and therefore does not cover discrimination based on citizenship or alienage, nepotism, alcoholism, or sexual orientation. 45A Am. Jur. 2d *Job Discrimination* § 2 (2012) (summarizing cases).

Title VII covers any type of employer "engaged in an industry affecting commerce who has fifteen or more employees for each working day in each of twenty or more calendar weeks in the current or proceeding calendar year." 42 U.S.C. § 2000e(b). Thus, private employers are covered as long as they meet the above requirements. In addition, Title VII is the exclusive remedy for victims of discrimination by the federal government unless it has been preempted by a later statute. *Brown v. Gen. Servs. Admin.*, 425 U.S. 820, 834-35 (1976). Federal employees are governed by 42 U.S.C. § 2000e-16, known as Section 717. Title VII, however, also contains limited exemptions for religious institutions and certain foreign corporations, § 2000e-1, private membership clubs, § 2000e(b)(2), and employers on or near Indian reservations, § 2000e-2(i); *see also* 1 *Employment Discrimination Coordinator: Analysis of Federal Law* §§ 12:21 to 12:25 (2011) [Emp. Discrim. Coord.] (discussing exempt employers). It is also important to note that the Civil Rights Act of 1991 limited the amount of damages recoverable under Title VII, but not § 1981. 42 U.S.C. § 1981a(b)(3), (4) (2012).

In addition to forbidding employment discrimination, Title VII prohibits retaliation against any employee "because he has opposed any practice made an unlawful employment practice by [Title VII], or because he has made a charge, testified, assisted, or participated in any manner in an investigation, proceeding, or hearing under [Title VII]." § 2000e-3(a). To establish retaliation, an employee must demonstrate "that his or her protected activity was a but-for cause of the alleged adverse action by the employer." *Univ. of Tex. Sw. Med. Ctr. v. Nassar*, __ U.S. __, 133 S. Ct. 2517, 2534 (2013).

B. SECTION 1983

Section 1983 imposes civil liability on state or local government officials whose actions "under color of" state law deprive any person within the United States of "any rights, privileges, or immunities secured by the Constitution and laws." 42 U.S.C. § 1983 (2012). Section 1983 does not create any new substantive legal rights. Rather, it provides a means for vindicating other rights under federal statutes and the Constitution. The statute therefore covers all bases for discrimination set out in other federal statutes like § 1981 and Title VII. Frederick T. Golder & David R. Golder, *Labor and Employment Law: Compliance and Litigation* § 4:9 (3d ed. 2010) [Golder]. Public employees have made a variety of constitutional claims under this statute, including claims based on the First Amendment, substantive and procedural due process, and equal protection. 1 Emp. Discrim. Coord. §§ 13:19, 13:19.50.

There are a number of restrictions on the types of individuals subject to suit under § 1983. For example, states and state agencies are not "persons" under § 1983. *Will v. Mich. Dep't of State Police*, 491 U.S. 58, 71 (1989). Federal officials are also excluded from the statute's coverage because they do not act under color of state law. *Wheeldin v. Wheeler*, 373 U.S. 647, 650 n.2 (1963). However, local government units and municipalities qualify as persons subject to liability. *Monell v. Dep't of Soc. Servs.*, 436 U.S. 658, 690 (1978).

Private employers are only subject to employment discrimination claims under § 1983 if their conduct constitutes "state action." *United States v. Price*, 383 U.S. 787, 794 n.7 (1966). This determination is based on several factors, including (1) the amount of public funding; (2) the extent of public regulation; (3) whether the private entity performs a traditionally "public function"; and (4) whether there is a "symbiotic relationship" between the state and the private entity. *Rendell-Baker v. Kohn*, 457 U.S. 830, 840-43 (1982). It is also important to note that the sovereign and personal immunity doctrines affect whether certain public entities and officials can be held liable under this provision. *See Quern v. Jordan*, 440 U.S. 332, 341 (1979) (state sovereign immunity); *Harlow v. Fitzgerald*, 457 U.S. 800, 807-08 (1982) (personal qualified and absolute immunities).

C. SECTION 1981

The most relevant provisions in § 1981 prohibit racial discrimination in making and enforcing contractual relationships. 42 U.S.C. § 1981(a) (2012). In 1991, Congress amended the definition of "make and enforce contracts" to include "the making, performance, modification, and termination of contracts" as well as "the enjoyment of all benefits, privileges, terms, and conditions of the contractual relationship." Pub. L. No. 102-166, 105 Stat. 1071 (codified as amended at 42 U.S.C. § 1981(b)). The statute's broad language prohibits all discrimination against, or in favor of, any race, including white persons. *McDonald v. Santa Fe Trail Transp. Co.*, 427 U.S. 273, 286-87 (1976). Section 1981 frequently applies to employment contracts where an employer engages in racially discriminatory conduct. 3 Emp. Discrim. Coord. §§ 119:9, 105:27. Courts have found that even at-will employment must be considered a contractual relationship under § 1981. *Humphries v. CBOCS West, Inc.*, 474 F.3d 387, 398 n.7 (7th Cir. 2007), *aff'd*, 553 U.S. 442 (2008); *see also Walker v. Abbott Labs.*, 340 F.3d 471, 475-78 (7th Cir. 2003) (noting that every circuit court to address the issue had held that at-will employment is a contractual relationship under § 1981, and to hold otherwise would contravene Congressional intent in passing the Civil Rights Act of 1991). The Supreme Court has further extended § 1981 by interpreting the term "race" broadly to include allegations of intentional discrimination based on ethnic characteristics or ancestry. *Saint Francis Coll. v. Al-Khazraji*, 481 U.S. 604, 613 (1987). However, plaintiffs cannot raise claims under this provision based solely on their country of origin or religion. *Pavon v. Swift Transp. Co.*, 192 F.3d 902, 908 (9th Cir. 1999); 1 Emp. Discrim. Coord. § 4:3.

Section 1981(c) explicitly provides for protection of these rights against impairment by both private employers *and* those acting "under color of State law" (state and local employers). 42 U.S.C. § 1981(c). As under § 1983, though, states themselves cannot be sued under § 1981. Likewise, immunity doctrines may protect individual state officials. *Pittman v. Oregon Emp't Dep't*, 509 F.3d 1065, 1071 (9th Cir. 2007) (pointing out that all the courts of appeals that have reached the issue have concluded that "states enjoy sovereign immunity under § 1981 in the absence of waiver"). Federal employees are excluded from coverage because Title VII was intended to be the exclusive remedy for discrimination against federal employers. *Brown*, 425 U.S. at 834-35. However, in contrast to § 1983, § 1981(c) has not been limited to suits against only those private employers whose conduct constitutes state action. *Runyon v. McCrary*, 427 U.S. 160, 173 (1976) (applying § 1981 to private, commercially operated nonsectarian schools, and noting that § 1981 "reaches private conduct").

D. IMPORTANT NOTE: INTERRELATION OF CLAIMS UNDER TITLE VII, SECTION 1981, AND SECTION 1983

There are a number of differences between these three statutes that affect when and how plaintiffs may use each one. This section begins with an overview of important distinctions to consider when deciding which claims a client may bring and then describes the concurrent applications of the statutes in pairs.

1. Important Distinctions

There are four significant distinctions an employment attorney must keep in mind when deciding whether to bring a claim under § 1981, § 1983, or Title VII. The first and most significant of these distinctions is whether the defendant employer is a public or private institution. Some government employees may bring suit under all three statutes, subject to the jurisdictional restrictions described below. Private sector employees have a more restricted set of options. Section 1983 only applies to private sector discrimination if the employer's conduct meets the "state action" requirement described above. Few private employees have access to this statute as a result. On the other hand, while Title VII applies to private employers, its provisions place several restrictions on the definition of "employer." Section 2000e(b) states that employers must be "engaged in an industry affecting commerce who has fifteen or more employees for each working day in each of twenty or more calendar weeks in the current or preceding calendar year." 42 U.S.C. § 2000e(b). Lastly, § 1981 applies to a broad range of private sector employees, 42 U.S.C. § 1981(c), but covers a narrower type of discriminatory conduct when compared to the other two statutes, 42 U.S.C. § 1981(a). Plaintiffs have a claim under § 1981 only if the discrimination is based on race, ancestry, or ethnicity.

A second important distinction under these statutes is between state or local and federal government employers. Title VII is the exclusive remedy for a federal employee for discrimination based on those characteristics covered by Title VII's provisions. *Brown*, 425 U.S. at 834-35. All of these statutes are available to redress discrimination by state and local government employers, subject to any restrictions described above.

Third, the statutes require distinct forms of proof. Under Title VII, a plaintiff may demonstrate a violation through either a disparate impact or a disparate treatment claim. 42 U.S.C. § 2000e-2(k); *McDonnell Douglas Corp. v. Green*, 411 U.S. 792, 802-04 (1973). Plaintiffs have the advantage of a comparatively easier standard of proof under this statute as a result. *Sims v. Mulcahy*, 902 F.2d 524, 538 (7th Cir. 1990). In contrast, §§ 1981 and 1983 require proof that the employer acted with discriminatory intent. *Gen. Bldg. Contractors Ass'n, Inc. v. Pennsylvania*, 458 U.S. 375, 388 (1982); *Washington v. Davis*, 426 U.S. 229, 239 (1976). Under either statute, intentional discrimination may be established through the direct or indirect method as articulated in *McDonnell Douglas*, 411 U.S. at 802-04. *Pilditch v. Bd. of Educ. of Chi.*, 3 F.3d 1113, 1116 (7th Cir. 1993); Ivan E. Bodensteiner, *§ 1981: Equal Rights Under the Law* (2008), *available at* LEXSTAT 42 US NITA 1981 (Lexis); 1 Emp. Discrim. Coord. § 7:5.

Fourth, there are several aspects of Title VII that generally distinguish it from the older civil rights statutes. Title VII requires a number of administrative proceedings that go beyond what §§ 1981 and 1983 require. 42 U.S.C. § 2000e-5; *see also Johnson v. Ry. Express Agency*, 421 U.S. 454, 460 (1975) (noting the filing of a Title VII charge and resort to that administrative machinery are not prerequisites for a § 1981 suit). These proceedings may delay the resolution of the case, but they may also help an individual plaintiff obtain more evidence through discovery. Golder, § 4:229. Title VII also offers claimants assistance in investigation, under § 2000e-8, § 2000e-9, and 29 C.F.R § 1601.16, and in obtaining court costs and attorney's fees, § 2000e-5(k). On the other hand, it has a shorter statute of limitations for administrative filings, § 2000e-5(e)(1), and Congress enacted a statutory cap on damages awards in the Civil Rights Act of 1991, § 1981a(b)(3).

2. Relationship between Sections 1981 and 1983

Sections 1981(c) and 1983 both expressly permit civil actions for discrimination committed "under color of" state law. However, the above distinctions between public and private and state and federal employers are particularly significant when deciding between filing suit under these two statutes.

Section 1981 is limited to a prohibition on racial discrimination in making and enforcing contracts. Section 1983 vindicates a more expansive category of rights (all federal rights conferred by federal statutes and the Constitution). Cases involving racial discrimination and contractual relationships are an area of overlap between these two statutes.

Prior to the enactment of the Civil Rights Act of 1991, the Supreme Court held that § 1981 does not create a private right of action to enforce its prohibitions against state actors and "§ 1983 constitutes the exclusive federal remedy for violation of the rights guaranteed in § 1981 by state governmental units." *Jett v. Dallas Indep. Sch. Dist.*, 491 U.S. 701, 733 (1989). Thus, plaintiffs with claims under § 1981 against state actors must enforce them through § 1983, with all the limitations that come with that statute. *Id.* There is some debate between the Ninth Circuit and the remaining appellate courts about the effect of the Civil Rights Act of 1991 on *Jett. See Pittman v. Oregon, Emp't Dep't*, 509 F.3d 1065, 1067-74 (9th Cir. 2007) (summarizing this debate); 1 Emp. Discrim. Coord. § 13:21. In *Federation of African American Contractors v. City of Oakland*, 96 F.3d 1204, 1205 (9th Cir. 1996), the court held that the 1991 Act's amendments to § 1981 allowed a direct cause of action against municipalities and superseded the *Jett* decision. Other circuits addressing the issue have disagreed with the Ninth Circuit and held that the 1991 amendments do not overturn *Jett* or create a cause of action against municipalities or other state actors. *Bolden v. City of Topeka*, 441 F.3d 1129, 1134 (10th Cir. 2006); *Oden v. Oktibbeha Cnty.*, 246 F.3d 458, 463 (5th Cir. 2001); *Butts v. Cnty. of Volusia*, 222 F.3d 891, 892 (11th Cir. 2000); *Dennis v. Cnty. of Fairfax*, 55 F.3d 151, 156 n.1 (4th Cir. 1995). Thus, in the majority of federal circuits, plaintiffs must still enforce their rights under § 1981 through § 1983.

3. Relationship between Title VII and § 1983

The legislative history of Title VII indicates it was not intended to act as the exclusive remedy for discrimination in nonfederal employment. *Johnson*, 421 U.S. at 459. As a result, plaintiffs may bring concurrent claims under Title VII and § 1983 as long as the § 1983 claims are based on violations of federal laws other than Title VII. *Johnston v. Harris Cnty. Flood Control Dist.*, 869 F.2d 1565, 1574 (5th Cir. 1989). For example, an employee could allege violations of independent constitutional rights like the First and Fourteenth Amendments. *See Carrero v. New York City Hous. Auth.*, 890 F.2d 569, 575 (2d Cir. 1989); *Ratliff v. City of Milwaukee*, 795 F.2d 612, 624 (7th Cir. 1986). However, a plaintiff cannot bring a § 1983 action complaining of misconduct that only violates Title VII and no other right that existed prior to Title VII's enactment. *Johnston*, 869 F.2d at 1574; *Day v. Wayne Cnty. Bd. of Auditors*, 749 F.2d 1199, 1204-05 (6th Cir. 1984). In addition, suits under § 1983 "cannot be based on the same factual grounds as those that constitute a violation of Title VII, because to do so would circumvent Title VII's comprehensive administrative remedial scheme." 3 Emp. Discrim. Coord. § 113:71 (citing *Foster v. Wyrick*, 823 F.2d 218 (8th Cir. 1987)). There is a continuing debate between and within the federal circuits as to whether a plaintiff is foreclosed from bringing a § 1983 claim based on discrimination if he or she failed to institute a corresponding Title VII action. *See Keller v. Prince George's Cnty.*, 827 F.2d 952, 962 (4th Cir. 1987) (holding a plaintiff is *not* foreclosed); *Thigpen v. Bibb Cnty., Ga. Sheriff's Dep't*, 223 F.3d 1231, 1239 (11th Cir. 2000) (same) (abrogated on other grounds). *But see Hughes v. Bedsole*, 48 F.3d 1376, 1383 (4th Cir. 1995) (holding a plaintiff *is* foreclosed).

4. Relationship between Title VII and § 1981

Plaintiffs can (and often do) bring concurrent claims under Title VII and § 1981. "[T]he two procedures augment each other and are not mutually exclusive," provided the employer's conduct can be described as discrimination based on race, ethnicity, or ancestry and related to making or enforcing contracts. *See Johnson*, 421 U.S. at 459. In particular, the remedies available under Title VII are coextensive with those available under § 1981. *Id.* There is some debate as to whether courts may consider § 1981 claims based on the same facts as a concurrent Title VII claim, but the majority of courts allow both claims to proceed. 1 Emp. Discrim. Coord. § 1:4. In fact, in some jurisdictions, the jury will determine fact issues common to both sets of claims. 3 Emp. Discrim. Coord. § 105:28. If the case falls within its express terms, § 1981 may be a better choice for the client in light of Title VII's administrative prerequisites, restricted definition of employer, statutory cap on damages, and shorter statute of limitations. Importantly, though, the Civil Rights Act of 1991 prevents a "double recovery" of damages under both Title VII and § 1981. 42 U.S.C. § 1981a(a)(1). Thus, if damages are recoverable under § 1981, they are unavailable to the plaintiff under Title VII.

E. AGE DISCRIMINATION IN EMPLOYMENT ACT OF 1967

The Age Discrimination in Employment Act of 1967 (ADEA) is a comprehensive federal statute enacted to eliminate discrimination in employment on the basis of age.[30] The explicit goals of the ADEA are "to promote employment of older persons based on their ability rather than age [and] to prohibit arbitrary age discrimination in employment." 29 U.S.C. § 621(b) (2012).

The ADEA makes it unlawful for an employer "to fail or refuse to hire or to discharge any individual or otherwise discriminate against any individual with respect to his compensation, terms, conditions, or privileges of employment, because of such individual's age."[31] 29 U.S.C. § 623(a)(1) (2012). This includes any discriminatory decision, even if no actual action is taken on that basis. *Nance v. Maxwell Fed. Credit Union*, 186 F.3d 1338, 1341 (11th Cir. 1999). The Act further prohibits limitations, segregation, or classification of employees on the basis of age that deprive individuals of employment opportunities or "otherwise adversely affect" an individual's "status as an employee." 29 U.S.C. § 623(a)(2). Employers cannot reduce employee wage rates in order to comply with these prohibitions. 29 U.S.C. § 623(a)(3). An additional provision prohibits discrimination "because [an employee] has opposed any practice made unlawful by this section, or because [an employee] has made a charge, testified, assisted, or participated in

---

[30] The Age Discrimination Act of 1975, 42 U.S.C. § 6101 (2012), and Executive Order 11141, Exec. Order No. 11,141, 29 Fed. Reg. 2477 (Feb. 12, 1964), supplement the ADEA's ban on age discrimination in employment by addressing more specific circumstances for programs and activities that receive federal assistance, federal contractors, and subcontractors. State age discrimination laws may also apply.

[31] The Supreme Court has held that this provision does not extend to discrimination against the "relatively young" compared to older employees. *Gen. Dynamics Land Sys., Inc. v. Cline*, 540 U.S. 581, 590 (2004). There is substantial case law discussing what constitutes unlawful employment actions.

any manner in an investigation, proceeding, or litigation under this chapter." 29 U.S.C. § 623(d). More detailed rules apply to employee pension plans, particularly for highly compensated employees. 29 U.S.C. § 623(i), (l), (m). The EEOC is responsible for additional rules and regulations that it considers "necessary or appropriate for carrying out this chapter" and "may establish . . . reasonable exemptions to and from any or all provisions." 29 U.S.C. § 628 (2012); *see also* 29 C.F.R. §§ 1625, 1626 (EEOC guidelines and procedures for claims under the ADEA).

The Act provides for several exceptions. First, employers may take otherwise prohibited action where (1) "age is a bona fide occupational qualification reasonably necessary to the normal operation of the particular business"; (2) "differentiation is based on reasonable factors other than age"; (3) the employer has a "bona fide seniority system"; or (4) the employer is observing "the terms of a bona fide employee benefit plan." 29 U.S.C. § 623(f)(1), (2); 29 C.F.R. §§ 1625.6-1625.8. Second, the Act establishes special rules for firefighters and law enforcement officers. 29 U.S.C. § 623(j). Third, the Act allows for compulsory retirement of employees at 65 years of age who were employed in a "bona fide executive or a high policymaking position" for the two immediately preceding years as long as they are entitled to at least $44,000 in retirement benefits. 29 U.S.C. § 631(c)(1) (2012); 29 C.F.R. § 1625.12(a).

Employees have a private right of action against employers for legal or equitable relief,[32] but an individual may not commence a suit until "60 days after a charge alleging unlawful discrimination has been filed with the Equal Employment Opportunity Commission." 29 U.S.C. § 626(d)(1) (2012). The charge must generally be filed with the EEOC within 180 days "after the alleged unlawful practice occurred." 29 U.S.C. § 626(d)(1)(A), (B); *see also* 29 C.F.R. § 1626.7 (timeliness of charge). Individuals cannot waive their right to bring an action under the ADEA unless that waiver is "knowing and voluntary." 29 U.S.C. § 626(f)(1). However, the Supreme Court has held that the ADEA does not abrogate states' Eleventh Amendment sovereign immunity, and therefore employees cannot directly bring suit against state entities. *Kimel v. Fla. Bd. of Regents*, 528 U.S. 62, 73 (2000).

Covered employers are those "engaged in an industry affecting commerce who has twenty or more employees for each working day in each of twenty or more calendar weeks in the current or preceding calendar year." 29 U.S.C. § 630(b) (2012). A separate and parallel section, § 633a, deals with age discrimination by federal government employers. 29 U.S.C. § 633a (2012). Specific prohibitions against age discrimination also apply to employment agencies, 29 U.S.C. §§ 623(b), 630(c), and labor organizations, 29 U.S.C. §§ 623(c), 630(d), (e).

---

[32] The Supreme Court has held that employees may bring a disparate impact claim, although its use is a bit more restricted than under Title VII. *Meacham v. Knolls Atomic Power Lab.*, 554 U.S. 84, 93 n.9 (2008); *Smith v. City of Jackson*, 544 U.S. 228, 240 (2005).

QUESTIONS AND EXERCISES

1) Review the regulations regarding help wanted notices and advertisements set out at 29 C.F.R. § 1625.4 (2012). Evaluate whether the following advertisements would violate the ADEA.

   a) Do you want to have a great time and make some money? Do you want to have a positive impact in the lives of children? Are you willing to be crazy fun and get down and dirty at work? If so, come join the staff at Camp Kidaround, a year-round after-school program. Hiring now! Must have college degree (preferably in early childhood education), must be familiar with recent literature in child development, and must submit to background check.

   b) Ladies and Gentlemen, Boys and Girls, step right up! Looking for fun, energetic bartenders and wait staff for busy college bar. Must be willing to work nights and weekends. Must enjoy deafeningly loud rock music and rowdy customers. The timid need not apply.

2) The ADEA only provides protection to individuals who have reached the age of 40. 29 U.S.C. § 631(a); 29 C.F.R. § 1625.2 (2012). In enacting the ADEA, Congress provided the following statement of findings and purpose:

   (a) The Congress hereby finds and declares that—

       (1) in the face of rising productivity and affluence, older workers find themselves disadvantaged in their efforts to retain employment, and especially to regain employment when displaced from jobs;

       (2) the setting of arbitrary age limits regardless of potential for job performance has become a common practice, and certain otherwise desirable practices may work to the disadvantage of older persons;

       (3) the incidence of unemployment, especially long-term unemployment with resultant deterioration of skill, morale, and employer acceptability is, relative to the younger ages, high among older workers; their numbers are great and growing; and their employment problems grave;

       (4) the existence in industries affecting commerce, of arbitrary discrimination in employment because of age, burdens commerce and the free flow of goods in commerce.

   (b) It is therefore the purpose of this chapter to promote employment of older persons based on their ability rather than age; to prohibit arbitrary age discrimination in employment; to help employers and workers find ways of meeting problems arising from the impact of age on employment.

29 U.S.C. § 621 (2012). In light of the purpose of the ADEA and the findings listed above, what is the rationale for a bright-line rule that only those who have reached the age of 40 are protected? Should that number be higher? Lower? The

Americans with Disabilities Act provides protection to those "regarded as" having a disability. 42 U.S.C. §12101(a)(1) (2012). Would it make sense to offer similar protection to workers who are "regarded as" being too old for a particular job? If so, why? If not, why not?

F. TITLE I OF THE AMERICANS WITH DISABILITIES ACT (AND THE ADA AMENDMENTS ACT OF 2008)

Title I of the Americans with Disabilities Act of 1990 (ADA), 42 U.S.C. § 12111-17 (2012)[33] makes it illegal for a covered entity to "discriminate against a qualified individual on the basis of disability in regard to job application procedures, the hiring, advancement, or discharge of employees, employee compensation, job training, and other terms, conditions, and privileges of employment." 42 U.S.C. § 12112(a). Under the ADA, a covered entity includes an "employer, employment agency, labor organization, or joint labor-management committee." 42 U.S.C. § 12111(2). In general, employers are covered if they have 15 or more employees during 20 or more calendar weeks of the current or prior year. 42 U.S.C. § 12111(5)(A).

The ADA requires employers to make reasonable accommodations[34] for qualified individuals[35] with a disability except when to do so would cause the employer undue hardship.[36] Under the ADA, an individual can establish that he or she has a disability if the individual:

(A) [has] a physical or mental impairment that substantially limits one or more major life activities of such individual;

(B) [has] a record of such an impairment; or

(C) [is] regarded as having such an impairment.

42 U.S.C. § 12102(1)(A)-(C). Although this definition might seem quite broad, a series of Supreme Court decisions in the late 1990s and early 2000s greatly

---

[33] Prior to the enactment of the ADA, most disability discrimination was governed by the Rehabilitation Act. Courts still use cases and administrative interpretations of the Rehabilitation Act when interpreting provisions of the ADA. Also, the Rehabilitation Act still has extreme relevance for employment discrimination lawyers, as it provides the only protection for federal employees claiming disability discrimination. (The ADA excludes the United States and any corporation wholly owned by the United States from the definition of "employer." § 12111(5)(B)(i).)

[34] Examples of reasonable accommodation include:

> (A) making existing facilities used by employees readily accessible to and usable by individuals with disabilities; and (B) job restructuring, part-time or modified work schedules, reassignment to a vacant position, acquisition or modification of equipment or devices, appropriate adjustment or modifications of examinations, training materials or policies, the provision of qualified readers or interpreters, and other similar accommodations for individuals with disabilities.

§ 12111(9)(A), (B).

[35] A qualified individual is one "who, with or without reasonable accommodation, can perform the essential functions of the employment position that such individual holds or desires." § 12111(8).

[36] According to the ADA, undue hardship is any "action requiring significant difficulty or expense." § 12111(10)(A). The ADA provides a list of factors to help a covered entity determine whether an action requires such difficulty or expense. § 12111(10)(B).

narrowed the scope of coverage under the ADA.[37] In direct response, Congress passed the ADA Amendments Act (ADAAA) of 2008. Although the ADAAA did not alter the general definition of disability in the ADA, the new Act did alter the way in which some key terms in the ADA should be interpreted. The Equal Employment Opportunity Commission (EEOC)[38] has summarized the major changes to the ADA, noting that the ADAAA:

- directs [the] EEOC to revise that portion of its regulations defining the term "substantially limits";
- expands the definition of "major life activities" by including two non-exhaustive lists . . . ;
- states that mitigating measures other than "ordinary eyeglasses or contact lenses" shall not be considered in assessing whether an individual has a disability;
- clarifies that an impairment that is episodic or in remission is a disability if it would substantially limit a major life activity when active;
- changes the definition of "regarded as" so that it no longer requires a showing that the employer perceived the individual to be substantially limited in a major life activity, and instead says that an applicant or employee is "regarded as" disabled if he or she is subject to an action prohibited by the ADA (e.g., failure to hire or termination) based on an impairment that is not transitory and minor; and
- provides that individuals covered only under the "regarded as" prong are not entitled to reasonable accommodation.

Notice Concerning the ADA Amendments Act of 2008, U.S. Equal Emp't Opportunity Comm'n, http://www.eeoc.gov/laws/statutes/adaaa_notice.cfm (last visited March 13, 2013).

Even after the enactment of the ADAAA, employers do have some defenses to liability under the Act. For example, the ADA (as amended) provides that a covered entity "may" have a "defense to a charge of discrimination" even where "qualification standards, tests, or selection criteria" have "screen[ed] out . . . or otherwise den[ied] a job or benefit to an individual with a disability" if the qualification standards, tests, or selection criteria are "job-related and consistent with business necessity." 42 U.S.C. § 12113(a). The covered entity must also show that acceptable "performance cannot be accomplished by reasonable accommodation." *Id.* Likewise, under what is known as the "direct threat exception" to the ADA, the fact "that an individual [might] pose a direct threat to the health or safety of other individuals in the workplace" is an acceptable qualification standard. § 12113(b).

---

[37] *See, e.g., Toyota Motor Mfg. Ky., Inc. v. Williams*, 534 U.S. 184, 198 (2002) (concluding that an individual must establish that an impairment "prevents or severely restricts the individual from doing activities that are of central importance to most people's daily lives . . . [and] must also be permanent or long term"); *Sutton v. United Air Lines, Inc.*, 527 U.S. 471, 475 (1999) (holding that the determination of whether an individual has an impairment covered by the ADA "should be made with reference to measures that mitigate the individual's impairment, including, in this instance, eyeglasses and contact lenses").

[38] The EEOC is the administrative agency charged with administering the ADA and the ADAAA.

G. TITLE II OF THE GENETIC INFORMATION NONDISCRIMINATION ACT

Title II of the Genetic Information Nondiscrimination Act (GINA) addresses discrimination based on genetic information (other than sex or age) in employment. An employer violates GINA if the employer "fail[s] or refuse[s] to hire, or to discharge, any employee, or otherwise . . . discriminate[s] against any employee" regarding "the compensation, terms, or privileges of employment of the employee" because of that employee's genetic information. 42 U.S.C. § 2000ff-1(a)(1) (2012). It is also unlawful "to limit, segregate, or classify . . . employees . . . in any way that would deprive . . . any employee of employment opportunities or otherwise adversely affect the status of the employee as an employee, because of genetic information with respect to the employee." 42 U.S.C. § 2000ff-1(a)(2).

In most cases, an employer may not attempt to acquire genetic information about an employee or his or her family members. 42 U.S.C. § 2000ff-1(b). Limited exceptions include (but are not limited to) situations in which an employer has made "inadvertent" requests or had made requests to comply with federal or state family and medical leave laws. 42 U.S.C. § 2000ff-1(b)(1), (3). Employers also do not violate GINA by purchasing "commercially and publicly available" documents that contain family medical history (except where those documents are found in court records or medical databases). 42 U.S.C. § 2000ff-1(b)(4).

Because there are limited situations in which it is permissible for employers to gain access to genetic information of employees, GINA provides explicit guidance regarding confidentiality of genetic information. 42 U.S.C. § 2000ff-5 (2012).

QUESTION

GINA explicitly provides that a disparate impact cause of action is not available for genetic discrimination claims. 42 U.S.C. § 2000ff-7(a) (2012). Given your understanding of the disparate impact theory, what reason might Congress have for providing such a limitation? Notwithstanding the explicit exclusion of disparate impact claims under GINA, Congress did provide that "6 years after May 21, 2008," a "Genetic Nondiscrimination Study Commission" must be established "to review the developing science of genetics and to make recommendations to Congress regarding whether to provide a disparate impact cause of action under [GINA]." 42 U.S.C. § 2000ff-7(b). Does this provision provide any insight as to why current legislation does not allow for a disparate impact claim under GINA?

H. PREGNANCY DISCRIMINATION ACT

The Pregnancy Discrimination Act (PDA) was enacted in 1978. It appeared in the form of an amendment to Title VII. The PDA makes clear that it is impermissible to discriminate (or retaliate) against a woman "on the basis of pregnancy, childbirth, or related medical conditions." 42 U.S.C. § 2000e(k) (2012). Under the statute, an employer is not required to pay for health insurance benefits covering abortion "except where the life of the mother would be endangered if the fetus were carried to term, or except where medical complications have arisen from an abortion." *Id.*

I. FAMILY MEDICAL LEAVE ACT

The Family Medical Leave Act (FMLA) requires employers to provide 12 weeks of unpaid[39] leave during a 12-month period[40] to employees for eligible medical reasons. 29 U.S.C. § 2612(a)(1) (2012). These reasons include (1) the birth of a child; (2) the adoption of a child or placement of a foster child; (3) the need to care for a parent, child, or spouse with a serious health condition; and (4) the inability to work due to the employee's own serious health condition. 29 U.S.C. § 2612(a)(1)(A)-(D); *see also Laro v. New Hampshire*, 259 F.3d 1, 9 (1st Cir. 2001) (specifying the four situations). The FMLA also offers leave for qualifying exigencies arising out of active duty in the Armed Forces. 29 U.S.C. § 2612(a)(1)(E). Covered employers include private employers and public agencies "engaged in [or affecting] commerce . . . who employ[] 50 or more employees for each working day during each of 20 or more calendar workweeks." 29 U.S.C. § 2611(4)(A)(i); 29 C.F.R. § 825.104 (2012).[41] To be eligible for leave, an employee must be employed for at least 12 months and at least 1,250 hours at a worksite where 50 or more employees are employed within 75 miles of the worksite. 29 U.S.C. § 2611(2)(A), (B); 29 C.F.R. § 825.110(a)(1)-(3).

Section 2601(b) lists several employment discrimination-related statutory purposes for the Act, including promoting equal employment for women and men and minimizing "the potential for employment discrimination on the basis of sex by ensuring that leave is available for eligible medical reasons and . . . for compelling family reasons, on a gender-neutral basis." 29 U.S.C. § 2601(b)(4) (2012). In light of that, the Act makes it "unlawful for any employer to interfere with, restrain, or deny the exercise of or the attempt to exercise, any right provided under this subchapter." 29 U.S.C. § 2615(a)(1) (2012). Employers also may not discriminate against any individual who "oppos[es] any practice made unlawful by this subchapter." 29 U.S.C. § 2615(a)(2); *see also* 29 U.S.C. § 2615(b)(1)-(3) (making unlawful interference with proceedings or inquiries related to the subchapter). Employees have a private right of action against employers for damages, interest, and other equitable relief. 29 U.S.C. § 2617(a) (2012); 29 C.F.R. § 825.400(a) (2012). The Secretary of Labor may also bring a civil suit. 29 U.S.C. § 2617(b)(1)-(3).

The Supreme Court has upheld the FMLA provisions for leave to care for family members as a valid abrogation of state sovereign immunity, and thus state

---

[39] A pending bill in the House would amend the FMLA so that four of the 12 weeks become paid leave for a federal employee. Federal Employees Paid Parental Leave Act of 2011, H.R. 616, 112th Cong. (2011).
[40] The DOL has set out four methods for determining the 12-month period. 29 U.S.C. § 825.200(b)(1)-(4).
[41] The relevant regulations for the FMLA can be found beginning at 29 C.F.R. § 825.100 (2012).

employees may bring suit against state employers for violations. *Nev. Dep't of Human Res. v. Hibbs*, 538 U.S. 721, 726-27 (2003). With regard to the "self-care" provision, § 2612(a)(1)(D), the federal circuits have uniformly held Congress did not validly abrogate state sovereign immunity because its findings related to gender-based discrimination provide a rationale for the family leave provisions, but not the personal medical leave provision. *See, e.g., Laro*, 259 F.3d at 16.[42] Instead, according to these courts, the self-care provision was intended to "protect families from economic dislocation caused by a family member losing his or her job due to a serious medical problem" and discrimination on that basis. *Id.* at 12.

J. EQUAL PAY ACT

The Equal Pay Act (EPA) is part of the Fair Labor Standards Act (FLSA). The EPA prohibits compensation discrimination on the basis of sex by public and private employers. 29 U.S.C. § 206(d) (2012).[43] Its provisions are enforced by the Equal Employment Opportunity Commission (EEOC) and not the Department of Labor (DOL), 29 C.F.R. 1621.1 (2012), although the DOL does offer policy statements regarding implementation of and exemptions from the FLSA in various industries, 29 C.F.R. §§ 775-800 (2012). The EPA has the "same basic coverage as the FLSA" and includes employers whose employees are "engaged in commerce or in the handling of goods that have moved in commerce" or "production of goods for commerce." 29 C.F.R. §§ 1620.1(a), (b), 1620.2, 1620.3 (2012). Men and women are covered equally. 29 C.F.R. § 1620.1(c). It includes labor unions to the extent they are employers, 29 U.S.C. § 206(d)(4), but not lawsuits against the union by members as members, *Koski v. Midwest Printing Co.*, No. 4-85-1523, 1986 WL 6099, at *2 (D. Minn. Mar. 25, 1986).

Discrimination under the EPA is judged based on the "equal work standard," which makes it unlawful for an employer to pay "wages to employees . . . at a rate less than the rate at which he pays wages to employees of the opposite sex . . . for equal work on jobs the performance of which requires equal skill, effort, and responsibility, and which are performed under similar working conditions." 29 U.S.C. § 206(d)(1). This standard is based on actual job performance and content rather than job titles, classifications, or descriptions. *Rodriguez v. SmithKline Beecham*, 224 F.3d 1, 7 (1st Cir. 2000); *Stopka v. Alliance of Am. Insurers*, 141 F.3d 681, 685 (7th Cir. 1998). Both male and female employees must separately demonstrate equal skill, effort, and responsibility, and failure to do so is fatal to a lawsuit. 29 C.F.R. § 1620.14(a). Employees of different sexes must be compared using particular individuals and not hypothetical employees. *Houck v. Va. Polytechnic Inst. & State Univ.*, 10 F.3d 204, 206 (4th Cir. 1993). Wages include all

---

[42] Other circuit court cases are *Nelson v. Univ. of Tex. at Dallas*, 535 F.3d 318, 321 (5th Cir. 2008); *Miles v. Bellfontaine Habilitation Ctr.*, 481 F.3d 1106, 1107 (8th Cir. 2007); *Toeller v. Wis. Dep't of Corr.*, 461 F.3d 871, 879 (7th Cir. 2006); *Touvell v. Ohio Dep't of Mental Retardation & Dev. Disabilities*, 422 F.3d 392, 400 (6th Cir. 2005); *Brockman v. Wyo. Dep't of Family Servs.*, 342 F.3d 1159, 1164-65 (10th Cir. 2003); *Hale v. Mann*, 219 F.3d 61, 69 (2d Cir. 2000).

[43] Title VII, 42 U.S.C. § 2000e-2(a)(1) (2012), the ADEA, 29 U.S.C. § 623(a)(1) (2012), and the ADA, 42 U.S.C. § 12112(a) (2012), also prohibit compensation discrimination.

forms of compensation "irrespective of the time of payment" or what the payment is called, which includes benefits. 29 C.F.R. §§ 1620.10, 1620.11(a).

Employers are not permitted to reduce the wages of any employee in order to comply with these obligations. 29 U.S.C. § 206(d)(1); *see also Hodgson v. Miller Brewing Co.*, 457 F.2d 221, 227 (7th Cir. 1972) (noting that the EPA "does not authorize courts to equalize wages merely because they find that two substantially different jobs are worth the same monetarily to the employer"). However, the statute does provide exceptions that permit pay disparities where the differential is based on a bona fide seniority system,[44] merit system,[45] incentive system, or factor other than sex.[46] 29 U.S.C. § 206(d)(1). Plaintiff employees can recover liquidated damages equal to the amount of back pay due just like other violations of the FLSA. 29 U.S.C. § 216(b) (held unconstitutional on unrelated Eleventh Amendment grounds by *Alden v. Maine*, 527 U.S. 706, 712 (1999)). These types of damages are recoverable directly from the employer. 29 C.F.R. § 1620.33(b).

K. EMPLOYEE POLYGRAPH PROTECTION ACT

The Employee Polygraph Protection Act (EPPA) governs the use of lie detector tests by "employer[s] engaged in or affecting commerce or in the production of goods for commerce." 29 U.S.C. § 2002 (2012); *see also* 29 C.F.R. §§ 801.1-801.75 (regulations governing the application of the EPPA). The EPPA makes it unlawful for employers to rely on such tests in four ways, two of which concern general use and two of which deal with discrimination. 29 U.S.C. § 2002(1)-(4). First, employers may not "directly or indirectly . . . require, request, suggest, or cause any employee or prospective employee to take or submit to any lie detector test." 29 U.S.C. § 2002(1). They also may not "use, accept, refer to, or inquire concerning the results of any lie detector test of any employee or prospective employee." 29 U.S.C. § 2002(2).

Subsections (3) and (4) of the statute prohibit discrimination against an employee for actions related to a lie detector test. Specifically, employers may not "discharge, discipline, discriminate against in any manner, or deny employment or promotion to, or threaten to take any such action against . . . any employee

---

[44] Such systems must be based on length of service and seniority standards must be applied on a sex neutral basis. 29 C.F.R. 1620.13(c); *see also Mitchell v. Jefferson Cnty. Bd. of Educ.*, 936 F.2d 539, 545-47 (11th Cir. 1991) (rejecting a seniority system which did not reflect the length of employment, and remanding case to district court to determine whether female plaintiff and male coworker performed "equal work" as defined by the EPA).

[45] This can mean a system of advancement of reward for merit, not a regularly evaluated written set of job descriptions. *Morgado v. Birmingham-Jefferson Cnty. Civil Def. Corps.*, 706 F.2d 1184, 1188 (11th Cir. 1983).

[46] The Supreme Court has stated this exception refers to a "bona fide job rating system" that does not discriminate on the basis of sex. *Washington County v. Gunther*, 452 U.S. 161, 171 (1981). Thus, this exception is different from a merit-based system because merit systems evaluate employee job *performance* while job rating systems evaluate and classify *jobs*. Empl. Discrim. Coord. § 26:19.

or prospective employee"[47]: (a) where that employee "refuses, declines, or fails to take or submit to any lie detector test"; (b) "on the basis of the results of a lie detector test"; or (c) because such employee "exercise[s] . . . any rights afforded by [the statute]," including the right to file a complaint or testify in an action under this section. 29 U.S.C. § 2002(3)(A)-(B), (4)(A)-(C). In such a lawsuit, an employee must establish discrimination using either the "pretext" framework from *McDonnell Douglas Corp. v. Green*, 411 U.S. 792, 802-804 (1973) or the "mixed-motive" model from *Price Waterhouse v. Hopkins*, 490 U.S. 228, 246-47 (1989) (plurality opinion). *Worden v. SunTrust Banks, Inc.*, 549 F.3d 334, 341-42 (4th Cir. 2008). It is improper for lie detector test results to be even one factor in a termination or hiring decision. *Id.* at 341. Thus, employers' ability to discriminate against employees on the basis of lie detector testing is extremely limited, and employers must pay attention to its prohibitions or face the risk of civil suits and penalties. 29 U.S.C. § 2005(a), (c); 29 C.F.R. § 801.40-801.43. In *Worden*, however, the employer was held not liable for discrimination under the EPPA where it terminated its former employee and proved it would have fired him even without knowledge of the results of two polygraph examinations. *Worden*, 549 F.3d at 343.

There are a number of significant exemptions. Importantly, the Act does not apply to "the United States Government, any State or local government, or any political subdivision of a State or local government. 29 U.S.C. § 2006(a). Likewise, other exemptions exist regarding those employed (including consultants and contractors) to aid in the government's national defense and security programs; those employed as FBI contractors; an employer conducting an "ongoing investigation involving economic loss or injury to the employer's business"; those employed in some types of security services; and those involved in drug security, theft, or diversion investigations. 29 U.S.C. § 2006(b)-(f). The EPPA also does not preempt any state or local laws that also prohibit lie detector tests or are more restrictive of their use in the workplace. 29 U.S.C. § 2009.

L. JURY SYSTEMS IMPROVEMENT ACT

The Jury Systems Improvement Act of 1978 makes it unlawful for any employer to "discharge, threaten to discharge, intimidate, or coerce any permanent employee by reason of such employee's jury service, or the attendance or scheduled attendance in connection with such service, in any court of the United States."[48] 28 U.S.C. § 1875(a) (2012). Employers must ensure the employee is aware she can report for jury duty without fear of reprisal. *Lucas v. Matlack*,

---

[47] The employer also cannot discriminate against a former employee because the employee has exercised any of her rights under the EPPA. 29 C.F.R. § 801.8(c) (2012). An example of such discrimination against a former employee would be providing an unwarranted negative job reference to a future prospective employer.
[48] A district court found an employee hired for a 13-month term appointment was "permanent" under this Act where the employer regularly renewed term appointments and the employee was only absent because she served on a jury, but limited its decision to those facts. *Madison v. District of Columbia*, 604 F. Supp. 2d 17, 20 (D.D.C. 2009).

Inc., 851 F. Supp. 225, 228 (N.D. W.Va. 1993); *Rogers v. Comprehensive Rehab. Assocs., Inc.*, 808 F. Supp. 493, 498 (D.S.C. 1992). Employers may require reasonable notice before an employee will be absent for jury duty, as long as a notice requirement is not used as a pretext for termination because of jury service. *In re Scott*, 155 F.R.D. 10, 12-13 (D. Mass. 1994). For example, in *In re Webb*, 586 F. Supp. 1480, 1483 (N.D. Ohio 1984), an employer was found liable for discrimination under the Act where the defendant employer referred to the grand jury and the employee's service on it in a highly derogatory manner, reduced the employee's hours from 40 to 26 while he served, terminated him, and made statements about his poor attitude and work performance that were directly contradicted by all other employees at the company. Similarly, the Eleventh Circuit found a supervisor intimidated or coerced an employee where he made hostile remarks about jury service, was angry about the employee's absences despite receiving advance notice, and subjected the employee to reprimands about the service. *Hill v. Winn-Dixie Stores, Inc.*, 934 F.2d 1518, 1526-27 (11th Cir. 1991) (superseded by statute on other grounds).

This Act has clear implications for employment discrimination, and employers must pay attention to the Act's proscriptions in order to avoid liability for damages like wages or lost benefits, an injunction from further violations, forced reinstatement of an improperly discharged employee, civil penalties of up to $5,000 per employee, or required community service. 28 U.S.C. § 1875(b)(1)-(3). Employers may face further costs if an individual claiming a violation of this Act applies to the district court in the district in which the employer maintains a place of business, the court appoints counsel to represent the employee, the employee prevails, and the court awards the employee a reasonable attorney's fee. 28 U.S.C. § 1875(d)(1), (2). Under these circumstances, the court may "tax a defendant employer, as costs payable to the court, the attorney's fees and expenses incurred on behalf of a prevailing employee where such costs were expended by the court pursuant to [§ 1875(d)(1)]."[49] 28 U.S.C. § 1875(d)(2). However, at least one circuit has held that an employee may not recover compensatory damages for emotional distress under this Act. *Shea v. Cnty. of Rockland*, 810 F.2d 27, 28 (2d Cir. 1987).

The basic exceptions to jury service for any employee still apply, though, and in the jury selection process a court may look at whether the employee's absence for a proceeding that is anticipated to last longer for thirty days will cause the employer "severe economic hardship." 28 U.S.C. § 1869(j) (2012).

---

[49] There is a minor split among district courts about whether the court may award a plaintiff employee attorney's fees where the counsel was not appointed by the court "upon finding probable merit in such claim" under § 1875(d)(1). The Northern District of Ohio has held that counsel must be appointed by the court to receive attorney's fees, *In re Webb*, 586 F. Supp. at 1485, while the District Courts for the District of Columbia and the Central District of Illinois have awarded attorney's fees outside of a court appointment on the basis of probable merit. *Jones v. Marriott Corp.*, 609 F. Supp. 577, 579 (D.D.C. 1985); *Flynn v. Am. Fire & Elec. Indus., Inc.*, 817 F. Supp. 63, 64 (C.D. Ill. 1993).

M. DRUG-FREE WORKPLACE ACT

The Drug-Free Workplace Act ("the Act") [50] applies only to federal contractors and federal grant recipients. 41 U.S.C. §§ 8102-06 (2012). It requires them to take certain actions to provide a drug-free workplace as a precondition of receiving a contract or grant from a federal agency.[51] Contractors are "the department, division, or other unit of a person responsible for the performance under the contract" with the federal government. 41 U.S.C. § 8101(a)(1) (2012).[52] "Grantees" are similarly the unit responsible for performance under a grant of federal funds. 41 U.S.C. § 8101(a)(8). Affected entities are further divided into "individuals" and non-individual employers. 41 U.S.C. §§ 8102(a), (b), 8103(a), (b). If the employer does not qualify as an individual, it must provide a statement notifying employees that it provides a drug-free workplace; establish a drug-free awareness program; and require employee compliance with the employer's statement. 41 U.S.C. §§ 8102(a)(1)(A)-(D), 8103(a)(1)(A)-(D). Employees must notify the employer of any "criminal drug statute conviction for a violation occurring in the workplace," and the employer must then notify the relevant contracting agency, sanction the employee, or require them to participate in rehabilitation. 41 U.S.C. §§ 8102(a)(1)(D)-(F), 8103(a)(1)(D)-(F). Contractors that fail to meet these requirements, make a false certification, or have an excessive number of employee convictions will be suspended, terminated, or debarred from future opportunities. 41 U.S.C. §§ 8102(b), 8103(b); 29 C.F.R. § 98.600-98.645 (2012) (describing the federal government-wide suspension and debarment procedures). However, the Act does not require contractors or grantees to actually conduct drug tests of their employees. Governmentwide Implementation of the Drug-Free Workplace Act of 1988, 54 Fed. Reg. 4946-01 (Jan. 31, 1989).

The Act is relevant to employment discrimination in light of the ADA's prohibition on discrimination against persons perceived as having an impairment, which may include a history of drug or alcohol abuse. The ADA does not permit employers to discriminate against former drug users or alcoholics in hiring or other employment practices. However, the ADA is explicit that employers can require employees to conform to the requirements of the Drug-Free Workplace Act. 42 U.S.C. § 12114(c)(3) (2012). It also explicitly excludes current illegal drug users from its protections. 42 U.S.C. § 12114(a).

---

[50] 41 U.S.C. §§ 8101-06 (2012). Congress recently amended the Drug-Free Workplace Act in a reorganization of Title 41 of the U.S. Code enacted on January 4, 2011. *See* Public Contracts – Enact Certain Laws, Pub. L. No. 111-350, 124 Stat. 3677 (2011). Congress made no substantive changes to the Act, but merely made some minor wording changes and relocated the definition section at the beginning of the relevant series of subsections. 41 U.S.C. § 8101 (2012). The original citation was 41 U.S.C. §§ 701-706 (relevant only as an aid to researching under the Act).

[51] Each federal agency has its own a set of regulations implementing this Act, although they are generally identical. The general Office of Management and Budget Governmentwide Guidance on requirements for grants and assistance for all federal agencies can be found at 2 C.F.R. §§ 182.5-182.40 (2012). For similar regulations for public contracts, see 41 C.F.R. § 60-741.24 (2012).

[52] Contracts "for the procurement of commercial items" as defined in 41 U.S.C. § 103 are excluded from these provisions. 41 U.S.C. § 8102(a)(1).

N. FAIR LABOR STANDARDS ACT

The Fair Labor Standards Act (FLSA)[53] was originally enacted in 1938. As the title of the FLSA suggests, the statute was designed to ameliorate "labor conditions detrimental to the maintenance of the minimum standard of living necessary for health, efficiency, and general well-being of workers." 29 U.S.C. § 202(a) (2012). The FLSA covers a broad array of fair wage issues, including issues related to minimum wage,[54] standards for payment of overtime, restrictions on child labor, and equal pay provisions.[55]

To be covered under the FLSA, a business must meet a set of very specific requirements. First, the business must qualify as an "enterprise." The term "enterprise" is defined as "related activities performed (either through unified operations or common control) by any person or persons for a common business purpose, and includes all such activities whether performed in one or more establishments."[56] Second, a business must have two or more employees engaged in commerce.[57] Third, a business must meet a dollar volume test. In order to meet this test, the business must have $500,000 in either annual gross volume of sales made or business done.[58]

When determining whether a business will count as a covered enterprise, the practitioner should note that several types of businesses will qualify for enterprise coverage without having to meet either the commerce or dollar amount tests. Specifically, hospitals, nursing homes, schools, colleges, universities, and public agencies fall into this category.[59]

Although coverage under the FLSA is quite broad, there are employees who are exempt from coverage. One of the most litigated exemptions involves the exemption of white collar employees. Under 29 U.S.C. § 213(a)(1) (2012), those employed "in a bona fide executive, administrative, or professional capacity" are exempt from the minimum wage and overtime requirements of the FLSA. Other types of employees exempt from both minimum wage and overtime requirements include:

- seasonal employees of amusement and recreational businesses (29 U.S.C. § 213(a)(3));
- fishing employees (29 U.S.C. § 213(a)(5));
- certain agricultural employees (29 U.S.C. § 213(a)(6));
- employees exempted by special orders (29 U.S.C. § 213(a)(7));
- seamen on foreign vessels (29 U.S.C. § 213(a)(12));

---

[53] 29 U.S.C. §§ 201-19 (2012).
[54] A pending amendment to the FLSA would establish a new minimum wage for tipped employees. *See* H.R. 631, 112th Cong. (2011).
[55] 1 Mark A. Rothstein, et al., Employment Law 487 (3d ed. 2004).
[56] 29 U.S.C. § 203(r)(1).
[57] 29 U.S.C § 203(s)(1)(A)(i).
[58] 29 U.S.C. § 203(s)(1)(A)(ii).
[59] 29 U.S.C. § 203(s)(1)(B), (C).

- domestic employees (29 U.S.C. § 213(a)(15));
- employees of small newspapers (29 U.S.C. § 213(a)(8));
- certain switchboard operators (29 U.S.C. § 213(a)(10)); and
- skilled workers in the computer field (29 U.S.C. § 213(a)(17)).

Another group of employees are exempt only from minimum wage requirements. For example, with some limitations, workers under the age of 20 can be paid less than minimum wage for the first 90 days of employment. 29 U.S.C. § 206(g) (2012). Yet other categories of employees are exempt from overtime provisions only. 29 U.S.C. § 213(b) (listing numerous exemptions).

The Wage and Hour Division of the DOL administers the FLSA.[60] Regulations interpreting the FLSA are found in the Code of Federal Regulations at 29 C.F.R. §§ 776-94 (2012).

O. IMMIGRATION REFORM AND CONTROL ACT

The Immigration Reform and Control Act (IRCA) was enacted in 1986 as an amendment to the Immigration and Nationality Act.[61] The law covers any "person or other entity" that hires, recruits, or refers an alien for a fee in the United States. 8 U.S.C. § 1324a(1)(A) (2012). The IRCA provides specific penalties for covered employers who discriminate against authorized aliens on the basis of national origin. Primary responsibility for enforcement of the IRCA rests with the Department of Homeland Security. Regulations interpreting the IRCA are found at 8 C.F.R. § 274a.1-.14 (2012).

P. NATIONAL LABOR RELATIONS ACT

Labor law (laws governing the relationship between employers, unions, and unionized employees) is generally outside the scope of this book. However, you should be aware that there are specific laws governing discrimination in the union context. The National Labor Relations Act (NLRA),[62] 29 U.S.C. §§ 151-69 (2012), for example, contains provisions prohibiting discrimination or retaliation against unionized employees (or those attempting to unionize). Section 157 of the NLRA gives employees the right to self-organize or join labor organizations. Section 158 enumerates the unfair practices of both employers and unions. Under that section, it is illegal to "discriminat[e] in regard to hire or tenure of employment or any term or condition of employment" in order "to encourage or discourage membership in any labor organization." § 158(a)(3). Retaliatory discharge or discrimination is also prohibited. § 158(a)(4). Importantly, discrimination on the

---

[60] 29 U.S.C. § 204(a).
[61] *See* 8 U.S.C. §§ 1324a-1324b (2012).
[62] The NLRA is administered by the National Labor Relations Board (NLRB), an independent federal agency created by Congress in 1935. *See* 29 U.S.C. § 153 (2012).

part of the labor organizations themselves is also prohibited. For example, it is unlawful for a labor organization:

> to cause or attempt to cause an employer to discriminate against an employee . . . or to discriminate against an employee with respect to whom membership in such organization has been denied or terminated on some ground other than his failure to tender the periodic dues and the initiation fees uniformly required as a condition of acquiring or retaining membership.

§ 158(b)(2).

Q. UNIFORMED SERVICES EMPLOYMENT AND REEMPLOYMENT RIGHTS ACT

The Uniformed Services Employment and Reemployment Rights Act, 38 U.S.C. §§ 4301-35 (2012) (USERRA), applies to any employer with employees who are or have been affiliated with any of the uniformed services, including the National Guard. Congress explicitly enacted USERRA in part "to prohibit discrimination against persons because of their service in the uniformed services." § 4301(a)(3). Under USERRA, an employee who has ever served or applied to serve in any uniformed service "shall not be denied initial employment, reemployment, retention in employment, promotion, or any benefit of employment by an employer on the basis of" the employee's membership or application for service in any uniformed service. § 4311(a). The employee only has to prove that the employee's membership or application for service was "a motivating factor" in the adverse employment action. § 4311(c)(1). If the employee is able to meet this burden, the employer has the opportunity to "prove that the action would have been taken in the absence of such membership [or] . . . application for service." *Id.* USERRA also contains provisions protecting employees from retaliation for opposing violations of USERRA or participating in investigations under the law. § 4311(b). USERRA is administered by the DOL's Veterans' Employment and Training Service.

R. OCCUPATIONAL SAFETY AND HEALTH ACT

The Occupational Safety and Health Act, 29 U.S.C. §§ 651-78 (2012) (the OSH Act) is the most important federal law governing on-the-job safety and health for employees. The OSH Act is administered by the Occupational Safety and Health Administration (OSHA), an agency within the DOL. Section 654 of the OSH Act requires employers to furnish employees with "employment and a place of employment which are free from recognized hazards that are causing or are likely to cause death or serious physical harm." (This clause is known as the "General Duty Clause" and is often used when more specific standards are not found in the regulations.) Detailed and complex regulations regarding workplace safety are set out at 29 C.F.R. §§ 1902.1 -1990 (2012). The OSH Act specifically prohibits discrimination by an employer against an employee for reporting a violation or exercising rights under the OSH Act. 29 U.S.C. § 660(c).

S. EMPLOYEE RETIREMENT INCOME SECURITY ACT

The Employee Retirement Income Security Act, 29 U.S.C. §§ 1001 *et seq.* (2012) (ERISA), covers any private retirement, health, and other welfare benefit plans (e.g., life, disability and apprenticeship plans) maintained by an employer or employee organization engaged in commerce. 29 U.S.C. § 1003. ERISA is a very long and complicated statute, and often law firms employ specific attorneys who specialize in employee benefits law to address ERISA and other benefits issues. Generally, ERISA establishes certain duties for plan administrators to disclose and report particular aspects of their plans to plan members and to the Secretary of Labor. ERISA also sets certain funding requirements for employee benefits plans and requires plan administrators (and their fiduciaries) to act prudently to safeguard the assets in the plan, to meet their fiduciary duties, and to treat plan members fairly. Just as with many other statutes, ERISA protects employees from discrimination or other adverse action based on their reporting of a violation of ERISA. 29 U.S.C. § 1140. ERISA is administered by the DOL, and ERISA regulations can be found at 29 C.F.R. § 2509 (2012).

T. HEALTH INSURANCE PORTABILITY AND ACCOUNTABILITY ACT

The Health Insurance Portability and Accountability Act of 1996 (HIPAA), 42 U.S.C. §§ 300gg to 300gg-28 (2012), arose as an amendment to ERISA. The law applies to employers or health insurance providers that run a group plan that covers 2 or more people. § 300gg-21. The non-discrimination provisions of HIPAA prohibit plan providers from discriminating against individuals based on their health status. In general, a health insurance plan provided by an employer "may not establish rules for eligibility . . . [or] continued eligibility . . . based on" the individual's (or a dependent of the individual's) "health status, medical condition, claims experience, receipt of health care, medical history, genetic information, evidence of insurability . . . [or] disability." § 300gg-1(a)(1)(A-H). An employer offering health insurance coverage under a group health plan may also not discriminate by making some pay higher premiums than others based on any "health status-related factor." § 300gg-1(b). HIPAA also limits employers' abilities to exclude individuals from health plans due to preexisting conditions. The DOL provides a useful information guide to the non-discrimination provisions of HIPAA, located at http://www.dol.gov/ebsa/faqs/faq_hipaa_ND.html (last visited April 2, 2013).

U. FEDERAL BANKRUPTCY CODE

The United States Bankruptcy Code contains provisions prohibiting discrimination by employers against those who have filed for bankruptcy. Public employers are covered by 11 U.S.C. § 525(a) (2012), which states:

> a governmental unit may not . . . deny employment to, terminate the employment of, or discriminate with respect to employment against, a person that is or has been a debtor under this title or a bankrupt or a debtor under

the Bankruptcy Act, or another person with whom such bankrupt or debtor has been associated, solely because such bankrupt or debtor is or has been a debtor under this title or a bankrupt or debtor under the Bankruptcy Act, has been insolvent before the commencement of the case under this title, or during the case but before the debtor is granted or denied a discharge, or has not paid a debt that is dischargeable in the case under this title or that was discharged under the Bankruptcy Act.

In contrast, private employers are covered by 11 U.S.C. § 525(b), which states that it is illegal for a private employer to:

> terminate the employment of, or discriminate with respect to employment against, an individual who is or has been a debtor under this title, a debtor or bankrupt under the Bankruptcy Act, or an individual associated with such debtor or bankrupt, solely because such debtor or bankrupt—(1) is or has been a debtor under this title or a debtor or bankrupt under the Bankruptcy Act; (2) has been insolvent before the commencement of a case under this title or during the case but before the grant or denial of a discharge; or (3) has not paid a debt that is dischargeable in a case under this title or that was discharged under the Bankruptcy Act.

QUESTIONS

1) Why might an employer legitimately fear hiring or retaining an employee who has filed for bankruptcy? What interests are served by providing protection for debtors?

2) As you may have noticed, the rules differ depending upon whether the employer is a governmental unit or a private entity. What are the key distinctions? Do these distinctions make sense from a policy standpoint? Why or why not?

3) Unlike other types of employment discrimination, where the law prohibits actions that were motivated *at least in part* by discriminatory beliefs, the bankruptcy code only prohibits discrimination where the employment decision occurred "*solely*" because of a debtor's status as a debtor or bankrupt individual. Why did Congress make this distinction? Do you think the requirement strikes the proper balance between debtor and employer interests? If not, how would you change the language of the statute to better address competing policy considerations?

V. FAIR CREDIT REPORTING ACT AND THE CONSUMER CREDIT PROTECTION ACT

Although even most laypeople are aware that consumer credit protection laws exist, very few people are aware that such laws might come into play in the employment discrimination arena. One such law is the Fair Credit Reporting Act, 15 U.S.C. §§ 1681-1681x (2012) (FCRA).[63] This Act is part of the larger Consumer Credit Protection Act (CCPA). 15 U.S.C. §§ 1601-93r (2012). The FCRA applies both to credit reporting agencies and to those who use their reports (including employers). Although employers are permitted to request credit reports of prospective or current employees, employers are limited in the ways in which they may use those reports. For example, § 1681b requires employers to first provide "clear and conspicuous" notice to the prospective employee that a credit report will be ordered for employment purposes, and the employee must agree in writing to allow access to the report. § 1681b(b)(2)(A). Furthermore, the FCRA forbids using a credit report to take an "adverse action" against an employee or prospective employee "based in whole or in part" on the credit report without providing a copy of the report and notifying the consumer of her rights under the FCRA. § 1681b(b)(3)(A). Under § 1681d, an employer who orders an "investigative consumer report" must (1) notify the employee that such a report has been ordered within three days; (2) inform her of the credit reporting agency's contact information; (3) advise her of her FCRA rights; and (4) upon request, describe the scope of the report. § 1681d(a), (b). Finally, when credit reporting agencies compile data for the public record that may make it difficult for a consumer to gain employment, the agencies must notify the consumer of that reporting. § 1681k(a).

Although not directly related to employment discrimination law, the larger CCPA, 15 U.S.C. §§ 1601-93r (2012), also contains provisions with which a good employment lawyer should be familiar. The provisions relevant to employment law involve garnishment of wages. *See* §§ 1671-77. The Wage and Hour Division of the DOL administers these provisions of the CCPA.[64] Section 1673 sets the maximum amount a creditor can garnish from an individual's wages. § 1673(a). Importantly, § 1674 prohibits an employer from terminating any employee whose wages have been garnished due to any one debt. § 1674(a). Employers who willfully violate § 1674 may be fined, imprisoned, or both. §1674(b).

QUESTIONS AND EXERCISES

A potential client has approached you regarding each of the situations outlined below. Review the facts of each scenario and determine whether the potential client has a cause of action based on any of the laws discussed above. If you are unsure whether a law is implicated, determine what additional information you need to make your assessment.

1) Steve, a 35-year-old African American man, was employed as a bartender. He claims that he was subjected to disparaging jokes about his race by his co-workers, and that he was terminated two weeks after complaining to his manager about the jokes. Steve occasionally worked over 40 hours per week,

---

[63] The Federal Trade Commission administers the FCRA along with the CCPA. The Federal Trade Commission's regulations are located at 16 C.F.R. §§ 600-98 (2012).
[64] The relevant regulations are located at 29 C.F.R. § 870 (2012).

but the employee manual includes this provision: "The employee and employer agree that only 40 hours per week will be counted as working time." Finally, Steve did not receive the same raises as female bartenders over the five-year period that he worked for his employer. The other two bartenders, both women, had the title of "head bartender," even though their responsibilities and reporting relationships are essentially the same as those of a bartender.

2) Shirley, a 41-year-old Korean woman, worked as a customer service representative for a telecommunications company for 11 years. An anonymous individual reported to management that Shirley was having an inappropriate relationship with her supervisor, and that the relationship led to Shirley being assigned to a coveted project. As a result of the allegation, Shirley was suspended. She was then reinstated after she was cleared of the allegation, but took three weeks of leave to cope with the stress of the situation. Before the allegation, Shirley worked a regular Monday through Friday shift from 8:00 a.m. to 5:00 p.m. When she returned to work, she was assigned to a Sunday through Thursday 11:00 a.m. to 8:00 p.m. shift. Shirley informed her supervisor that her work assignment was unacceptable because she was a single mom. As an alternative, she was offered a Saturday through Wednesday 10:00 a.m. to 7:00 p.m. shift that was also unacceptable. Shirley was disciplined and eventually terminated when she did not work all of her assigned shifts. Prior to her termination, Shirley overheard a supervisor discussing their employer's plan to save money by "weeding out" longer tenured supervisors to replace them with college graduates who could be hired for a lower salary and without benefits.

3) Anita, a 36-year-old Caucasian woman, was employed as a paralegal for a mid-sized law firm for 10 years. For most of her employment, she received outstanding performance evaluations and merit raises. After both of her sisters developed breast cancer, she decided to undergo genetic testing. The genetic testing revealed a mutation that put her at a higher risk of developing breast cancer. Based on the testing, Anita decided to undergo a preventative mastectomy. During the months after she returned to work, she began receiving negative performance reviews. She was ultimately terminated after taking 10 days off for a second procedure related to the preventative mastectomy. Two months after her termination, she was notified that her insurance claims had been denied because her employer's insurance did not cover procedures for individuals with genetic mutations.

4) Richard, a 27-year-old Argentine citizen, applied for a position as a pizza deliveryman. The application included a "Background Check Disclosure Form" requesting that the applicant authorize a background check, along with a release from any liability related to the background check. Richard was hired and worked for several weeks before he learned that he was not scheduled for any hours. When he asked a manager about the schedule, the manager told him that there was a problem with his application. The manager speculated that the problem was related to his immigration status, and asked Richard whether he was in the United States legally. Richard later received a letter

stating that the employment offer had been withdrawn and his application denied based on the results of the background check.

5) Amy is a 32-year-old Native American who was employed as a public school teacher for three years. During the first two years of Amy's employment, she received good evaluations. At the end of the second year, Amy complained to the principal that the Special Education teachers were not properly monitoring their students. Following Amy's complaint and at the beginning of her third year, the principal conducted a formal classroom observation that resulted in a negative assessment. In addition, the principal accused Amy of excessive absenteeism and poor attendance. Amy's absences were a result of bronchitis, and she submitted documentation of her diagnosis to the school for each of her absences. Amy was terminated at the end of her third year of teaching.

II. STATE STATUTES AND LOCAL ORDINANCES

Although federal law provides many protections for employees suffering from discrimination in the workplace, an effective employment lawyer must be aware that state and local laws prohibiting employment discrimination often provide more protection than their federal counterparts. State anti-discrimination laws cannot narrow the protections and remedies offered by federal statutes or the U.S. Constitution. However, state and local laws may offer protection to a wider range of protected groups. For example, state statutes and local ordinances may offer protection against discrimination based on sexual orientation, political action, marital status, and other categories not traditionally covered by federal anti-discrimination laws.

State and local laws may also provide more protection for employees working for small employers. Recall that many federal laws define "employer" based upon the number of employees working for the employer. State and local laws often cover employers with far fewer employees. Finally, state statutes may provide for a broader range of remedies or have different exhaustion requirements or statutes of limitations.

COMMON LAW CLAIMS IN EMPLOYMENT DISCRIMINATION LAW

Although most employment discrimination law is statutory, employees often bring concurrent tort or contract claims under state law. Plaintiffs may choose to do so for several reasons. First, a plaintiff may have failed to exhaust administrative remedies within the time frame necessary to file a claim under federal or state anti-discrimination laws. Second, as you may recall, many employment discrimination statutes, particularly federal statutes, limit coverage only to employers who have a certain number of employees. Employees working for smaller employers may be forced to file suit only under state anti-discrimination statutes or to file contract or tort claims. Third, the remedies available under a given statutory scheme likely differ from those remedies available in a claim arising in tort or contract. This section briefly discusses some common tort claims that appear in employment discrimination lawsuits.

I. INTENTIONAL INFLICTION OF EMOTIONAL DISTRESS (REFERRED TO IN SOME JURISDICTIONS AS THE "TORT OF OUTRAGE")

One claim often brought in conjunction with employment discrimination lawsuits is a claim for intentional infliction of emotional distress (IIED). The Restatement (Second) of Torts describes IIED as follows: "[o]ne who by extreme and outrageous conduct intentionally or recklessly causes severe emotional distress to another is subject to liability for such emotional distress, and if bodily harm to the other results from it, for such bodily harm." Restatement (Second) of Torts § 46(1) (1965). The Illinois Supreme Court, following the definition found in the Restatement (Second) of Torts § 46, set out the elements commonly required in a claim for IIED:

> First, the conduct involved must be truly extreme and outrageous. Second, the actor must either *intend* that his conduct inflict severe emotional distress, or know that there is at least a high probability that his conduct will cause severe emotional distress. Third, the conduct must in fact cause *severe* emotional distress.

McGrath v. Fahey, 126 Ill. 2d 78, 86 (1988). Although almost every state recognizes IIED as an independent cause of action,[65] and most use the definition as set out in the Restatement, a claim for IIED is generally disfavored. Courts, therefore, set a high bar for recognizing a claim. For example, when determining whether challenged conduct is "extreme and outrageous" enough to sustain a claim, the Restatement has provided that conduct must have "been so outrageous in character, and so extreme in degree, as to go beyond all possible bounds of decency and to be regarded as atrocious, and utterly intolerable in a civilized community." *Hoy v. Angelone*, 554 Pa. 134, 154 (1998) (quoting § 46 cmt. d). Thus, "liability clearly does not extend to mere insults, indignities, threats, annoyances, petty oppressions, or other trivialities." *Id.* (same). Courts have set a similarly high bar for showing that the distress was severe enough. For example, the Illinois Supreme Court noted that "[t]he law intervenes only where the distress inflicted is so severe that no reasonable man could be expected to endure it. The intensity and duration of the distress are factors to be considered in determining its severity." *McGrath*, 126 Ill. 2d at 86 (quoting Restatement (Second) of Torts § 46 cmt. j). Many courts will also require "competent medical evidence" to support a claim of emotional distress. *See, e.g., Hoy*, 554 Pa. at 151 n.10.

II. NEGLIGENT INFLICTION OF EMOTIONAL DISTRESS

An employee is arguably even less likely to be able to establish a claim for negligent infliction of emotional distress (NIED). As is apparent by the name of the tort, the key difference between a claim for IIED and NIED is the lack of an intent requirement in the latter claim. Although negligence might seem easier to establish than intentional conduct, in most employment discrimination cases, demonstrating negligence is likely difficult or impossible. Recall that almost every available employment discrimination claim involves an assertion of intentional conduct on the part of one or more actors. (A disparate impact claim is, of course, an exception, and there are certainly other exceptions to this rule.) For example,

---

[65] The concept of the tort as being an "independent cause of action" means that plaintiffs need not offer another legal violation or injury on which the IIED claim must piggyback. A small number of states, like Pennsylvania, have not expressly recognized a claim for IIED as an independent tort at the state supreme court level. Nevertheless, even in those states, most lower courts recognize IIED as an independent cause of action.

one Illinois state appellate court declined to find that a terminated employee had established a claim for negligent infliction of emotional distress, stating that "[w]here the purported emotional distress has been caused by *intentional* acts committed by a defendant, the plaintiff does not state a cause of action for *negligent* infliction of emotional distress." *Brackett v. Galesburg Clinic Ass'n*, 293 Ill. App. 3d 867, 872 (1997) (citation omitted).

Recall that any type of negligence claim requires four elements: duty, a breach of that duty, causation, and harm. *See Corgan v. Muehling*, 143 Ill. 2d 296, 306 (1991) (citation omitted) (noting that a complaint alleging a negligent act "must set out facts that establish the existence of a duty owed by the defendant to the plaintiff, a breach of that duty, and an injury proximately caused by that breach"). Thus, another key issue in an emotional distress claim sounding in negligence is whether the defendant-employer had a duty to protect the plaintiff-employee from the alleged harm. According to the Illinois Supreme Court, to determine whether a defendant should have a duty to the plaintiff in a negligence action, "a court will look at various policy considerations, such as the likelihood of harm, the gravity of the injury, the burden [on the employer] of guarding against the injury, and the relationship between the parties." *Id.* (citation omitted)

III. FALSE IMPRISONMENT

A false imprisonment claim is another tort commonly alleged by plaintiffs in employment actions, particularly in sexual harassment actions. Generally, in a sexual harassment case, plaintiffs will file suit under Title VII and its state (and perhaps local) counterpart. Under Title VII and many state laws, however, the manager or supervisor committing the actual acts of sexual harassment may not be sued directly. Rather, the plaintiff must sue the employer itself. A false imprisonment claim, however, may be brought against the harasser individually. This allows the plaintiff both the opportunity to join additional defendants and, from a psychological standpoint, to actually find a measure of justice against the actual perpetrator of the harassment. For example, in *Moore v. Sam's Club*, 55 F. Supp. 2d 177, 187 (S.D.N.Y. 1999), a female employee sued her employer after her supervisor allegedly sexually harassed and raped her. She sued Sam's Club under Title VII and the New York Human Rights Law. She also alleged several state law claims against both her employer and her supervisor. The supervisor argued that the false imprisonment claim against him should have been dismissed because the plaintiff-employee failed to allege "that she was threatened or intimidated" or "that the confinement, if any, lasted for any prolonged period of time." *Id.* at 187. The court rejected this argument, noting that "[t]he elements of a cause of action for false imprisonment are: (1) the defendant intended to confine plaintiff; (2) the plaintiff was conscious of the restraint; (3) the plaintiff did not consent to confinement; and (4) the confinement was not otherwise privileged. *Id.* (citing *Parvi v. Kingston*, 362 N.E.2d 960 (1977)). The court emphasized that false imprisonment occurs with "the unlawful detention of the person of another, for any length of time, whereby he is deprived of his personal liberty." *Id.* (quoting *Kajtazi v. Kajtazi*, 488 F.Supp. 15, 18 (E.D.N.Y. 1978)). The court refused to dismiss the false imprisonment claim as to the supervisor because the complaint had alleged that the defendant supervisor made "unwelcomed verbal remarks and physical contacts, including pulling her close to him and attempting to kiss her, pinning her against a filing cabinet, [and] trying to place her hand on his genitals." *Id.* (citing Complaint at 11).

While false imprisonment is one claim that may be brought against individual defendants, it may be more difficult to get some courts to impose liability on a *company* for the intentional torts of its employees. For example, in *Moore*, Wal-Mart moved for summary judgment on the false imprisonment claim against it because "[the supervisor's] allegedly tortious conduct was not within the scope of his employment and . . . [Wal-Mart was] therefore not liable for his actions on a respondeat superior theory." *Id.* at 195. The court noted that "the intentional torts of employees related to sexual misconduct" generally "arise from personal motives and do not further an employer's business, even when committed within the employment context." *Id.* (citations omitted). Thus, the court entered judgment on behalf of Wal-Mart on the false imprisonment claim and other state law claims. *Id.*

IV. ASSAULT AND BATTERY

Assault and battery can arise as companion claims in employment discrimination cases, particularly those involving sexual harassment. Although sexual harassment can occur without assault or battery, many sexual harassment cases do, in fact, involve both assault and battery. Therefore, any plaintiff alleging sexual harassment where the defendant's involved unwanted touching, groping, or other sexual contact of any sort should consider adding common law or statutory claims for assault and battery.

V. NEGLIGENT HIRING, SUPERVISION, OR RETENTION; FAILURE TO TRAIN

A negligent hiring, supervision, or retention claim is a claim generally brought by a plaintiff-employee against an employer who allegedly failed to protect the employee from torts committed against the plaintiff by other employees. For example, under Florida law, a claim for negligent retention or supervision may be available "when, during the course of employment, the employer becomes aware, or should have become aware, of problems with an employee that indicates [the employee's] unfitness, and the employer fails to take further action such as investigation, discharge, or reassignment." *Medina v. United Christian Evangelic Ass'n*, No. 08-22111-CIV, 2009 WL 653857, at *5 (S.D. Fla. Mar. 10, 2009) (internal quotations omitted). Importantly, "the underlying wrong allegedly committed by an employee in a negligent supervision or negligent retention claim must be based on an injury resulting from a tort which is recognized under [the] common law." *Id.* (quoting *Scelta v. Delicatessen Support Servs., Inc.*, 57 F. Supp. 2d 1327, 1348 (M.D. Fla. 1999)). Therefore, this type of claim is a companion claim usually brought where the plaintiff-employee is also alleging that he or she suffered a tort like common law assault or battery at the hands of a fellow employee or supervisor.

Another growing area of liability involves employer liability for a failure to train managers and supervisors regarding anti-discrimination laws. Both federal and state courts have found employers liable for a failure to train supervisors regarding compliance under a range of federal and state anti-discrimination statutes. Administrative decisions have similarly concluded that a failure to train may result in liability for an employer. In an interesting administrative decision arising in California, the Fair Employment and Housing Commission concluded that a law firm was liable for failure to train its managers even though the underlying harassment and discrimination claims brought by a paralegal at the department ultimately failed. *Dep't of Fair Emp't & Hous. v. Lyddan Law Grp., LLP*, No. E-200607-A-1082-00-rs, 2010 CAFEHC LEXIS 4 (Cal. F.E.H.C. Oct. 19, 2010). The Commission concluded that "respondents . . . fail[ed] to take all reasonable steps to prevent discrimination or harassment [under Cal. Gov. Code § 12940, subd. (k)]." *Id.* at *2. The opinion did clarify, however, that the aggrieved employee had no private cause of action for the violation. Rather, the Commission concluded that "the prosecution of an independent . . . violation [of subdivision (k) was] . . . exclusively the province of the DFEH [Department of Fair Employment and Housing]." *Id.* at *3.

Finally, in the context of claims against municipalities (an issue largely outside the scope of this book), it may be possible to establish a violation of 42 U.S.C. § 1983 (2012) by a municipality that failed to train or supervise its employees who committed violations of anti-discrimination laws.

QUESTIONS AND EXERCISES

A potential client has approached you regarding each of the situations outlined below. Review the facts of each scenario and determine whether the potential client has a cause of action based on any of the tort or contract claims discussed above. If you are unsure whether a claim is implicated, determine what additional information you need to make your assessment.

1) Janine was employed as a realtor for approximately one year. Four months before her termination, Janine learned that she had been diagnosed with colon cancer. Janine notified her supervisor of her diagnosis the same day, and told her supervisor that she wanted to keep her job as normal as possible. Her supervisor told Janine that her job could not be guaranteed, and refused to allow Janine to adjust her hours or let her work remotely to accommodate her surgery or treatment schedule. When Janine returned to work following surgery, her supervisor told her that she would have lost her job except that an employee from another office covered for her while she was out. Her supervisor also stated that Janine would not be allowed personal telephone calls

at work, including from her physicians or nurses. While Janine was hospitalized after experiencing complications following chemotherapy, she received a phone call from her supervisor, who informed her that her employment was terminated.

2) Ethan was employed as a marketing executive for a food crafting company. Ethan's immediate supervisor frequently told vulgar jokes and sexually explicit stories, and on one occasion, had Ethan come to her home for a performance review. Ethan told management that his supervisor's behavior was making him uncomfortable at work. Management gave Ethan some advice about how to deal with his supervisor, but did not tell Ethan about the company's complaint procedure. When Ethan learned about the procedure on his own and approached management about his intent to file a complaint, management recommended that Ethan not file a complaint because it could make it difficult to get a raise or promotion. Ethan decided to file a complaint anyway, and after his supervisor learned about the complaint, she gave him a poor review. Ultimately, Ethan's supervisor was fired as a result of Ethan's complaint, but Ethan was also terminated due to poor performance.

3) Tim is employed as a receptionist at a hair salon. His supervisor regularly made sarcastic comments about Tim's work and criticized Tim's personal life. The supervisor mocked Tim for being a man working in a hair salon, made fun of the house Tim purchased, criticized his wife's job, and screamed in his face whenever she thought Tim had made a mistake. His supervisor also occasionally slapped Tim on the rear when criticizing Tim's work. The supervisor's behavior caused Tim to experience anxiety attacks and depression. Tim complained to the salon manager, who concluded after an investigation that the supervisor's behavior did not "rise to the level of illegal harassment," but recommended that the supervisor take classes to improve her management style.

4) Samantha was employed as a nurse. During her employment, she received consistently favorable performance evaluations. One year ago, her male supervisor began giving her less desirable shifts. Instead, he gave the more desirable shifts to another nurse with whom he was having a relationship. At the end of one of Samantha's shifts, she went to the locker room to change. Her supervisor entered the dressing room and, while she was changing, prevented Samantha from leaving the room while he berated her for failing to enter a medication order into a patient's chart. (The patient was actually the patient of another nurse.) Samantha filed a complaint with management over the supervisor's creation of a hostile working environment.

The material in this first part of the book serves as a broad overview of the framework of governing law in the employment discrimination arena. Of course, the list of possible laws and concepts included in Part I is not exhaustive, but it should provide a good background for approaching any problems arising in this particular area of law.

PART

II

RESEARCH STRATEGY AND PRESENTATION OF RESEARCH RESULTS

What is research? Is it a mechanical activity or a fluid process? How can one transition from being a novice legal researcher to a master legal researcher? How do you start a new research project? How do you know when you are finished? This part of the book aims to answer these questions.

WHY IS RESEARCH DIFFICULT?

More often than not, novice legal researchers believe they are having difficulty learning research for mechanical reasons. Specifically, novice legal researchers believe they can become better researchers simply by becoming more proficient with using terms and connectors or natural language searching on Westlaw or Lexis. The bad news is that becoming a good legal researcher is more difficult than simply learning how to do a better Boolean search[1] or how to navigate the new, user-friendly interfaces offered by WestlawNext and Lexis Advance. The good news is that conducting effective legal research is much more interesting

---

[1] *See* Carol McCrehan Parker, *Writing Is Everybody's Business: Theoretical and Practical Justifications for Teaching Writing across the Law School Curriculum*, 12 Legal Writing: J. Legal Writing Inst. 175, 188 (2006).

than the mechanical process imagined by most novice legal researchers. Perhaps Justice Frankfurter put it best when he noted over eighty years ago that

> Research requires the poetic quality of the imagination that sees significance and relation where others are indifferent or find unrelatedness; the synthetic quality of fusing items theretofore in isolation; above all the prophetic quality of piercing the future, by knowing what questions to put and what direction to give to inquiry.

Felix Frankfurter, *The Conditions for, and the Aims and Methods of, Legal Research*, 15 Iowa L. Rev. 129, 134 (1930) (originally read as a paper at a 1929 meeting of the Association of American Law Schools in New Orleans, Louisiana).

Good legal research requires mastery of several key skills, only one of which is the proper use of online databases. First, the researcher must know how to effectively and efficiently use all available resources, including paid online services, free open web sources, and paper resources. Second, the researcher must have a sound strategy for choosing the resources and the approach to use for a given project. Third, the researcher must develop the ability to approach legal problem-solving creatively and analytically. Specifically, the researcher must be able to ask the right questions at the outset of a research project, choose the right legal concepts to research, and adapt to what he or she is learning through the research process to refine the question asked. Finally, the researcher must be able to organize material in a way that allows others to see what areas the researcher has covered and how updated the research is.

In short, legal research is a complex, creative, and analytical process. It involves methodical planning and strategy. Effective legal research also involves constant analysis and reanalysis of the goals and progress of the research. The first two chapters of the research component of this book will provide advice regarding how to conduct effective legal research in a manner that is generally applicable to any field of law. Chapter 5 addresses basic legal research strategy, and Chapter 6 provides specific guidance on using various research tools.

The next two chapters address more specific questions an employment discrimination lawyer should ask (Chapter 7) and good research resources specific to employment discrimination law (Chapter 8).

After working through the reading and the exercises in this section, you should feel confident that you have developed both a sound methodology for approaching any research problem and a foundation for approaching legal research specifically in the area of employment discrimination law.

CHAPTER
5

DEVELOPING A BASIC STRATEGY FOR RESEARCHING ANY LEGAL ISSUE

I. INTRODUCTION

I remember embarking on one of my first major legal research assignments. As I worked through the problem, I experienced a profound sense of frustration and hopelessness. I remember thinking two things simultaneously: "There must be a better way!" and "If anyone finds out how stupid I am, they will NEVER hire me."

The issue involved hostile work environment sexual harassment in the Fifth Circuit. The issues were fascinating. Could a female employee establish a claim for hostile work environment harassment where her supervisor made lewd remarks to her on an almost daily basis (and occasionally propositioned her) if the female employee also regularly told lewd jokes in the workplace and had recently been promoted? What if the female employee said she only told the jokes because she felt like her job was in jeopardy if she didn't fit in with the otherwise all-male workplace? What defenses were available to the employer?

I did what I thought every good lawyer would do. I started with a secondary source. First, I went to a national encyclopedia, *American Jurisprudence*. After wading around in the index, I found material on sexual harassment under Title VII, so I had a basic understanding of the key Supreme Court cases and the relevant statute. I even discovered the difference between hostile work environment harassment and quid pro quo sexual harassment. However, the case citations were all over the country. I knew I needed relevant Fifth Circuit law, and I knew I might also be able to use state cases applying Fifth Circuit law. So I jumped to

Westlaw,[2] where I ran a terms and connectors search for "sexual harassment" in the all federal and state law cases database. Thousands of results came up. THOUSANDS. I tried "sexual harassment" /s "hostile." Still, I had thousands of results. I switched to a natural language search and typed in "sexual harassment hostile work environment female employee." I got fewer results, but the cases were from all over the country, and many seemed wholly irrelevant to my legal issues. Hours and hours later, I was frustrated, tired, and nowhere near finding answers to the assigned legal questions.

So what did I do wrong? In a nutshell, I did nearly everything wrong. Here are a few key areas in which my research failed miserably:

1. I started with a secondary source, which was a good decision. But then I made a bad choice when selecting what type of secondary source would be most useful. Selecting an appropriate secondary source is addressed in this chapter, and Chapter 8 includes a list of specific useful secondary sources for the lawyer practicing employment discrimination law.

2. My searches were in over-inclusive databases,[3] so I forced myself to wade through a lot of irrelevant (non-binding) authority. Moreover, in general, if you are searching using one of the classic systems, larger databases cost the client more money to search in, so the client won't be happy with an unnecessarily broad search.[4]

3. The terms I used in my searches were ineffective because I never skimmed any deeper than the very surface of the relevant legal issues. I treated the research question as simply one of law: What is hostile work environment sexual harassment? However, a client wishing to sue for sexual harassment (or defend itself in such a lawsuit) is not likely to ask you to research "what is a definition of hostile work environment sexual harassment," and this question is all that my searches were designed to find. I should have spent time at the outset identifying the type of question I was being asked (how to apply the law to a given set of specific facts), and whether I was being asked multiple questions. In fact, the assignment

---

[2] When the authors began learning to perform legal research, only the classic versions of Westlaw and Lexis were available. However, similar searches in WestlawNext or Lexis Advance would prove equally fruitless. As of September 2013, Lexis has begun phasing out its use of Lexis.com in law schools. Law firm attorneys may continue to access and use Lexis.com, depending on the firm's contract with Lexis. During this transitional period, if a source is available on Lexis.com but not on Lexis Advance, you can access Lexis.com through Lexis Advance by selecting the Research tab at the top of the screen, then "Lexis.com."

[3] The reference to "databases" is a reference to the way material is primarily organized in the classic systems. This text covers both classic Westlaw and Lexis.com and WestlawNext and Lexis Advance. Although many law firms, government employers, and public interest organizations are transitioning to using solely the new platforms, other workplaces remain on the classic systems. Until Westlaw and Lexis fully transition to the new systems and retire the old ones, students will need to be flexible enough to research effectively on all four platforms.

[4] Under the classic systems, the larger the database, the more expensive the search. However, under a transactional pricing model (where the user is charged per search rather than by time), it will not cost the user extra to read documents within that search. Under the new systems, one can search a large amount of material without paying more money for doing so. Rather than charging different amounts for different databases, WestlawNext and Lexis Advance allow users to search broadly and then narrow using a number of filters. This process does not cost the user more money. Instead, users are charged when they click on documents in the search. In essence, the pricing models are near mirror images of each other. Effective researchers know the pricing models so that they can research in the most efficient and inexpensive way for clients.

did call for multiple separate inquiries. To answer the question asked, I needed to research the following:

    a. What is required to establish hostile work environment sexual harassment under Title VII in the Fifth Circuit? Do the *specific facts of this case* support a finding of hostile work environment harassment?

    b. Is an employer strictly liable for hostile work environment harassment? If not, when is an employer liable for actions taken by one of its supervisory employees? (Put another way, what defenses are available to an employer?) Do the employer's *specific actions in this case* satisfy its burden of showing it took appropriate action to avoid liability?

    c. Is the lawsuit against the employer, the supervisor, or both? If it is against the supervisor, can supervisors be held liable under Title VII?

  4. More importantly, though, I did not start with a sound research strategy. I jumped in without planning the research, and I ended up wasting hours of time looking at the wrong materials in the wrong databases.

The remainder of this chapter and the next chapter discuss how to avoid these pitfalls and develop a solid research methodology appropriate for use with any assignment.

II. DEVELOPING A SOUND (AND GENERALLY APPLICABLE) RESEARCH STRATEGY

This section provides a basic research template you can use to approach any legal question you are assigned.

A. STEPS TO EFFICIENT AND EFFECTIVE LEGAL RESEARCH

Step One: Know the issue(s) you have been asked to research.

You may receive a research project in a number of different ways. An attorney may give an assignment orally or in written form (memorandum, e-mail, instant message, text, etc.). Or you could be asked to interview a new or existing client to ferret out the important issues yourself. If you are interviewing a client or receiving instructions orally, you must listen carefully, take good notes, and ask clarifying questions where necessary. If you receive an assignment in written form, carefully read the assignment and identify questions you need to pose to the client or assigning attorney *before* contacting them.

Later portions of this chapter discuss how to effectively receive an assignment and to identify the relevant issues.

Step Two: **Make sure you have all relevant background material, and read it carefully.**

Sometimes, you will be asked to research a pure question of law. For example, an assigning attorney may ask you to prepare a client education bulletin that summarizes the changes to disability discrimination law brought about by the passage of the ADA Amendments Act of 2008. You need no client documents to answer that question.

More often than not, though, you will be asked to research questions whose answers are tied to an existing case or to activities in a client's workplace. Because the assigning attorney or client may not tell you there are relevant documents, you should take the initiative to think about what you need and to ask for it.

If you are asked to do research in an ongoing case, make sure you get the relevant documents. What you need will depend on the type of research you are doing and the purpose for that research. Examples:

- *Your assignment is to update and revise your client's mandatory arbitration agreement.* You will need a copy of the old policy, and it will also help to retrieve sample arbitration agreements from treatises or other sources.
- *Your assignment is to draft a 12(b)(6) motion in a case alleging race discrimination under Title VII.* You will need a copy of the Complaint in the case, as a 12(b)(6) motion alleges that the Complaint has failed to allege a claim upon which relief can be granted. As you may remember, a 12(b)(6) motion can only rely on the pleadings in a case.
- *Your assignment is to file an appeal to the intermediate appellate court from a verdict against your client in a genetic discrimination lawsuit that went to trial under a state anti-discrimination statute.* You will need the entire client file, including all pleadings, discovery documents, trial transcripts, the judge's order, and other trial documents. If the assigning attorney does not provide these materials, ask for them.
- *You represent plaintiffs in employment discrimination matters. A prospective client asks whether she has a good case against her employer for hostile work environment sexual harassment.* Of course, you'll have to interview the client to get the relevant facts. You'll also need to discover whether the employer had a sexual harassment policy. If so, you will need a copy of the policy. This may be a stand-alone policy or part of an Employee Handbook.

Step Three: If you are relatively unfamiliar with the subject matter you are researching, consult a relevant secondary source to get background information and additional research references.

Once you have been practicing for a while, you will have a basic background understanding of many issues you'll be asked to research. If you have a basic framework for a problem (you know the relevant statute, a key case or two, and the elements of the claim at issue), you can probably go directly to primary authority. However, for most issues, a secondary source can be quite useful for providing the background information and leading you to relevant primary authority.

Of course, using a secondary source will only be a useful first step in your research if you carefully select a source that is both authoritative and relevant. A source is authoritative if it is likely to provide accurate information. The most authoritative sources are well-known treatises, A.L.R. annotations, national and state legal encyclopedias, government publications (like the EEOC Compliance Manual), and law review articles. Among these materials, treatises are more likely to be useful if they are well-known and written by experts in the area. Early on in practice, it is difficult to decide what the best treatise or secondary source to use might be. This book provides a long list of authoritative and useful treatises and describes the basic substance of those treatises. In practice, this list should be quite useful. You can also ask the assigning attorney or a law librarian whether there is a good treatise in your area of inquiry. The least authoritative background sources are Wikipedia articles, blog postings, and law firm client education websites. While these materials may in some situations provide accurate summaries of basic background law, you will have to perform additional research to verify the accuracy of the material you find from these sources.

A secondary source is most relevant if it is subject-matter-specific and contains references to primary authority *in your jurisdiction*. So, for example, while *American Jurisprudence* (a national encyclopedia, also known as *Am. Jur.*) would likely have material on sexual harassment law under Title VII, it may not cite cases from the relevant jurisdiction. Moreover, the analysis of your issue will be less detailed than you would find in a treatise dedicated to federal employment discrimination law generally or sexual harassment law specifically.

AN OVERVIEW OF ACCURATE AND AUTHORITATIVE SECONDARY SOURCES

Relative Quality of Source	Sources for Researching State Law Issues	Sources for Researching Federal Law Issues
Best Sources Look here first for the most authoritative, accurate, and relevant material.	• State government websites • State law encyclopedias • Subject-matter-specific treatises • A.L.R. annotations • Law review articles (for unresolved issues of law and policy arguments)	• Federal government websites • A.L.R. annotations[5] • Law review articles (for unresolved issues of law and policy arguments)
Acceptable Sources Look here only if "best sources" yielded no helpful results. Material on this list will be authoritative and accurate, but it may not include references to *relevant* binding authority.	• National encyclopedias (*American Jurisprudence* or *Corpus Juris Secundum*) • Legal dictionaries • Thesauri	• National encyclopedias (*American Jurisprudence* or *Corpus Juris Secundum*) • Legal dictionaries • Thesauri
Least Useful Sources Material on this list is not guaranteed to be authoritative or accurate. You may find useful material here, but you will have to look to more authoritative materials and primary sources to check the accuracy of the material you find in sources on this list.	• Law firm websites • Interest or advocacy group websites • Human resources websites • Wikipedia • Individual blogs • Employment discrimination discussion groups or message boards	• Law firm websites • Interest or advocacy group websites • Human resources websites • Wikipedia • Individual blogs • Employment discrimination discussion groups or message boards

---

[5] *American Law Reports* covers both state and federal issues. In the earlier volumes (A.L.R., A.L.R. 2d, and A.L.R. 3d), state and federal issues were included in the same volume. A.L.R. 4th-6th only cover state issues, while A.L.R. Fed. and Fed. 2d cover federal issues and those international law issues affecting only the United States. *A.L.R. International* covers issues of international law, even issues not affecting the United States. *A.L.R. International* is the only volume that includes references to cases from non-English-speaking jurisdictions.

Step Four: Incorporate what you have learned from the secondary source(s) (terms of art, for example) into a more refined statement of the issue or issues you have been asked to research. If possible, begin to develop an outline of relevant issues or sub-issues.

In Step One, you identified the issue or issues you were asked to research. For example, you might have written down the following issue statement:

> *Under Title VII [relevant law], can Susan Smith, a waitress at Hooters, establish a claim for sexual harassment [legal question], where . . . [relevant facts you've gotten from the client or the assigning attorney]?*

When you looked in a secondary source, though, you identified that she could not establish quid pro quo sexual harassment because she had not suffered a tangible employment action. Rather, her best case was for hostile work environment harassment. Through your reading in the treatise, you discovered that she must show the harassment was unwelcome as well as severe or pervasive. Moreover, you also discovered that the employer could raise an affirmative defense.

At this point in your research, you would be able to complete better research if you identified the component parts of the question you started with. Also, your searches in primary authority will be more effective if you add the terms of art you're learning from your research in secondary sources (severe, pervasive, etc.).

So, at this stage, you would likely refine your overall research question to ask whether:

> *Under Title VII [relevant law], can Susan Smith, a waitress at Hooters, establish a claim for hostile work environment sexual harassment [legal question], where . . . [relevant facts you've gotten from the client or the assigning attorney]?*

You should also list all the relevant sub-issues. Here is an example of the list you might create as you learn about the various sub-issues in your legal analysis:

1. What is "severe" harassing behavior, and do the facts of this case support a finding that the harassment was severe?
2. What is "pervasive" conduct, and do the facts of this case support a finding that the harassment was pervasive?
3. What does it mean for conduct to be "unwelcome"?
4. Did the employer take legally-sufficient measures to prevent and correct the harassment?
5. Did the employee fail to take advantage of sexual harassment policies put in place for employees' safety?

As you continue to research your issues, you may find these legal questions break into still more issues and sub-issues. Continue to refine your outline as you learn about the legal and factual issues.

Your research might also lead you to decide that you do not have enough of the relevant facts in your client's case. Keep a list of those facts so you can find out answers from your client or the assigning attorney.

Step Five: Research primary authority, starting with constitutions, statutes, and regulations, and then moving to cases (binding before persuasive).

Make sure you first discover whether the problem is governed by a statute or constitutional provision. If you are researching a statutory problem, you can use the annotated statute to lead you to some relevant cases. Make sure you read the relevant statute or constitutional provision in its entirety. If the cases have fully explored the applicability of the statute, then you can use the cases to analyze how the statute operates. However, if you are dealing with a newer statute, a term that has not yet been defined, or an ambiguity in the statute, you may have to look to methods of statutory interpretation other than cases to help analyze the statute. Sometimes the plain language of the statute will answer your legal question. More often than not, though, you'll need to turn to the legislative history of the statute, the canons of construction, or cases from non-binding jurisdictions to help inform your analysis.

Many areas of employment discrimination law are administered by various federal agencies. Those agencies have often provided interpretive guidance in the form of regulations. Sometimes, courts in the relevant jurisdiction will have adopted the agency interpretation. If so, that interpretation is binding. Otherwise, the regulations are highly persuasive, though not binding, authority.

The next chapter of this book provides information regarding conducting legislative history research and regulatory research.

Step Six: Fill in your outline of issues and sub-issues with relevant primary authority. Find 1-2 cases for general propositions of law. Once you have supported the basic propositions of law with binding authority, look for factually analogous cases for each issue and sub-issue (unless you're researching an issue of pure law).

Look again at the list of questions regarding hostile work environment sexual harassment. Take those questions and develop an outline. Leave room to fill in cases as you find relevant case support. Example:

Outline:

Hostile Environment Sexual Harassment

Overall rule regarding Title VII sexual harassment: Cite to major Supreme Court opinions (and perhaps 1-2 binding circuit court opinions).

Elements:

Based on Sex: List a case to provide support for the fact that this is a requirement. If necessary, include cases with analogous facts on this specific sub-issue to help you analyze whether the plaintiff in this case can establish the harassment was based on sex.

Severe or Pervasive enough to create a hostile environment: List 1-2 cases that provide definitions of "severe" and "pervasive." Importantly, then look for opinions that have applied these definitions to cases with analogous facts on this specific sub-issue.

Unwelcome: List 1-2 cases that provide definitions of "unwelcome." Importantly, then look for cases with facts similar to those in your client's case on this specific sub-issue.

Employer defenses: List 1-2 cases for the general rule regarding what defenses are available to an employer at this point. Then list cases with specific facts that help you analyze whether the employer in this case can establish a defense.

Step Seven: Make sure all cases are still good law for the points for which you are using them.

Make sure you check that your cases are still good law by using Keycite (Westlaw) or Shepard's (Lexis). Remember that a case may have been criticized or overruled on a point unimportant to your specific research question or by a court outside of your jurisdiction. If the point for which you are using a case has not been overruled, criticized, or distinguished by a higher court in your jurisdiction, it is "good law" for your purposes.

B. TROUBLESHOOTING YOUR RESEARCH

Particularly in the early days of your practice, you will likely find many research projects complex and frustrating, though mastering the techniques in this book should give you a huge leg up in the process of mastering good research strategies and techniques.

Here are some suggestions for moving past the most common causes of frustration in legal research.

1. What if I'm finding no cases (or too few cases)?

Nothing is more frightening or frustrating than sitting down to research a problem for a client or another attorney and coming up completely empty-handed. If this happens, one of two things has occurred:

- It really is true that there are no cases on the issue you have been asked to research. The issue is one of first impression.
- You are doing something wrong.

Of course, it's the second possibility that terrifies even the most experienced attorney. I remember observing a Sixth Circuit oral argument during a summer internship in law school. An attorney made what I thought was a really creative and interesting argument on behalf of his client. I was just thinking that I hoped I would one day be as smooth as the attorney I was observing when one of the Judges interrupted him to ask, "Doesn't the _____ case preclude that line of reasoning?" The attorney had not found the case cited by the Judge, and an awkward time was had by all. I learned a valuable lesson that day. Being a bright, creative, accomplished attorney requires more than the ability to speak persuasively and develop interesting policy arguments. Good attorneys sweat the small stuff. Good attorneys start by developing solid legal research and writing skills, as a persuasive argument or a complex legal analysis built on a crumbling foundation is worthless.

So what might have gone wrong? First, you may have simply misunderstood the research project and the specific question asked. Go back and read your notes to make sure you understand the question and that you got enough information from the assigning attorney to approach the project effectively. If you still believe you understand what you have been asked to do but just cannot find relevant information, then you have probably simply chosen an incorrect database[6] or the wrong terms to search. Usually the latter situation occurs when a novice legal researcher is unfamiliar with relevant terms of art in a given area of law. Your best bet is to take a step back and look at the secondary sources again. Use the secondary sources to find discussion of your issue, and carefully read the discussion to identify relevant terms of art. Those terms will likely be the ones appearing in cases on your issue (and in indexes, tables of contents, and annotations in statutes).

Then, use finding tools to lead you to relevant cases rather than jumping directly to natural language searching or terms and connectors searching. Start with topical searching in Westlaw or Lexis, or use the index in a paper digest or other secondary source. Use an annotated statute to help you find relevant cases on various issues and sub-issues if the issue is a statutory problem.

Another possibility is that you really have misunderstood the research project. If this is the case, you will probably have to return to the assigning attorney to ask some follow-up questions. Before you do this, make sure you take a few minutes to collect your thoughts and organize your questions so you do not waste the attorney's time with multiple follow-up conversations.

A final possibility is that you have found the relevant law, but you have not been provided with all of the relevant facts necessary to answer the legal question. Again, you may need to have a follow-up conversation with the client or the assigning attorney to gain additional information. Before you schedule a follow-up meeting, though, first check the client file to make sure you can't find the information on your own.

---

[6] On WestlawNext and Lexis Advance, you can search within a given source, in a specific jurisdiction, or other similarly limited database. You can also do terms and connectors searching just as you would do in the classic systems. In addition, you can use the universal search bar to search all materials at once and then filter by jurisdiction, date, headnote, additional focused search terms, and the like.

2. What if I find too many cases? Do I include them all?

In a word, no. Some issues have been exhaustively litigated, and you may find hundreds or thousands of relevant cases. It would be impossible to even read all the cases, let alone thoughtfully analyze them. Here are the types of cases you must include:

- Seminal cases cited by nearly all other decisions.
- The most analogous cases.
- The cases your opponent is likely to rely upon (so you can distinguish them).

Finding the seminal cases is usually easy. These are the cases cited over and over again. They are often discussed in secondary sources, and you may even find them extensively cited in less reliable free internet resources. A good example is the *McDonnell Douglas* case, which established the burden-shifting proof structure used in most employment discrimination cases.[7]

Choosing the relevant analogous and distinguishable cases is harder. Again, look for frequently-cited cases, as these are cases likely to be cited by your opponent. Then, make sure you are searching in the narrowest database possible (Lexis.com or Westlaw Classic) or filtering by relevant jurisdiction (Lexis Advance or WestlawNext). If you need Fifth Circuit law on an issue, for example, do not waste your time combing through the law of all federal circuits. Only look beyond Fifth Circuit law if you cannot find anything on point in the binding jurisdiction. Likewise, if you need California state law on an issue, do not look in a federal/state combined database (Lexis.com or Westlaw Classic) or filter by federal and state cases (Lexis Advance or WestlawNext) unless California cases do not provide an answer and you hope to find Ninth Circuit cases interpreting California state law.

Finally, it is appropriate to use terms and connectors searching or a focus-within-results feature in this situation, so you can narrow down a larger pool of cases to find the most relevant ones. Remember, though, that one case may be very helpful on one sub-issue but fail to discuss another sub-issue in depth. Thus, as you narrow down a large pool of cases, you may find you need different sets of cases to discuss varying issues.

3. I have started my research, and it is clear that I'm missing some key information necessary to analyze the legal question. What do I do?

When an attorney or client provides you with information regarding a claim or research project, they may or may not know the law well enough to provide you with all the facts necessary to effectively analyze the claim. If this is the case,

---

[7] *McDonnell Douglas Corp. v. Green*, 411 U.S. 792 (1973).

you'll have to collect additional information from the assigning attorney or client. As mentioned above, first check the client file or do other research if the missing piece of information is something you can easily discover without turning to someone else. If you must schedule a follow-up meeting, make sure you have listed all the questions you have in advance so you do not waste others' time.

4. I've hit a dead end. I think I've gone down the wrong path entirely. What do I do?

Another extremely frustrating situation for the novice researcher is starting a research project, finding useful material early in the research process, and then hitting a wall. What went wrong?

If you started out on the right path, go back to where you think you veered off course. Re-read the secondary sources to make sure you have not missed key terms of art or legal issues. Make sure you have the correct statute, if the problem is a statutory one, and make sure you are looking in the appropriate database or filtering out irrelevant material. You can also consult a law librarian if you have access to a law library with a staff of librarians.

If you believe you are simply having difficulty with the mechanics of using Westlaw or Lexis (crafting an effective search, finding a relevant database, or using the filtering capabilities of the new systems), use the live support function on those services to ask an online question, or call a Westlaw or Lexis reference attorney and ask for help.

If you cannot get your research back on track, you may have to return to the assigning attorney for guidance. As long as you have been thorough in attempting to solve the problem on your own first, the assigning attorney will likely be happy to provide additional guidance. It is always better to ask for help than to waste hours of time running down the wrong path.

5. As I read through the cases, I've gotten a bit confused about the background legal framework. Should I continue reading cases? Return to the assigning attorney?

A number of things may have gone wrong in your research to lead you to feel like this, so you will need to troubleshoot your confusion. If you are feeling as if you do not understand the basic background law, one of several things could be happening:

First, you may actually have gone down the wrong path entirely. If this is the case, refer to the advice for this scenario above.

Second, you actually have found the basic legal framework for your issue, and you understand the rules. However, you haven't found cases with precisely the same fact pattern as yours. If this is what is troubling you, you may be expecting to find the "perfect" case, one that likely does not exist. If you have the correct legal framework, and you have a set of cases analyzing the application of the relevant legal rules, see if those cases are analogous enough that applying the reasoning of those cases to your client's facts makes sense. The ability to creatively analogize the facts of your client's case to those in similar, but not identical, precedent cases is part of what it means to be a great attorney.

Third, you have tried to jump into the primary sources too early. Return to secondary sources when necessary to redirect your research or refine your understanding of a new area of law.

6. *How do I know when I'm finished?*

The best clue that you are nearing the end of a research project is when you start encountering the same cases and statutes over and over again. Once you get to a point where every search yields things you have already looked at, you are probably nearing the end of your research project.

When you start seeing diminishing returns in your searching, ask yourself whether you have been thorough in your research. If so, you can comfortably stop. You have been thorough if you have followed the steps suggested by this book. In short, make sure you have checked relevant and authoritative secondary sources; researched primary authority (binding before persuasive) until you have found cases to answer all issues and sub-issues; and checked to make sure your authorities are still good law. If you have kept a good log of your research process, you'll be able to assure yourself (and anyone else) that your process was sound and that you did not miss anything.

III. TYPES OF ASSIGNMENTS AND MODES OF PRESENTING RESEARCH RESULTS

The next material we will cover involves research on employment discrimination topics. However, you cannot perform good research unless you understand the purpose for your research and how you will present your results. For example, will your research be used for preventative purposes, like counseling clients on compliance issues? Or will your research be used to help a client decide whether to file suit or to defend a client in an existing lawsuit? Are you being asked to give objective advice or provide a persuasive argument? Is the question purely legal, or does it require analysis of the facts of given cases and how they compare to your client's facts? Does the assigning attorney want you to provide a formal internal written memorandum of your findings, a persuasive court document, a client advice letter, or an oral report?

You should have learned how to write a basic legal memorandum in your first year legal writing, reasoning, and research course. Unless you have taken advanced courses, it is likely that your legal writing experience has been confined to drafting one or more memos, each focused on applying the law to a given set of facts. Most first year students receive assignments in the form of a written memo from an associate attorney or partner.

However, in practice, you may receive assignments in a number of ways, including orally or via e-mail. You may be expected to get the relevant facts by interviewing a client or reviewing a set of pleadings and discovery documents in a case. Furthermore, you may be asked to respond in a typical formal office memorandum, or you may be expected to return your research results orally or in e-mail form. Finally, the typical "apply the law to the facts" memorandum is not the only type of memorandum you'll be asked to draft in practice.

This section begins by providing brief suggestions for how to most effectively communicate research results if you are asked to provide your results orally, via e-mail, or through a short informal office memorandum. The section concludes with a list of the key types of memos you might be asked to draft in practice with suggestions for presenting material clearly and professionally.

A. MODES OF RECEIVING ASSIGNMENTS

1. Oral Assignments

Whenever you go to an assigning attorney's office, bring a pad of paper and a pen. Never trust an oral assignment to your memory.[8] Take notes, and ask good questions. Attorneys hate having to write off wasted research time more than they dislike answering a few questions at the outset of a research project.

Before you leave the assigning attorney's office, make sure you know (1) what you've been asked to research and for what purpose your research will be used (objective analysis, advocacy, client education or advice, etc.); (2) what jurisdiction's law is relevant; (3) roughly how much time the attorney believes the assignment will take; (4) when the assignment is due; and (4) in what format the assigning attorney would like to receive the finished product (formal or informal memorandum, e-mail, oral report, etc.).

It never hurts to send out a quick confirmation e-mail after receiving an assignment. You can write something as simple as this: "You have asked me to research whether our client has a claim under X statute. The due date for this assignment is March 5th. If you have other issues you would like me to research, just let me know." Another very useful thing to include in a confirming e-mail or in your initial discussion with the attorney is a statement of the assumptions you are making. That way, if you have made certain incorrect assumptions about the

---

[8] It's also a very good idea to keep a pen and a piece of paper in a location you can easily reach from your desk. Attorneys in practice frequently drop by unexpectedly to give assignments orally, and you want to be prepared to take down pertinent information without making a busy attorney wait for you to get organized.

facts or the purpose of your research, the assigning attorney can identify those incorrect assumptions and correct them before you waste a lot of billable hours building your research on a faulty foundation.

If you come up with new questions as you are researching, it is fine to go back to the attorney and ask them. In fact, you will likely really impress an assigning attorney if you discover an easier way to solve a client's problem or a complexity in the law about which the attorney was unaware. Just make sure you respect the time of others. Make sure you have fully thought out your question before posing it to the assigning attorney (which you can do via e-mail or in person, depending on the preference of the assigning attorney). If you come up with a question, take a step back and make sure you do not have other questions. Try to pose them all in one e-mail or conversation so you do not fill an attorney's in-box with serial questions in separate e-mails.

2. Via E-Mail

You may also receive assignments from an attorney via e-mail. If the question is a simple one, you can probably perform the assignment without going through the process of asking follow-up questions and meeting the attorney for a face-to-face meeting.

Example: What is the statute of limitations under the Lilly Ledbetter Fair Pay Act?

If the attorney e-mailed you the question, you can probably respond via e-mail, though of course write a memo if that is the custom with the assigning attorney who sent you the e-mail.

Or, if you work in-house or communicate regularly with in-house attorneys and human resource professionals, you may receive "quick" legal questions by e-mail (or telephone). It is perfectly acceptable to respond with an e-mail (or phone call) noting that you will get back to the client shortly with the answer. After you have been practicing for a short time, you may find that you begin to know the answers to some simple questions off the top of your head. However, unless you are absolutely certain, quickly look up the answer anyway just to confirm your advice is accurate and up-to-date.

3. Client Interview

Another very common way that a research project can develop is through an interview with a client. Two different types of interviews will lead to research and writing projects. First, you may conduct an initial client intake interview. From that interview, multiple research issues and writing projects may develop. Second, you may conduct follow-up interviews with an existing client. New issues will often arise from those follow-up conversations.

Detailed suggestions about effective client interviewing are beyond the scope of this text. For your purposes at this point, the important thing to remember is how conducting a client interview is similar to or different from receiving an assignment from a senior attorney.

Similarities:

- *Take notes and ask questions.* Just like when you receive an assignment from a senior attorney, you should take notes and ask good questions while interviewing a client. However, a client will likely be more emotionally involved in a case than an assigning attorney, particularly if the client is an individual plaintiff rather than a business. Thus, while you need to make sure you get all the relevant facts, it is equally important that you listen carefully and allow the client to tell his or her story.

- *Make sure you have relevant information and documents.* You will still need to discern (1) what you need to research and for what purpose your research will be used; (2) what jurisdiction's law is relevant; (3) roughly how much time you need to spend on the assignment; (4) when the assignment needs to be completed; and (5) what format the final document or documents should take (client letter, complaint, motion, etc.). However, you will not be able to ask the client the answers to these questions. You will have to identify the relevant legal issues, the jurisdiction, and what documents are necessary to prepare. You will become better at this as you gain experience. If you have questions, ask more senior attorneys around you. Also remember that the client may not want (or be able) to spend more than a certain amount of money. Keep this in mind as you strategize about how you will proceed with any research or writing projects.

- *Follow up with a confirmation message.* You should follow up your conversation with a client with a confirmation message indicating what steps you plan to take, what issues you think are raised by the client's situation, and when you will get back in touch with the client. Make sure you summarize the facts as you understand them, and tell the client to inform you if you are incorrect. Note that your legal advice could change if the facts change.

- *Return to ask additional questions if necessary, but respect the client's time.* If you identify new questions or areas of concern, you should go back to the client to clarify the facts, ask additional questions, get copies of relevant documents, and the like. If you come up with a question, take a step back and make sure you do not have other questions. Try to pose them all in one e-mail or conversation.

Differences:

- *Particularly with clients unfamiliar with the law, you have to lead the interview and tell the client what information you need.* For example, if you represent employment discrimination plaintiffs, your clients will usually not be sophisticated in business and legal matters. (An exception would be some executive and professional employees or human resource professionals.) Most plaintiffs in employment law matters have a general understanding of the law of discrimination, but they will not have any of the detailed knowledge necessary to analyze whether they can establish a successful case of employment discrimination. Rather, when a client comes to you, they will come with a belief that they have been wronged, and they will want to tell their story. You should let them tell the story, but you will also have to guide them. It is your job to identify the legal issues and to ask the factual questions for which you need answers. You cannot expect the client to know that the precise dates of incidents of sexual harassment might matter, for example, or that the precise statements a potential defendant made would need to be related verbatim. Corporate clients may be more aware of basic legal requirements, and so you may not need to do as much guiding in the interview process. However, do not assume a more sophisticated client knows everything. If the client knew all the answers, they would not have hired a lawyer.

■ *If you are dealing with a client in an ongoing case, regularly inform the client about the status of the matter.* When another attorney gives you a project, that attorney will assume you will contact him or her if you have a problem. Just the opposite may be true for a client. If you do not contact a client regularly with updates, the client may treat the silence as evidence of a problem. In fact, one of the most common complaints made by clients to state bar associations is that a lawyer has failed to keep the client reasonably informed about the status of a matter. This failure is an ethical violation.

B. TYPES OF RESEARCH AND ANALYTICAL WRITING AS-SIGNMENTS

1. *Typical 1L Research Assignment*

In the typical objective research memorandum assignment in a first-year legal writing, research, and analysis class, students are expected to take a client's fact pattern and apply the law to those facts. For example, a student may be asked to research whether a terminated employee has a claim for discriminatory discharge under a state discrimination statute given a certain set of facts. In order to answer the question, the new lawyer or student must find the relevant statute and regulations (if any) as well as cases interpreting the statute. The memorandum consists of a brief explanation of the overall background law governing the question, but the majority of the memorandum is devoted to a prediction of how a court will likely treat the specific facts of your client's case under the statute, particularly in light of analogous or distinguishable cases.

Although you have likely already drafted at least one "apply-the-law-to-the-facts" memorandum, this book provides a brief reminder of some of the key considerations for drafting a clear analysis of this type of problem. A rough form for this type of memorandum might look like this:

SECTIONS IN A FORMAL "APPLY-THE-LAW-TO-THE-FACTS" MEMORANDUM

Statement of Issue(s) Presented
(or Question Presented)

Short Answer (or Conclusion)

Statement of Facts

Discussion

A legal reader, of course, expects to see specific information in each of these sections. Detailed guidance on how to craft clear, concise, analytical material in this type of memorandum is listed below.

Statement of Issue(s) Presented (or Question Presented)

In a Statement of Issue(s) Presented involving the application of law to a specific set of facts, most legal readers prefer to see the following information in this order:

1. The governing law;
2. The relevant legal question addressed by the memorandum; and
3. The relevant facts in your client's specific case (only those key facts necessary to answer the legal question).

Example:

> *Under either Title VII or California law [governing law], can an employee establish a claim of hostile work environment sexual harassment against her employer, a small radio station employing seven employees [relevant legal question], where the employee's co-worker repeatedly left sexual notes and pornographic pictures on the employee's desk, circulated false rumors about the employee's sex life to other employees, and tried to force the employee to have sex in the break room after locking the door and turning out the light [relevant facts]?*

Usually, though not always, the Statement of Issue(s) Presented is just one sentence. If a question gets too complex and seems unreadable, the writer has a couple of solutions. First, the writer can organize the question as an enumerated list.

Example:

> *Under either Title VII or California law, can an employee establish a claim for hostile work environment sexual harassment against her employer, a radio station employing seven employees, where the employee's co-worker: (1) repeatedly left sexual notes and pornographic pictures on the employee's*

*desk; (2) circulated false rumors about the employee's sex life to other em-
ployees; and (3) tried to force the employee to have sex in the break room
after locking the door and turning out the light?*

Second, the writer can move to a multi-sentence format. Usually, this involves
writing one or two clear sentences establishing the relevant facts and then finish-
ing with a clear statement of the relevant legal question.

Example:

> *Our client, one of seven employees at a radio station in California, has
> complained about her supervisor's behavior at work. Specifically, the supervi-
> sor repeatedly left sexual notes and pornographic pictures on the employee's
> desk, passed around false rumors about the employee's sex life to other em-
> ployees, and asked the employee for sex in the break room after locking the
> door and turning out the light. Given these facts, can the employee establish a
> claim for hostile work environment sexual harassment under either Title VII
> or California law?*

Short Answer (or Conclusion)

A good Short Answer provides the reader with a clear understanding of your
prediction of the outcome of the legal question, along with a few key reasons for
your prediction. For most legal issues, a paragraph is enough to provide the detail
necessary for your reader at this stage. Because most legal readers are busy (and
perhaps even impatient), it is best to start your Short Answer with a clear "yes,"
"no," "probably yes," or "probably no." Then follow with a few brief sentences
explaining why you have come to that conclusion. Do not simply list black letter
statements of law. Explain why the law compels the result you have predicted,
given the specific relevant facts in your client's case.

Statement of Facts

Your Statement of Facts should be detailed enough to provide the context
necessary for a reader to understand your legal analysis in the Discussion section.
It is helpful to the reader if you start the Statement of Facts with a short, one or
two sentence introduction to the relevant parties and the issue addressed in the
memorandum.

After you have done this, tell the story. Make sure all details are accurate. If
you are working from your notes of a client interview, check the notes frequently.
If you are working from the record in a case, keep the file close at hand. When
possible, cite to where you found the relevant facts.[9]

---

[9] While citations to the record are not usually necessary in an internal memorandum, you will have to provide
those citations if you later turn your memorandum into an advocacy piece to file with a court. Save yourself
some time and avoid doing the same research twice by including the references the first time you prepare an
analysis of the legal issues.

Although you may draft a preliminary Statement of Facts before finalizing your Discussion section, revisit the Statement of Facts before turning in a memorandum. Every fact you needed in your Discussion section should appear in the Statement of Facts. You may also find that, after writing the Discussion section, several facts you initially thought were relevant can be eliminated from the Statement of Facts.

Students often ask how long a Statement of Facts should be. That is a nearly impossible question to answer. If you have written in a clear, concise fashion, and you have included every fact necessary to the legal analysis (and deleted those facts unnecessary to the analysis), you can be fairly certain your Statement of Facts is a proper length.

Lastly, consider the order of information in the Statement of Facts. Often, chronological order makes the most sense. This is the way we are used to hearing stories. Some of the more artful movies that you have seen may jump all over the place chronologically (remember *Memento*?). While this might be entertaining in a movie, think about how difficult it is to follow the story line when you have to keep jumping back and forth in time to get bits and pieces of the relevant facts. Busy legal readers are not looking for intellectually challenging entertainment. They are looking for efficient and accurate analysis.

Of course, in some situations, chronological order may not be the most logical order for information. If you are drafting a memorandum dealing with multiple legal issues, you may wish to group facts according to the issues to which they are relevant, or some other organizational scheme might present itself. This is fine, so long as you are certain you are presenting material in the most logical and readable way for your audience.

Discussion

The Discussion section is, of course, the heart of the memorandum. Here, you provide all of the relevant law and the analysis of how that law applies to your client's situation given the specific facts of the case.

The best legal memoranda have both sound analysis and clear organization. Make sure your memorandum has a solid predictive thesis paragraph and is well-organized at both a macro-level and a micro-level.

The Thesis Paragraph

To help a busy legal reader, start with a thesis paragraph that sets out the overall background law and provides a clear prediction of the result. A good basic thesis paragraph (or paragraphs) should contain the following elements, preferably in this order:

1. **A statement of the legal issue addressed in the memorandum.** This can be stated either as a legal conclusion or as a simple issue statement.

   Legal conclusion: Our client, Ms. Tracie Turner, can likely establish a claim for retaliatory discharge under the Minnesota Whistleblower Act.

   Simple issue statement: Our client, Ms. Tracie Turner, would like to know whether she can establish a claim for retaliatory discharge under the Minnesota Whistleblower Act.

2. **A statement of the relevant legal standards governing the analysis.** If your problem is a statutory problem, it is most helpful to the reader to start with the relevant language of the statute. Then follow with the basic law governing the area.

   Example: Under the Minnesota Whistleblower Act, an employer may not ... In order to establish a prima facie case under the Minnesota Whistleblower Act, an employee must establish that she engaged in statutorily protected conduct, that she suffered an adverse employment action, and that she suffered the adverse employment action because she engaged in protected conduct.

   Note that you probably do not have to provide the details on what constitutes "statutorily protected conduct" or how one shows "causation" in the thesis paragraph. This level of detail can wait until the heart of your discussion section.

3. **A very brief application of the law to your client's facts and a clear prediction of the likely outcome based on those facts.** If you need additional facts to answer the question, note what facts you need and what steps you have taken or will take in order to get the necessary information.

   Example: Ms. Turner should be able to establish a prima facie case for retaliatory discharge under the Minnesota Whistleblower Act. She can establish that she engaged in statutorily protected conduct because her complaints about suspected race discrimination in the workplace constituted good faith reports of an actual or suspected violation of law. She can show she suffered an adverse employment action because. . . . She can show causation because. . . .

Organizing the Discussion Section at the Macro-Level

Once you have set out a clear thesis paragraph, you should provide a detailed analysis of the legal issues presented by your client's unique situation. How you organize material depends on the question you are answering, though some general principles will help ensure a logical, analytically-sound flow to your memorandum. First, take time to organize your memorandum on a macro-level. If you are dealing with a legal issue that follows the *McDonnell-Douglas* burden shifting proof structure, for example, your reader will likely find it easiest to follow a Discussion section divided into subsections based on the three aspects of the proof structure: a prima facie case, a rebuttal, and proof of pretext.

SAMPLE MACRO-ORGANIZATIONAL FORMAT FOR MINNESOTA WHISTLEBLOWER ACT ANALYSIS

DISCUSSION

Thesis paragraph material.

   I.   Prima Facie Case
   II. Legitimate Reasons (Rebuttal)
   III. Proof of Pretext

Second, even within these subsections, you may find you need additional divisions. For example, in a case involving retaliatory discharge under the Minnesota Whistleblower Act, the prima facie case consists of establishing that the employee engaged in protected conduct, suffered an adverse employment action, and that the adverse employment action was the result of the protected conduct. Each of these three aspects should have its own subsection. Otherwise, the analysis will likely become muddled and hard-to-follow. So, a modified organizational format might look like this:

MODIFIED MACRO-ORGANIZATIONAL FORMAT FOR MINNESOTA WHISTLEBLOWER ACT ANALYSIS

DISCUSSION

Thesis paragraph material.

   I.   Prima Facie Case
      a. Statutorily Protected Conduct
      b. Adverse Employment Action
      c. Causal Connection between the Statutorily Protected Conduct and the Adverse Employment Action
   II. Legitimate Reasons (Rebuttal)
   III. Proof of Pretext

In fact, even some sub-subsections may need division. For example, to prove that an employee has engaged in statutorily protected conduct, that employee must show that she made a report in good faith regarding a violation about which she believed her employer had no prior knowledge.

The report must also be to a supervisor or co-worker, though sometimes it must be made to an outside agency. Moreover, in order to show causation, the employee must show both close timing between the statutorily protected conduct and the adverse employment action as well as employer knowledge that the employee engaged in statutorily protected conduct. So, one possible[10] completed macro-organizational format for the problem might look like this:

"FINAL" MACRO-ORGANIZATIONAL FORMAT FOR MINNESOTA WHISTLEBLOWER ACT ANALYSIS

DISCUSSION

Thesis paragraph material.

I. Prima Facie Case
   a. Statutorily Protected Conduct
      i. Protected Good Faith Report (Appropriate in Form and Substance)
      ii. To a Proper Recipient who did not have Prior Knowledge of the Violation
   b. Adverse Employment Action
   c. Causal Connection between the Statutorily Protected Conduct and the Adverse Employment Action
      i. Close Timing Between the Relevant Events
      ii. Employer Knowledge of the Employee's Protected Conduct
II. Legitimate Reasons (Rebuttal)
III. Proof of Pretext

The best time to develop this macro-outline is as you are researching the legal issues. As you find the basic analysis, start creating the outline. As you find cases that discuss specific issues and sub-issues, plug them into your outline. You will likely discover that much of the analysis and organization is complete before you are even finished researching.

Organizing the Discussion Section at the Micro-Level

One final aspect of organization unique to the "apply-the-law-to-the-facts" memorandum is the act of comparing the facts of prior cases with those in your client's case. Novice lawyers often gravely underestimate the power of clear analogies and distinctions to a fact-based legal analysis. If you keep in mind the necessary micro-organizational elements for this type of analysis, you will be able to express complex legal concepts as they relate to your client's facts in a way that is easy to follow and persuasive to the reader.

---

[10] Note that this is only one option. The point is not that there is only one right way to organize a complex legal analysis. The point is that it is the job of the person expressing the complex analysis in writing to do so in a way that makes it easy for the reader to comprehend the analysis and prediction.

Let's return to the Whistleblower Act problem above. Take the sub-issue of employer knowledge of the employee's protected conduct in the causation element of the prima facie case. Often, a novice lawyer will be tempted to write an analysis that looks like this:

Ms. Turner can likely show that her employer had knowledge of her protected activity. In order to establish causation, an employee must show that the employer had "actual or imputed" knowledge of her protected reports. CITE. Ms. Turner cannot show actual knowledge, because she wrote her complaint about suspected race discrimination at the company in an anonymous note to the supervisor. However, she can likely show imputed knowledge. Her handwriting is distinct, and the supervisor had seen it before. Moreover, other employees were discussing the fact that they thought she was the complainer. Therefore, the supervisor likely had imputed knowledge that Ms. Turner was the whistleblower.

What's wrong with this? The writer has clearly thought through the relevant facts. The writer also establishes that she is aware of the basic rule on employer knowledge. But what does it mean to establish "imputed" knowledge? Is this self-evident, or should the writer have explained this concept a bit better?

As you know, judges make decisions in cases based on what prior binding cases have done on similar issues. What's missing in the above micro-organizational analysis of the issue of employer knowledge is a thorough analysis of the relevant analogous precedent cases.

A more useful and analytical approach includes the following elements:

MICRO-ORGANIZATION OF A SINGLE LEGAL ISSUE OR SUB-ISSUE

1. State the issue (perhaps as a conclusion).
2. State the basic law governing resolution of the issue.
3. Set out clear, fact-specific examples from precedent cases to illustrate how the law actually works in similar situations.
4. Address your client's facts, drawing clear, precise comparisons to precedent cases and distinguishing cases where necessary.
5. Predict the result on the discrete sub-issue you are analyzing.

Of course, an apply-the-law-to-the-facts memorandum is only one type of research project you will be asked to perform in practice. The remainder of this sub-section addresses how to approach other types of research projects.

2. The "Find the Cases (or Statutes)" Memo

Another type of memorandum may simply require you to find and summarize cases on a given legal topic. The assigning attorney may have identified an issue that commonly arises for many clients and may want a summary of available law on the topic. Or the assigning attorney may have a vague notion of the state of the law in a given area and ask you to confirm that by summarizing the key cases in the area. Alternatively, the assigning attorney or client may want an update of recent cases decided on an issue during a particular term. In such a situation, the standard memorandum format should be modified.

It may still be helpful to provide a Statement of Issue(s) Presented or at least a short paragraph introducing the topic of the memorandum. If you can summarize your key findings based on a synthesis of all the material you found, you can also include a Short Answer. For the most part, though, you will just be summarizing the relevant cases or statutory provisions.

Examples of a "Find the Cases (or Statutes)" assignment

■ A partner walks by you in the hallway and says, "Congress recently enacted the Lilly Ledbetter Fair Pay Act of 2009. Can you summarize the main provisions of the Act as well as any key cases decided under the Act so far?"

■ Another attorney in your office prepared a memo (dated March 1, 2006) summarizing the cases in California discussing same-sex harassment under Title VII or the corresponding California state statute. The attorney hands you a copy of the memorandum and asks you to make sure there are no additional cases to add to the memo.

■ The Human Resources Director for one of your clients calls and asks you to summarize the relevant statutes and regulations governing religious harassment in the workplace.

■ An attorney asks you to summarize the employment discrimination cases decided during the last two terms of the United States Supreme Court.

Variation: You may also receive a similar assignment, one in which you are told to "find a case that says x, y, or z." In other words, an attorney or client may ask you to find a case in a specific jurisdiction that stands for a specific legal proposition. This usually occurs when an attorney or client has a particular legal position they want to advance. You may get this type of assignment in one of two forms. First, the attorney may speak to you directly or send you an e-mail asking you to find such a case. Second, the attorney may hand you a piece of a memorandum or brief with the statement of law already in it, followed by a note to "find a citation for this point."

Realize that such a case may or may not exist. In practice, I used to refer to this as the "needle in a haystack" assignment. The attorney or client hopes such a case exists, because it would be very helpful for advocating a certain position. Such wishful thinking, however, cannot make a case materialize. So what does a young attorney do with an assignment like this? Start in the binding jurisdiction. Look to see if you can find a case that says what the assigning attorney or client wants it to say. If not, see if you can at least find something close. If not, then check outside jurisdictions. It's fine to go back to the attorney or client and say that no case exists, as long as you have thoroughly researched the issue.

If, while searching for the "needle in a haystack" case, you find another way to solve your client's problem, bring that to the assigning attorney's attention. Sometimes, although you cannot solve the problem in the way the attorney initially hoped, you can provide a solution that is as good or better.

3. Pure Legal Questions: Surveys of State or Federal Law

You may also be asked to summarize the law in a given area for a set of jurisdictions. For example, you may be asked to provide a summary of the key cases on same-sex harassment by state or by federal circuit. With such an assignment, it makes the most sense to start with a Statement of Issue Presented or introductory paragraph, followed by a Discussion section that simply lists each case and provides a brief summary.

As far as organizing the list of cases, you have several options. If the cases are all over the map in what they say, it is probably best to simply list the cases by state.

SAMPLE FORMAT FOR A SURVEY OF THE LAW WHERE NO TRENDS IN THE LAW ARE APPARENT

Introductory Paragraph or Statement of Issues Presented

This memorandum surveys the treatment of depression as a disability under various state and federal anti-discrimination statutes.

Federal Law
Summarize the law . . .
State Law
   Arkansas
   Summarize Arkansas law.
   California
   Summarize California Law.
   . . .

However, if you find that all the states apply one of a limited number of possible rules, you might consider grouping states according to the rules they follow. The reader will also appreciate a Short Answer that summarizes the various positions taken by the states.

SAMPLE FORMAT FOR A SURVEY OF THE LAW WHERE STATES CAN BE GROUPED ACCORDING TO THE RULE THEY FOLLOW

Statement of Issue Presented: This memorandum summarizes the law in all fifty states regarding the availability of a claim for genetic discrimination under state law.

Short Answer: The majority of states have concluded that.... In other states, however.... A limited number of states have failed to address the issue....

Discussion:

States that recognize a claim for genetic discrimination

In each sub-section, you should organize the states alphabetically and then provide a summary of key cases and statutory provisions governing your issue.

States that do not recognize a claim for genetic discrimination

States that have not addressed the issue of genetic discrimination

---

Variation:

Initially, you may be asked by an attorney to advocate for a specific position for a client. What if you discover that courts in the relevant jurisdiction have not yet addressed the issue? First, you'd have to tell the assigning attorney that the issue is one of first impression. Then, you may be asked to use cases from other jurisdictions (and reasoning from those cases) to craft an argument that your jurisdiction should adopt a specific rule or interpretation. If you have quickly surveyed the various positions in other jurisdictions, you may discover that you are able to say that the majority of states have adopted the rule you want the court to adopt, or that the courts that have adopted the rule you advocate had better reasoning.

4. Other Types of Pure Legal Questions

Pure legal questions come up in practice all the time. These questions can arise in several categories:

    a. Summaries of New Cases or Statutes
    b. Updates of the Law
    c. Questions about Remedies
    d. Questions about Procedural Issues

As with the state or federal law surveys, you should start with either an introductory paragraph or a Statement of Issue Presented. If the question lends itself to a short summary of your conclusions, you can also include a Short Answer.

Examples of Assignments involving Pure Legal Questions:

- *Summaries of New Cases or Statutes*
  Summarize the major changes made to the ADA in the ADA Amendments Act of 2008.
- *Updates of the law*
  The assigning attorney gives you the firm's client education bulletin that was designed to inform clients about how to comply with the ADA. The date on the document is January 15, 2007. Update that memorandum to reflect changes made to the ADA by the recently-enacted ADA Amendments Act.
- *Questions about Remedies*
  Are punitive damages available under Title VII?
- *Questions about Procedural Issues*
  What is the statute of limitations for bringing a religious discrimination claim under Title VII?

5. Pure Questions of Fact

Purely fact-based questions also arise in legal practice. The answer to these factual questions may be necessary to help predict the outcome in a legal matter or to determine what strategy to take in a lawsuit.

Examples:

- How many lawsuits have been filed against Wal-Mart in the last two years? How often has Wal-Mart taken those lawsuits to trial (rather than settling)?
- Who is the CEO of Target? Have any lawsuits been filed against the CEO?
- What is the sexual harassment policy in place at Best Buy?

C. MODES OF PRESENTING RESEARCH RESULTS

As discussed earlier in this chapter, the one common format for presenting research results is the formal research memorandum. However, depending upon where you work (and for whom you work), you may be expected to present your research results in different, and often less formal, formats. While this text provides suggested formats that should serve you well in practice, it is important for you to determine the expected format in your particular work place.

I. Formal Memorandum

As discussed earlier in this chapter, formal memoranda generally include the following sections:

- Memorandum Header
- Statement of Issue(s) Presented or Question(s) Presented
- Conclusion or Short Answer
- Statement of Facts (if you're dealing with a fact-based question)
- Discussion

The Memorandum Header looks like this:

MEMORANDUM

To: Joe Smith
From: Susan Jones
Date: April 7, 2010
Re: *Gibson v. Hooters* – Under Title VII, is being Female a Bona Fide
        Occupational Qualification for Working as a Server at Hooters?

While the Memorandum header may seem self-explanatory, you should keep in mind a couple of things. First, the "Re" line matters. While you do not have to include the level of detail included in the example above, you should include a brief summary of the subject of your memorandum. The *Gibson v. Hooters* file may end up including many memos on various legal topics. Someone trying to go back and find a specific memo will find it much easier to locate if you include the topic in your header. In many firms, you will also be expected to include the client identification number or the case number in the "Re" line.

Second, the "Date" line matters. Consider the following situation. You start researching the above legal issue on March 31, 2010. You find the relevant cases, and you Shepardize or Keycite them to make sure they are still good law. Then you write your memo, and you date it April 7, 2010, the date you turned it in. Someone reviewing your research will assume that the law in your memorandum is up-to-date as of the date in your header. But if you Shepardized or Keycited the cases when you found them (say on March 31 and April 1), you are being misleading, as an entire week has gone by, during which cases you have cited may have been criticized, distinguished, or overruled. Shepardize or Keycite the cases on the date listed on your memorandum.

■ **PRACTICE NOTE ON LANGUAGE:** When you write a legal memo, do not use contractions. Also, avoid using slang or inserting yourself into the analysis ("I think, I believe, etc.). However, you should write in clear, concise language, avoiding unnecessary legalese (hereinafter, heretofore, the "said" agreement, and similar words). Do, however, use terms of art when necessary. When you have to use a term of art, define it, and use it consistently throughout the document. Elegant variation (using synonyms to avoid using the same term over and over), something encouraged in other disciplines, has no place in legal writing.

2. Informal Memorandum

Often, an assigning attorney may say they do not want a formal memorandum. Instead, the assigning attorney may say, "Don't write more than a couple of pages on this issue," or "Just give me a bulleted list of the major issues." When an assigning attorney asks for something "informal," though, remember that "informal" does not mean "unprofessional." You should still include a clear header for the memo, and you should continue to follow the language pointers mentioned above.

What makes an informal memorandum different? Often, what the attorney means is simply "Write something short," usually by deleting many of the formal sections (Question Presented, Short Answer, etc.). The attorney probably just wants the memo to include what you would have included in the Discussion section of a formal memorandum. Even so, it's best to start with a clear thesis paragraph that summarizes your prediction, and then to include your brief analysis of the legal issue.

Even if you are asked to provide a bulleted list, help your reader by beginning with a short introductory paragraph to summarize what is included in the list. If it would be helpful to the reader, include topical headings or subheadings.

3. E-Mail

When you provide an answer to a legal question in an e-mail, remember that a business e-mail is more formal than an e-mail you might write to a friend or family member. Start with a greeting ("Dear Ms. Jones:"), and then include your legal analysis. Finish with a signature line. While your language does not need to be quite as formal as in a legal memorandum (contractions are probably fine), you should still write as if you are writing a business letter rather than a personal letter. Avoid slang, abbreviations, etc.

If you work regularly with in-house counsel or human resource professionals, you may develop a close enough relationship to use first names in your correspondence. Even then, make sure the rest of your communication is professional and businesslike.

4. Oral Report

In practice, you may be asked to perform a quick research project (or even a complex research project) and report your results orally rather than in writing. While this might seem simpler than preparing a memorandum, presenting results orally poses an entirely different set of problems. This section provides a few suggestions for organizing your research results and presenting those results in a coherent, professional way.

First, presenting results orally does not mean presenting them informally or less thoroughly than you might otherwise have done. To keep yourself organized and on track, it is often useful to develop a short outline of your analysis as you go along, even if you do not plan to turn that outline into a memorandum at the end of your research. Create a folder for your research so you can file your outline and (perhaps) any copies of relevant cases. So, for example, let's say you are addressing a hostile work environment sexual harassment claim under California law. If you were unfamiliar with basic sexual harassment law, you would probably start in a treatise or encyclopedia. You discover the following basic overview from *California Jurisprudence*, a legal encyclopedia:

> To establish a prima facie case of hostile work environment sexual harassment, the plaintiff must prove:
>
> - The plaintiff belonged to a protected group
> - The plaintiff was subject to unwelcome sexual harassment
> - The harassment complained of was based on plaintiff's sex
> - The harassment complained of was sufficiently pervasive so as to alter the conditions of plaintiff's employment and create an abusive working environment
> - Employer responsibility
>
> A plaintiff bringing a hostile environment claim does not need to show loss of a tangible job benefit, but only that the harassing conduct was severe and pervasive enough that it affected the plaintiff's working conditions. Whether the sexual conduct complained of is sufficiently pervasive to create a hostile or offensive work environment must be determined from the totality of the circumstances. The plaintiff must prove that the defendant's conduct would have interfered with a reasonable employee's work performance and would have seriously affected the psychological well-being of a reasonable employee and that plaintiff was actually offended. When evaluating a sexual harassment claim, a reasonable employee is one of the same sex as the complainant. Factors that can be considered in evaluating the totality of the circumstances include:
>
> - The nature of the unwelcome sexual acts or works
> - The frequency of the offensive encounters
> - The total number of days over which all of the offensive conduct occurs
> - The context in which the sexually harassing conduct occurred
>
> In determining what constitutes "sufficiently pervasive" harassment, acts of harassment cannot be occasional, isolated, sporadic, or trivial. The plaintiff must show a concerted pattern of harassment of a repeated, routine or a generalized nature.
>
> A violent sexual assault can be the basis of a claim for sexual harassment under a hostile work environment theory, since harassment is defined to include physical harassment such as an assault.

41 Cal. Jur. 3d Labor § 75 (citations omitted). Using this information, you have a basic outline of issues you will need to research as well as some relevant California statutes and case citations to start with. You should write down the

issues (each element of the prima facie case, any sub-elements, etc.), and jot down relevant cases and a comparison to your client's facts as you go along.

Either keep copies of all relevant cases or at least provide citations for relevant cases. Check all cases to ensure that they are good law. Keep track of when you Shepardized or Keycited cases;[11] you will need to do this right before you go to present your results to the assigning attorney.

When you go to present your results to the assigning attorney, be prepared with the following information:

1. *The process by which you researched the problem.* While you won't necessarily tell the assigning attorney this information, it's good to have it in case you get asked the panic-inducing question, "Are you sure you found everything?"
2. *A brief summary of your prediction.* A good way to do this is to draft a very brief "Statement of Issue(s) Presented" and "Short Answer" for the issue as if you were drafting an actual memorandum.
3. *An outline of your analysis, broken down by issue and sub-issue.* Under each issue, list the relevant cases, a word or two about those cases to jog your memory, and a short prediction of how your client's facts stack up against those in analogous cases.

If you prepare in this manner, you will likely have anticipated all the tough questions the attorney might ask. Moreover, you will have organized materials to refer to if you forget a case name or a relevant legal principle. Finally, you will save yourself a lot of time and wasted client dollars if, a few months later, the assigning attorney says "Remember that quick issue I asked you to research a few months ago? The client wants to proceed with a lawsuit. Can you write up those results in a memo for me to give the client?"

---

[11] Consider how useful these dates can be. If you (or another attorney) are asked a year later to research the same (or a similar) issue, you know you only have to Shepardize or Keycite from the date you last did so for the first research project.

THE MECHANICS OF GOOD RESEARCH

I. INTRODUCTION

The last chapter provided a solid research methodology for approaching any legal issue you might be asked to explore. Having read that chapter, you now have a template for approaching legal research questions thoughtfully and efficiently. You should also have tools for troubleshooting your own research and for presenting your research results in the most useful and professional format possible.

The research portion of this book began with research process and strategy because that is where students and new practitioners struggle the most. Of course, research also requires a less creative (but equally-important) step: knowing what sources exist, identifying the correct source to use in a given situation, and using the source correctly.

If you had good training in your first year of law school, you will have had a basic introduction to the *mechanics* of researching in secondary sources, researching cases and statutes on Westlaw and Lexis, and updating your research using Shepard's or Keycite. You should also know how to research both primary and secondary sources in paper resources, including using tables of contents and indexes to find material. While this book assumes you have had this basic introduction, internalizing basic knowledge requires constant reinforcement of new skills. Therefore, this chapter begins with a short reminder of some key skills you should already have mastered. Moreover, even if your school does not require it, you should take as many Westlaw and Lexis training courses offered by the representatives at your school as you can, and you should take an advanced legal research course if it is offered.

Employment lawyers regularly perform types of research rarely taught in the first-year curriculum. These types of research include researching regulations and agency guidance, performing legislative history research, researching past jury awards and settlements so you can evaluate the likely value of a case (for settlement negotiation or client advice), and researching companies and businesses. Because knowing how to perform these types of research is crucial to becoming a good employment lawyer, this chapter addresses these more advanced types of research.

II. REMINDER OF BASIC RESEARCH SKILLS

A. START WITH A SECONDARY SOURCE FOR BACKGROUND

If you search in online databases, make sure you know what materials are included in those databases. For example, Westlaw is the only online source for *Corpus Juris Secundum*. Conversely, all Matthew Bender treatises are available exclusively on Lexis. Use an index to find relevant material in a book, or peruse a table of contents online. Do not rely on word searches at this stage, as you are unlikely to know what words are relevant.

B. MAKE SURE YOU ARE USING PAID ONLINE RESEARCH SERVICES EFFECTIVELY

Even when you move to primary authority, start with a topical search (or a digest search if you are working in paper resources). You are almost always better off starting with a topical search than starting with a terms and connectors search. If you are using Westlaw, you can search by key number or headnote. Lexis also provides the ability to search by topic. For most sources, you can access the table of contents to find relevant information, a strategy likely to help you narrow in on relevant material faster than plugging in ineffective search terms.

Only use terms and connectors searching to focus your research after you have a basic idea of the contours of the governing area of law. You can always focus on specific terms after you have discovered relevant terms through secondary source research and topical and table of contents searching on Westlaw or Lexis.[12]

---

[12] Because Westlaw and Lexis are the two most commonly-used commercial databases, this text focuses on those services for the most part. However, because Westlaw and Lexis are so expensive, other more limited commercial databases have been created for users needing more cost-effective resources. If you end up working as a solo practitioner or in a small firm, you may find that, for cost reasons, you will use one of the more limited databases like Loislaw, Lexis One, or VersusLaw. Another recent addition to the commercial legal research market is Bloomberg Law, a service planning to compete at the level of Westlaw and Lexis. Bloomberg offers a Labor and Employment "Practice Center" that includes primary materials and some helpful secondary sources. Most significantly, BNA materials will be available exclusively on Bloomberg Law beginning in 2013. Another helpful resource is the ability to retrieve court filings through the government's *Public Access to Court Electronic Records* (PACER) service, something already directly accessible to the public.

Even once you have found good terms to use in a search, make sure you know the rules for searching with terms and connectors before you start plugging away at your research. You should know what each connector means (the rules on Westlaw and Lexis are not the same) as well as the order in which the computer will process the connectors you enter. If you are not certain of both of these things, you do not know what material you are asking the computer to retrieve. Specific guidance on effective use of terms and connectors is available on the website.

If you are using Lexis.com or Westlaw Classic, make sure you are searching in an appropriate database. The appropriate database is usually the smallest possible database necessary to retrieve binding authority on your issue.[13] If necessary, you can then expand to look for persuasive authority if little or no binding authority exists.

Do not wait until you have collected a stack of cases to Shepardize or Keycite those cases. When you find a case that seems useful, make sure it is good law immediately. That way, you won't waste a lot of time building your research on the foundation of an overruled case. Moreover, Shepard's and Keycite are great tools for expanding your research by finding additional cases that have discussed your case on specific points for which you need more support.

C. STAY ORGANIZED, AND METHODICALLY TRACK YOUR PROGRESS

Always keep track of what sources you have visited, what terms you searched, and what materials you have reviewed. That way, you will be able to quickly pick up where you left off if you get pulled away from a project mid-stream. You will also be able to convince any skeptical outsiders that your research was thorough and effective.

Both Lexis and Westlaw track your search history, though those results do not remain forever. Moreover, your search history will not reflect free internet resources, other paid resources, and paper resources you reviewed. Therefore, do not rely solely on your electronic research trail to remind you what ground you have covered.

PACER "is an electronic public access service that allows users to obtain case and docket information from Federal Appellate, District and Bankruptcy courts, and the U.S. Party/Case Index via the Internet." http://pacer.psc.uscourts.gov/pacerdesc.html (last accessed December 13, 2012). Unlike PACER, Bloomberg offers expanded search functionality that allows keyword searches of federal dockets. Finally, Bloomberg also has transactional resources such as sample documents and clauses. Alternatively, Lexis Advance offers access to CourtLink, which will retrieve court filings as well as attorney, judge, and witness litigation profiles.
[13] As discussed in other parts of this book, Lexis Advance and WestlawNext allow you to run broad searches (without incurring additional costs) and then use filters to narrow down to relevant information. You can, however, still access specific source databases within the newer systems.

III. RESEARCHING REGULATIONS AND AGENCY GUIDANCE

A. RESEARCHING REGULATIONS

In many areas of employment discrimination law, both federal and state legislatures have given agencies the authority to create regulations designed to implement the relevant statutory schemes. Regulations promulgated by agencies are generally treated as binding authority by a court as long as the court believes (1) the regulations do not conflict with the language or intent of the statute they have been designed to implement; and (2) the agency did not exceed the limited rule-making authority granted to it by the legislature. (This, of course, gives courts a lot of leeway.) Regulations often provide more detailed information than the statutes themselves, and they can therefore be very helpful in interpreting otherwise vague or general statutory language.

1. Researching Federal Regulations

a. General Research

The Code of Federal Regulations (CFR) contains the "general and permanent rules" established "by the executive departments and agencies of the Federal Government."[14] The CFR "is divided into 50 titles that represent broad areas subject to Federal regulation," and each Title is updated once a year according to the following schedule:[15]

- Titles 1–16: Updated January 1
- Titles 17–27: Updated April 1
- Titles 28–41: Updated July 1
- Titles 42–50: Updated October 1

CFR titles are divided into chapters, and chapters are divided into sections and sub-sections. Most regulations related to employment discrimination law appear in Title 29 (Labor). However, some regulations may appear in other Titles. For example, Title 41 (Public Contracts and Property Management) addresses discrimination issues arising with government contractors and subcontractors.

Until the CFR is updated, new materials appear in a daily publication called the *Federal Register*. The "*Federal Register* is the official daily publication for rules, proposed rules, and notices of Federal agencies and organizations, as well as executive orders and other presidential documents."[16]

---

[14] www.gpo.gov/help/index.html#about_code_of_federal_regulations.htm (last accessed February 19, 2013).
[15] *Id.*
[16] www.gpo.gov/fdsys/browse/collection.action?collectionCode=FR (last accessed February 19, 2013).

The CFR and the *Federal Register* are available in print versions as well as on-line. You can access both publications on Westlaw and Lexis. You can also access free versions in a couple of ways. One way is through the Government Printing Office's Federal Digital System. You can access that system by going to www.gpo.gov/fdsys/ (last accessed February 19, 2013). Once there, you can also find a link to sign up for a daily e-mail update of the *Federal Register Table of Contents*.[17] You can also access the post-1994 Federal Register at www.FederalRegister.gov (last accessed February 19, 2013). The Office of the Federal Register maintains this site, and it arguably has a better search function than the site maintained by the Government Printing Office.[18]

You should always update your federal regulatory research to determine whether the regulations you are relying on have been repealed or amended since the last time the CFR was updated. The process for updating your regulatory research differs depending upon whether you are doing your research in print or online. If you are researching in print, the process is a bit more difficult. The government publishes a resource called the *List of CFR Sections Affected* (LSA). The LSA "lists proposed, new, and amended Federal regulations that have been published in the *Federal Register* since the most recent revision date of a CFR title. Each LSA issue is cumulative and contains the CFR part and section numbers, a description of its status (e.g., amended, confirmed, revised), and the *Federal Register* page number where the change(s) may be found."[19] Once you have found a regulation relevant to your research situation, you should look it up in the LSA. However, the LSA is only published on a monthly basis, so if you are doing your research in print, you will also have to refer to the *Table of CFR Parts Affected* (located on the back of the most recent issue of the *Federal Register*) to determine whether your regulation has been altered or repealed in the past month. The *Table of CFR Parts Affected* provides citations to the relevant location in the *Federal Register* where you can view changes to the relevant regulation(s).

If you are researching online, updating is automatic. Commercial databases (Westlaw, Lexis, Loislaw, etc.) update regulations continually. The government also prints a version of the CFR that is updated daily, the *e-CFR*.[20] While it is an unofficial version of the CFR, it is a very useful resource. When you access an *e-CFR* web page, the current update status will be listed at the top of the page.

You can also access the LSA on the *FDSys* website. While the LSA is only a monthly publication, the LSA on *FDSys* also provides users the ability to browse all "final and proposed rules that affect the CFR . . . [that] have been published in

---

[17] www.gpo.gov/fdsys/browse/collection.action?collectionCode=FR (last accessed February 19, 2013).
[18] The version of the Federal Register maintained by the Government Printing Office is an official version. The version listed at FederalRegister.gov is "an unofficial HTML version of the *Federal Register* known as Federal Register 2.0 . . . Each HTML rendering . . . includes a direct link to the official PDF rendering on FDsys." www.federalregister.gov/learn/tutorials (last accessed February 19, 2013).
[19] www.gpo.gov/fdsys/browse/collection.action?collectionCode=LSA (last accessed February 19, 2013).
[20] Located at www.ecfr.gov (last accessed February 19, 2013).

the Federal Register within the past 24 hours, week, month, or within a specific date range."[21]

Another useful resource is a government website located at www.Regulations.gov. On this website, you can access regulatory information for almost 300 agencies. The website allows you to do the following:

1. Search for a regulation such as a proposed rule, final rule[,] or *Federal Register* . . . notice[;]
2. Submit a comment on a regulation or on another comment[;]
3. Submit an application, petition[,] or adjudication document[;]
4. Sign up for e-mail alerts about a specific regulation[;]
5. Quickly access regulations that are popular, newly posted or closing soon-directly from the homepage[; and]
6. Subscribe to RSS feeds by agency of newly posted [*Federal Register*] notice[.][22]

EXERCISES

1) Take the tutorial located at http://www.regulations.gov/#!help. This tutorial covers the most common uses of the website, including how to find a regulation, how to submit a comment on a regulation, how to find a comment on a regulation, and how to subscribe to e-mail alerts. Search for a regulation on an employment discrimination topic, and set up an e-mail alert.

2) Look on the EEOC website or use the search function on www.regulations.gov to discover a proposed rule on any employment discrimination topic. Once you have selected a proposed rule, read current comments on that rule. Do any additional research you feel is appropriate to make your own determination regarding whether the proposed rule should be adopted. Prepare a memorandum with the following information:

☐ A summary of the key elements of the proposed rule (and attach a copy of the proposed rule to the assignment);

☐ An overview of the reasons why the agency felt it needed to create a proposed rule (to respond to a recent court opinion, to clarify existing regulations, etc.);

☐ A research log describing the other research you did to educate yourself regarding the rule and its merits; and

☐ An explanation of your analysis regarding whether the rule should be adopted, written in the form of a public comment you would feel comfortable posting online.

---

[21] www.gpo.gov/help/index.html#about_federal_register.htm (last accessed February 19, 2013).
[22] http://www.regulations.gov/#!aboutProgram (last accessed February 19, 2013).

b. *Short-cuts to Finding Regulations on Employment Discrimination Topics*

Probably the best way to narrow down your regulatory research quickly is to start that research on the website of the agency in charge of the relevant statute. While the regulatory materials on agency and executive department websites are not official versions, the agency will have already collected the relevant regulations and other policy guidance in one place. Once you identify the relevant regulations, you can update them using official versions of regulations and updating materials.

You can also use the commercial databases to find regulations by overall legal topic. On Lexis.com, you simply select "Searching by Source" and then take the following path: Legal > Area of Law by Topic > Labor & Employment > Find Statutes & Regulations. In Lexis Advance, you can similarly click on Browse Topics > Labor & Employment Law. From there, you can access materials in a given employment law area. If you click on a topic, Lexis Advance offers the option to get documents within that sub-topic, add the sub-topic to your search, create a "favorite" for that sub-topic, or create an alert for that sub-topic. Creating an alert will allow you to receive updates regarding new material on your topic either via e-mail or online (when you log on to Lexis Advance). You can also share updates with colleagues and limit the update to specific types of documents (cases, statutes, regulations, secondary sources, and the like).

Westlaw Classic offers an option where you can add subject-matter tabs to your display. From the main research screen, click on the "Add a Tab" link on the upper right-hand part of the display. Then click on the tab called "Add Westlaw Tabs." Several tabs are quite useful for employment lawyers. In the "General" tabs, you will see a tab for Westlaw's "Regulations Suite." If you scroll down to the "Topical" tab options, you will see other tabs related to employment law, including "Employment Practitioner" and "Labor & Employment."

In WestlawNext, you can also use the Browse by Content links to get to materials on Proposed & Adopted Regulations. If you click on Proposed & Adopted Regulations > Labor & Employment, WestlawNext will then allow you to browse the ten most recent documents or run a search solely in regulations on labor and employment law topics.

EXERCISES

1) Access the relevant federal government agency or executive branch website(s) dealing with age and disability discrimination in the workplace (these may or may not be the same agencies). From the government website(s), find the regulations governing age discrimination and disability discrimination in the workplace. If the website allows you to create an alert regarding new regulations in this area, do so. Be prepared to explain what you found.

2) If you have not already done so, create tabs on Westlaw Classic for "Labor & Employment," "Employment Practitioner," and the "Regulations Suite." Choose a question related to employment discrimination law that you have found from recent news articles, and research the statute and regulations governing that area using materials you find in these three tabs. Explain in a short memorandum what you find as well as how useful you found each tab.

2. Researching State Regulations

The process for researching state regulations is generally the same as it is for federal regulations. While each state has its own method for compiling regulations, most states start by publishing regulations in a publication similar to the Federal Register and then codifying the regulations in an official state code of regulations later.

Again, the easiest way to find regulations relevant to employment discrimination law issues is probably to go directly to the relevant state agency website. For example, the Illinois Department of Human Rights is the agency charged with administering the primary non-discrimination law in Illinois, the Illinois Human Rights Act. From their web page, www2.illinois.gov/dhr/Pages/default.aspx, you can access the full text of relevant statutes, proposed rules, and sections of the administrative code relating to discrimination.

Most state regulatory information is also available on commercial databases like Lexis and Westlaw. On the classic systems (Lexis.com and Westlaw Classic), you can easily access all of a given state's materials in one location by creating a tab for the given state and then accessing material from the state tab. For example, on Lexis.com, the relevant link on the California page is to "Statutes, Regulations, Administrative Materials & Court Rules."

In Westlaw Classic, you can easily access administrative materials by state simply by creating a tab for the relevant state and then looking for administrative materials within that section. Through the Regulations Suite tab, you can also access employment law regulation tracking (a full-text database of proposed and newly-enacted rules and regulations) for a specific state by clicking on "More Sources" in the Employment Regulations Suite.

You can also easily access state regulations in Lexis Advance or WestlawNext by using the Browse by State functions in either system and linking to regulations there.

If you are having difficulty locating a particular state's regulatory materials, one good resource is www.administrativerules.org. On this site, the National Association of Secretaries of State has collected links to administrative materials by state. Remember, though, that it is often easier to start by going directly to the website of the relevant agency dealing with your particular issue. The links in www.administrativerules.org are to the entire regulatory scheme for a state and are not divided by topic. Another useful website is Cornell's Legal Information Institute, located at www.law.cornell.edu/. From that portal, you can link to free versions of the United States Code (U.S.C.), the CFR, and state statutes and administrative agencies by topic, among other materials.

B. ADDITIONAL SOURCES OF AGENCY-CREATED INTERPRETIVE GUIDANCE

Agencies often provide additional interpretive guidance in the form of letter opinions, memoranda of understanding, compliance manuals, fact sheets, and agency decisions. Much of this material can be located directly on the website of the relevant government agency. For example, the EEOC provides regulatory and policy guidance through its website, www.eeoc.gov. While these materials are merely persuasive authority, an agency's policy guidance is a good place to start if you are trying to determine how the agency might handle a given situation.

■ **PRACTICE NOTE:** Agencies of the federal government handle discrimination charges by their employees internally. However, the EEOC hears appeals from decisions issued by government agencies. Those appeals are catalogued and searchable on the EEOC website beginning with decisions issued in July 2000.

If you are unable to locate agency decisions or other agency guidance on the relevant agency's website, you have a couple of other options for locating this material. First, specialized loose-leaf services provide agency decisions, among other materials.[23] Second, you can use a commercial database to locate these materials.

On Lexis.com, it is helpful to first set up a tab in the "Search by Source" area for "Labor & Employment." To do so, link to Legal > Area of Law – By Topic > Labor & Employment. Just above the search path, you will see a small link to create a sub-tab.

You can also access agency decisions and other agency materials in Westlaw Classic. You can find them by searching topically through the database directory. However, you will find it even easier to access administrative decisions and materials if you have added the tabs for "Labor & Employment" and the "Regulations Suite." In the Regulations Suite, you will find a link to "Multistate Regulations

---

[23] In fact, loose-leaf services are often the best place to start employment law research. The two major publishers offering labor and employment-related loose-leaf services are the Bureau of National Affairs (BNA) and the Commerce Clearing House (CCH). For example, BNA and CCH both publish the EEOC Compliance Manual, a resource that includes detailed policy guidance as well as an EEOC Decisions Finding List. For more focused research of EEOC agency decisions, you can look to the *CCH EEOC Decisions* resource, available as a loose-leaf service. In addition to print versions, BNA resources are available on Westlaw, while CCH resources are available on Lexis. BNA resources are now also available via Bloomberg Law, and they may soon only be available there.

Suite – Agency Decisions."[24] Under the Labor and Employment tab, look to the "Administrative Decisions and Materials" section. Remember to click the "show all" link so that you see the full list of administrative materials available. Under the Employment Practitioner Tab, you can access state or federal regulatory materials under the heading, "Administrative Decisions and Guidance."

In WestlawNext, you can also start by linking into the specific content heading, "Administrative Decisions & Guidance." You can then either use the universal search bar to search across all federal and state administrative decisions and guidance or further filter by federal material, specific state, or topic.

The preceding suggestions are useful for finding agency materials if you are still trying to determine the relevant regulations applicable to your research situation. However, Westlaw's "Regulations Plus" feature is quite useful if you have already located the relevant federal regulation and simply want to find related agency and court documents. When you enter a citation for a specific regulation on Westlaw, the "Regulations Plus" feature will appear on the left-hand column of your screen. This feature provides links to prior versions of the regulation as well as cases, agency decisions, and administrative materials related to your regulation.

Finally, in either Westlaw or Lexis, you can access limited administrative materials, including agency decisions, if you Shepardize or Keycite a statute or regulation.

IV. PERFORMING LEGISLATIVE HISTORY RESEARCH

A. INTRODUCTION

Reviewing the legislative history of a statute is one method of statutory interpretation available to attorneys and policymakers. The legislative history of a statute includes every document created during the legislative process, from a bill's initial introduction to its passage into law. To compile a complete legislative history, then, you need to look for a statement of the bill's purpose; statements of the bill's sponsors regarding the bill's purpose and meaning; the original bill presented (and any amended versions before the bill reached its final enacted form); committee reports, prints, and hearings; records of any floor debates; and presidential signing statements, if any.

As you might imagine, compiling a legislative history is a painstaking and time-consuming process. The good news is that, for two reasons, it is rarely

---

[24] Some material may be outside your employer's pricing plan. If so, you should get a warning so that you do not inadvertently incur unexpected charges.

necessary to do so. First, compiling a statute's legislative history is a tool for discerning legislative intent. Therefore, it is only relevant when you determine that the applicability or interpretation of a statutory provision is uncertain even after reading the relevant statute, its regulations, and any court or agency opinions interpreting the statutory provision. Second, for many laws (including those specifically dealing with employment discrimination topics), compiled legislative histories already exist.

Therefore, if you are doing statutory research, first determine whether the language is clear. If not, research the regulations and any agency guidance, and also review court opinions interpreting the relevant statute. If these sources do not provide an answer, turn to legislative history research to discern legislative intent. At this point, check to see if a legislative history has already been compiled for your statute.

B. LOCATING COMPILED LEGISLATIVE HISTORIES

Compiled legislative histories already exist for many employment law-related statutes. You can locate those legislative histories fairly easily if you know where to look.

First, you can find legislative histories for federal laws in two different print publications: (1) *Federal Legislative Histories: An Annotated Bibliography and Index to Officially Published Sources*, compiled by Bernard D. Reams, Jr. (Westport, Conn.: Greenwood Press, 1994); and (2) *Sources of Compiled Legislative Histories: A Bibliography of Government Documents, Periodical Articles, and Books, 1st Congress-108th Congress*, Nancy P. Johnson, (Littleton, Colo.: Fred B. Rothman & Co., 2007). This second publication is also available on *HeinOnline* if you have access to it.

Second, both Westlaw and Lexis provide access to some compiled legislative histories.[25] Access legislative history material on Lexis.com (including a limited number of compiled legislative histories) using the following path: Search by Source > Legal > Federal Legal – U.S. > Find Statutes, Regulations, Administrative Materials & Court Rules > Legislative History Materials. This information includes the volume of the CIS Index that has compiled legislative histories.

On Lexis Advance, access the legislative history for a particular statute by entering the statutory section in the search box and selecting Search. Then, use post-search filters to narrow your results: select Legis > Content Type/More > Legislative Histories or Congressional Record.

---

[25] ProQuest Congressional is also a good source for creating your own legislative history, as discussed below.

On Westlaw, you will find the Arnold & Porter Legislative History collection as well as the U.S. GAO legislative history collection. On WestlawNext, access either source by entering the source name in the search box. Alternatively, both sources can be found using the Legislative History link on the main page. On Westlaw Classic, access the Arnold & Porter database by searching in the U.S. Federal Materials folder in the Directory. Each statute's legislative history in the Arnold & Porter database is listed by name. Access the U.S. GAO legislative history collection by clicking on the Legislative History link in the U.S. Federal Materials Folder. You will then see a link to the U.S. GAO materials. To access a specific statute's legislative history, you either need to know the public law number or the statute's citation in Statutes at Large. Otherwise, you can run a word search in the database.

Third, some loose-leaf services covering a particular area of law will also compile the legislative history of the law in that area. Check major employment discrimination loose-leaf services on specific employment discrimination laws to see whether those services provide a compiled legislative history. Moreover, some large law firms have compiled legislative histories for major laws, and those legislative histories may be available in print and online via Westlaw or Lexis. If you have access to a good law library, ask a librarian what sources for compiled legislative histories are available.

Fourth, if you have access to the *U.S. Legislative History Database* on *HeinOnline*, you can search for existing compiled legislative histories on federal employment-related statutes by searching the *U.S. Federal Legislative History Title Collection*. Compiled legislative histories included in this database include regular legislative history materials as well as additional materials related to the legislative history of a given document.

Fifth, a case interpreting the statute may have collected all the material already. While the case might not address your particular issue, it may have collected the relevant materials.

C. COMPILING YOUR OWN LEGISLATIVE HISTORY

One very good source for compiling your own legislative history is ProQuest Congressional (http://congressional.proquest.com). While you can find much of this information for free by searching on FDSys (www.fdsys.gov), THOMAS (www.thomas.gov), or Congress.gov (www.congress.gov), the materials available on ProQuest Congressional (formerly LexisNexis Congressional) are more comprehensive (and, in many cases, are collected from an earlier date).

SAMPLE OF LEGISLATIVE HISTORY MATERIALS AVAILABLE ON PROQUEST CONGRESSIONAL

Published hearings abstracts and indexing (can use abstract numbers to get the full text of a document you need)	From 1970
CIS legislative histories	From 1984
Full text of bills	From 1989
Bill tracking	From 1989
Congressional testimony and hearings	Testimony: From 1988 Hearings: From 1970
Congressional committee reports	From 1990
Congressional committee prints	From 1993 (though only includes a small percentage of committee prints)
Full text of congressional record	From 1985
Most House and Senate documents	From 1995

The CIS Index is also available on Lexis.com[26] and as a print volume (print volume published yearly since 1984, and microfiche available back to 1970). It provides three kinds of volumes: the index, abstracts, and legislative histories. Using the CIS Index, which has multiple finding aids, you can find relevant documents to compile a full legislative history for any law passed from 1970 – present.

Another good resource for compiling your own legislative history is *United States Code Congressional & Administrative News* (USCCAN). This pamphlet, arranged by Congress and published monthly (cumulated annually), is available in print, online, and in Westlaw's Legislative History Database. USSCAN provides incomplete legislative history information. However, it generally includes the most important documents, like the full text of the laws and the relevant committee reports.

If you are doing legislative history research in Westlaw Classic, one of the best things you can do is first set up tabs for both federal and state legislative history materials.

Clicking on any step in the congressional lawmaking process will lead you to a search screen and the databases most relevant to that part of the process. This makes searching for relevant legislative material quite simple. Remember, though, that the legislative materials on Lexis, Westlaw, THOMAS, and FDSys are less comprehensive than those found in print and in ProQuest Congressional. This may or may not matter depending upon the statutory provision you are researching and the reason you are researching it.

---

[26] As of August 2013, the CIS Index is not available on Lexis Advance.

Clicking on a state leads you to relevant legislative materials in that state. An important thing to know as a researcher is that, while state legislative histories generally contain the same types of materials as federal legislative histories, not all state documents are published, and there are fewer useful finding tools for state legislative history. Before even attempting to locate state materials in a commercial database, try state government websites and subject-matter loose-leaf services. Also know that it is much more common to see arguments based upon legislative history when dealing with a federal statute than a state statute, so make sure you do not spend hours trying to compile a state legislative history before determining that your client or the assigning attorney wants you to spend the time and money on the project.

EXERCISES

1) List the Arnold & Porter legislative history titles that deal with employment discrimination statutes. Choose one of these statutes, and note the materials available in the compilation.

2) Look at THOMAS. List the available legislative history materials, including the dates a particular type of material became available. Compare this list to the legislative history materials available at www.Congress.gov.

3) With a partner, choose one of the following laws, and answer the question set below.

Lilly Ledbetter Fair Pay Act of 2009

ADA Amendments Act of 2008

The Civil Rights Act of 1991

☐ What is the public law number for the Act? What is the citation in the Statutes at Large?

☐ Can you locate an existing legislative history for the Act? Remember to check all sources of compiled legislative histories. If so, how did you find it? What materials are contained in the compiled legislative history?

☐ Does USSCAN provide any legislative history material for the Act? If so, describe how you found it and what you found.

☐ If you do not find a compiled legislative history for your Act and USSCAN does not provide all the materials you need, identify what types of documents you need. How will you go about finding the relevant documents?

V. RESEARCHING FOR CLAIM EVALUATION AND TRIAL PREPARATION

As an attorney, you will often be expected to estimate the monetary value of a claim (and its likelihood of success). Your first step in claim evaluation is, of course, to analyze the legal merits of the claim itself given your client's specific situation. Once you have determined how likely it is that your client will succeed based on the law, you may find it useful to expand your research to include a factual investigation of the companies and people involved in the dispute, from the parties and likely witnesses to the presiding judge and the attorneys handling the case.

When gauging whether to settle a case or to spend the time and money to go to trial, you will also find it helpful to research jury awards and settlements in similar cases. Numerous resources exist for performing research for the purpose of claim evaluation and trial preparation. This section covers a few of those key resources.

A. RESEARCHING INFORMATION RELATED TO COMPANIES AND PEOPLE

1. Free (or Nearly Free) Resources

You will primarily accomplish this type of research by working in public records databases. If you need to find out information about an individual or company, it is often easiest to start by running a simple search on a search engine like Google. Doing so may lead you to professional affiliations, licenses, and property ownership information. At the very least, you will likely locate where the person is living or where the company is incorporated, giving you a smaller world in which to search public records.

Many agencies provide public records data online, though you will sometimes have to actually go to the office of the relevant agency to make a document request. Usually you will have to pay a small fee for printing or mailing. Many states also offer online access to birth certificates, death certificates, marriage licenses, and divorce records through *VitalChek* (www.VitalChek.com).

Although VitalChek is a useful service, in many situations it is faster and less expensive to go directly to the relevant courthouse or administrative building to retrieve public records. The same records may be available directly from the agency (in person or by mail) or online through a third-party vendor like Vital-Chek. In some cases, the time it takes to receive a record as well as the cost of the record will vary widely depending upon how you access the record. For example, in Oklahoma, you can order a birth certificate using three methods: (1) appearing in person to request a copy at the Oklahoma State Department of Health Vital Records Service; (2) mailing a request to the Oklahoma State Department of Health Vital Records Service; or (3) ordering a birth certificate online through VitalChek. If you appear in person, the cost is $15.00, and you will receive a copy of the record within an hour. If you mail in the request, you will pay $15.00 (plus the cost of a self-addressed stamped envelope), and you will receive a copy of the record within four weeks. If you order through VitalChek, you will pay $25.95 plus shipping charges, and you may receive your records in as quickly as a few days or as long as 30-60 business days, depending upon the agency and the method of delivery you have chosen.

EXERCISE (CHOOSE ONE)

1) Research to determine whether the state in which you were born allows you to order birth certificates online or whether you have to make an in-person or written request. Order a certified copy of your own birth certificate using the most cost-effective and practical method for doing so.

2) If you are married, order a copy of your marriage license using the most cost-effective and practical method for doing so.

A good starting point for researching property ownership and sales is www.netronline.com/public_records.htm. From this site, you can choose a jurisdiction and locate where real estate documents are housed and whether you can access them online. Another online source for public records is located at http://publicrecords.searchsystems.net/. From that site, you can search "property, criminal, court, birth, death, marriage, divorce records, licenses, deeds, mortgages, corporate records, business registration, and many other public record resources."[27] While the site states that it provides free public records, some of the reports require payment of a small fee.

2. Commercial Databases

a. Westlaw Classic and WestlawNext

Although Westlaw has migrated most materials from Westlaw Classic to WestlawNext, you still have to access most public records through Westlaw Classic. WestlawNext does not have the level of security necessary to house many public records documents. The migration should occur over the next one or two years. Until then, you can still link to public records from WestlawNext. However, if you click on the public records link in WestlawNext, it will simply send you to Westlaw Classic to do your research.

Currently, one of the best ways to access relevant information on people and companies on Westlaw Classic is through the *Employment Practitioner* tab. Westlaw has collected key resources for researching companies, people, and expert witnesses there. If you create an *Employment Practitioner* tab, you will see entire sections on "Information on People," "Information on Companies," "Profiler-Professional," and "Court Documents."

---

[27] http://publicrecords.searchsystems.net/ (last accessed May 14, 2013).

The *Information on People* section allows you to search to determine an individual's assets, criminal record, professional licenses, and other information. You can also determine whether an individual has filed any lawsuits (or been sued) and what the nature and outcome of those lawsuits was.

In the *Information on Companies* section, you can search through corporate records and business registrations, prior lawsuits, and the like.

Westlaw Profiler helps you investigate judges, attorneys, arbitrators, and expert witnesses. When you search for an individual using *Westlaw Profiler*, you will get background information including cases the individual you are researching has been involved with as well as briefs and depositions involving the individual. From a cost perspective, one thing you should be aware of is that you incur a charge for using *Westlaw Profiler* even if it returns no results. You can also search through expert witness filings in the *Court Documents* section.

Westlaw's *Business Citator Reports* service permits a researcher to compile a due diligence report on a company. The service collects information from the United States and the United Kingdom on the relevant company. Unfortunately, this service is unavailable to academic subscribers (except perhaps in some business-related clinics), so most students cannot access it. However, it is a research tool of which you should be aware.

Finally, if you want to review *all* of the types of public records available in Westlaw, the best way is to access the list of public records databases through the Directory.

EXERCISES

1) From the *Employment Practitioner* tab, run a search for any criminal records for Bernard Madoff. Summarize what information you find there.

2) Choose the CEO of a major company, and search through at least two of the public records databases available in the *Information on People* section of the *Employment Practitioner* tab. Print reports of what you find.

3) Go to the Westlaw Classic Directory and search for public records databases that would help you research people or companies. List them. Some will likely be outside your subscription package, but you should be able to at least see the database names.

4) Choose a public figure and determine whether they have been involved in any lawsuits. If so, list the number of lawsuits and their subject matter.

b. Lexis.com and Lexis Advance

Conducting research regarding people and companies is relatively simple on Lexis.com. First, in the *"Search by Source"* window, you can link to a tab for *"Public Records."* Just like Westlaw, Lexis.com offers numerous categories of public records. You can click on several links from the main source page to find "a person, a business, assets, licenses, filings, and environmental site records," to name a few. If you click on the link for public records generally, you will find expanded lists of materials available in the various categories. Remember that there will often be a "view more" link next to a category that will expand the subcategories that may be available. Lexis Advance also offers public records through the Public Records tab in the far upper-left corner of the screen.

EXERCISES

1) Look in the Public Records tab on Lexis.com or Lexis Advance. Review all available sources. What records do you think would be most useful for you if you were representing a corporate defendant in a sexual harassment lawsuit and were compiling data on the plaintiff? Be prepared to explain your reasoning.

2) Using the same materials, list the types of public records information you would like to gather on a defendant corporation if you are representing plaintiffs in a race discrimination class action lawsuit.

Another useful Lexis.com resource for litigators is *"Litigation Workflow."* You can access the *Litigation Workflow* part of Lexis.com by taking the following path: Search > All > Legal > Area of Law – By Topic > Litigation Workflow. Once there, you can add *Litigation Workflow* as a sub-tab on your main page. *Litigation Workflow* organizes material based on the stage of the case you are in. When you are in the claim evaluation stage, a great resource for researching people and companies is under the *Early Case Assessment* link in the *Litigation Workflow* area. There, you will find links to research companies; witnesses and individuals; judges, arbitrators, and mediators; and attorneys and law firms. You can also look at information useful to assessing damages and drafting or evaluating proposed jury instructions. Lexis.com has collected multiple databases for researching people and companies in one location, and you can select whether to search one database or multiple databases.

Both Lexis.com and Lexis Advance offer the *Litigation Profile Suite*. From there, you can research judges, expert witnesses, and attorneys. On Lexis.com, you can access the *Litigation Profile Suite* by clicking on the "More" tab on the home screen at Lexis.com. On Lexis Advance, you can access it by clicking on the drop-down menu in the far upper-left corner of your screen. You can narrow your search for judges and attorneys by jurisdiction. You can further narrow your search for expert witnesses by area of expertise.

Finally, you should be aware of the *CourtLink* service offered by Lexis.com. *CourtLink* allows you to search federal, state, and local court records. You can gather and analyze data on attorneys, judges, and opposing counsel. While *CourtLink* provides many useful services, the most useful one for case evaluation is probably the strategic profile option. *CourtLink Strategic Profiles* searches through over 20 years of court records data and allows you to track "the litigation activity of an opposing party, attorney, law firm or judge assigned to a case—including prior litigation, background records and previous rulings by judges—to help assess the likely outcome or resolution of your case and sharpen your legal strategy."[28] *CourtLink* may be accessible by clicking on the "More" tab on the home screen at Lexis.com. If not, you can access it by clicking on Public Records > Find Filings > Civil & Criminal Court Filings & Regulatory Actions > Court Records. You can also access *CourtLink* directly without going to the Lexis.com website by going to http://courtlink.lexisnexis.com (last accessed May 15, 2013).

CourtLink Strategic Profiles will also allow you to determine what kinds of lawsuits a litigant or prospective litigant has recently been involved in. You can set alerts to track new activity for a particular judge, litigant, attorney, or witness. *CourtLink Alerts* incur an extra charge, but in a refreshing change of pace for commercial legal databases, the specific amount of these charges is prominently displayed. Currently, dockets from *CourtLink* are available on Lexis Advance. However, *CourtLink Strategic Profiles* are only available on Lexis.com.

EXERCISES

1) Access the *Early Case Assessment* materials in *Litigation Workflow*. If you want to search for a witness or individual, what databases will Lexis.com search for information?

2) Access *CourtLink*. Summarize its capabilities. Given what you already know about public records data you can retrieve from other sources, what services on *CourtLink* are better retrieved using other (cheaper) methods? What services are unique to *CourtLink*?

3) Consider a situation in which you are approached by an individual seeking to sue Wal-Mart for race discrimination under Title VII. Using *CourtLink Strategic Profiles,* run a "litigant" strategic profile on Wal-Mart for a three-month period. Note how many employment-related lawsuits the company has been involved in during your chosen time period.

4) Using the *Litigation Profile Suite*, find an expert witness in your area with expertise in employment discrimination cases. Summarize the types of cases in which the expert has been a witness (and for what side).

---

[28] http://law.lexisnexis.com/courtlink (last accessed May 15, 2013).

5) Using the *Litigation Profile Suite*, find a state or federal judge in your area. Explore the information available about the judge. Determine what percentage of cases the judge handles that involve labor and employment issues. Determine how many verdicts in that area have been for plaintiffs versus defendants as well as what the average jury awards have been (if the information is available).

c. A Note on Unpublished Opinions and Claim Evaluation

This book assumes the reader has a basic understanding of how to research cases. However, one very important issue related to case law is not generally covered in basic research classes. Unpublished opinions are often not citable for the legal propositions contained in them. Therefore, legal researchers often dismiss unpublished opinions wholesale. However, unpublished opinions can be quite useful in claim evaluation. If you are attempting to determine how many times a company has been sued for employment discrimination or whether a plaintiff has filed lawsuits in the past, for example, you want to include unpublished opinions in the mix.

Moreover, other facts about people, companies, or situations in an unpublished opinion may be crucial to your case. Recently, for example, an individual wrongfully convicted of murder in Michigan was exonerated, in part due to evidence found in an unpublished opinion in another case that another individual had committed the crime.

When you search through cases on Westlaw or Lexis, unpublished federal opinions are included in your search results (unless you specifically filter them out). Federal unpublished opinions are also (ironically) published in a print volume called the *Federal Appendix*. Some states will make unpublished opinions available either electronically or in print. However, if you are in a state that does not do so, you will probably have to pass on researching unpublished opinions unless your case investigation leads you to a specific unpublished case. If you know the specific case, you can go to the courthouse directly and retrieve the unpublished opinion from the court clerk.

B. RESEARCHING JURY AWARDS AND SETTLEMENT AGREEMENTS

When trying to determine how much a case is worth, it is often helpful to research jury awards and settlement agreements in similar cases. How often were plaintiffs successful in such cases? What was the average jury award or settlement amount?

I. *Available Jury Verdicts and Settlements on Lexis and Westlaw*

Jury verdict information is easy to locate on either Lexis or Westlaw.[29]

Lexis Advance

In Lexis Advance, access jury verdict information by selecting the Research tab at the top of the screen, then "Verdict & Settlement Analyzer." Enter your search terms in the search box, and select the appropriate jurisdiction and practice area. Your search will produce a report with graphs, charts, and a list of citations. Selecting a citation will direct you to a document summarizing the case and the award.

You may also access jury verdict information using the main search box: enter your search terms and narrow the content type to "Jury Verdicts and Settlements." You may then narrow your results by jurisdiction and practice area. Your search will retrieve a list of citations leading to summaries of each case and award. To view the "Verdict & Settlement Analyzer" Report for your search, select the "LexisNexis Verdict & Settlement Analyzer" at the beginning of your results.

Lexis.com

In Lexis.com, one entry point for this material is through the *Litigation Workflow* tab. Choose "Early Case Assessment," then "Damages Evaluation." This allows you to research the typical value of a certain kind of injury in a given jurisdiction. Alternatively, locate jury verdicts and settlements under "Expert Witness Analysis, Jury Verdicts & Settlements" on either the *Litigation Practice* or *Legal* tab. All of the verdicts and settlements available on Lexis are compiled here. You can search all verdicts, just federal verdicts, or state verdicts by state.

WestlawNext

In WestlawNext, access jury verdict information by choosing the "Jury Verdicts & Settlements" link under the main search box. You can search all verdicts, federal verdicts by jurisdiction, state verdicts by state, or verdicts by topic. Alternatively, to produce a report with relevant jury verdict information, select "Case Evaluator" on the right side of the screen. Narrow your search by case type, jurisdiction, injury type, damages, company, or industry. This search will generate a report with verdict and settlement trends, including awards by county and party, the largest awards, and award analysis. The report also includes verdict and settlement summaries and court documents.

---

[29] Neither Lexis nor Westlaw provide comprehensive coverage of jury verdicts and settlement agreements, so you are only getting a selection of verdicts. More verdicts are available at the state level than at the federal level. Most of the verdicts catalogued on Lexis and Westlaw are there because the litigants themselves submitted the verdicts for publication in the commercial databases.

Westlaw Classic

In Westlaw Classic, you can easily locate available jury verdicts and settlements by going through the database directory. In the directory, the following path leads you to the relevant materials: Directory > U.S. State Materials > Jury Verdicts, Settlements & Judgments. Once you have found the listing of available materials, you can limit your search to verdicts and settlements by circuit, region, state, or topic. If you regularly research in a particular state, it is helpful to create a tab for that state. If you do so, available jury verdicts for that state are easily accessible from the state tab.

2. Other Sources for Jury Verdict and Settlement Information

Because Westlaw and Lexis do not offer comprehensive databases of jury verdicts and settlements, you may find you want to do research beyond what is offered on these commercial databases.

While some print resources are available, most of them focus on awards and settlements in personal injury cases. BNA does offer a database of selected verdicts in employment discrimination cases. The database, *Employment Discrimination Verdicts and Settlements*, is available online for a fee. Depending upon the size of the organization for which you work, you may or may not have access to this resource. However, you are much more likely to have access to BNA's weekly newsletter, *Employment Discrimination Report*, available through BNA or Bloomberg Law. Many firms subscribe to the newsletter, which provides coverage of legal developments in employment discrimination law. Verdicts of note are published there.

Several other sites offer paid access to jury verdicts. For state-specific jury verdicts, you can go to a site maintained by the National Association of State Jury Verdict Publishers at www.juryverdicts.com. Once there, you can link to the jury verdict publishers in a particular state and subscribe to the one you need.

Another fee-based option is www.VerdictSearch.com. For a fee, you can subscribe to a large database of jury verdicts and settlements. You can also pay a fee to have Verdict Search perform a specific search for you; prices are listed prominently on the website.

EXERCISES

1) Spend some time reviewing the options for researching jury verdicts and settlements through Lexis Advance's Verdict & Settlement Analyzer Report.

2) Using Lexis Advance, research average jury awards or settlements in Title VII sexual harassment cases in the Sixth Circuit.

3) Westlaw Classic offers a specific database for labor and employment verdicts and settlements. Locate that database, and research settlements and verdicts in

age discrimination lawsuits. What types of damages have been awarded? What is the range of monetary awards to a successful plaintiff? Compare the information available through this database to the information available through WestlawNext's labor and employment verdicts and settlements database.

4) If your library subscribes to the BNA Employment Discrimination Reports or Verdicts and Settlements, take some time to familiarize yourself with these resources. Come to class prepared to discuss how and when you might find them useful.

5) Access www.juryverdicts.com. Research the resources available for researching jury verdicts and settlements in one of the following states: Louisiana, Oregon, California, New York, or Texas. Provide the following information:

    a) What is the name of the service(s) in your chosen state?

    b) What is the scope of the database (types of verdicts, numbers of verdicts, date range for verdicts, etc.)? If the information is available, list the cost of the subscription.

VI. RESEARCHING EXISTING STATUTES AND PENDING LEGISLATION

A. RESEARCHING EXISTING STATUTES

1. *Background Information*

Statutes are the result of legislation passed by federal or state legislatures. Statutes are the highest form of primary authority; only constitutions take precedence over them. Thus, when a legal area is governed by a statute (as much of employment discrimination law is), a court deciding an issue in that area is bound to do no more than interpret what the governing statute means and apply it to the case at hand.[30]

When a legislature first enacts a new law, the statute is assigned a *public law number* and is published in its own separate pamphlet (called a *slip law*). To cite to a slip law, you cite to its public law number. You will rarely, if ever, have to research slip laws.

> ▪ **EXAMPLE:** The slip law version of the ADA Amendments Act of 2008 is P.L. 110-325 (meaning this was the 325th law passed by the 110th session of Congress).

All slip laws for an entire session of Congress are then published together as *session laws*. Session laws are compiled in the publication *United States Statutes at*

---

[30] An exception arises in the small number of cases where the very issue is the constitutionality of some provision of a given statute. Because constitutions are higher primary authority than statutes, a court can analyze and determine that a portion of a statute is unconstitutional.

Large. Session Laws are published chronologically rather than topically (though you can search for topics using an index).

> ■ **EXAMPLE:** The ADA Amendments Act appears in *United States Statutes at Large* along with all other laws passed by the 110th Congress. Its session law citation is 122 Stat. 3553 (page 3553 of the 122nd volume). It appears just after P.L. 110-324, a law dealing with compensation to disabled veterans, and just before P.L. 110-326, a law addressing secret service protection for prior Vice Presidents.

Laws are organized topically for the first time when they appear in a jurisdiction's code. For this reason, you will almost always be doing statutory research in a code rather than by looking through slip laws or session laws.[31] A statutory code includes every statute that is currently in force in a given jurisdiction. The official federal code is the United States Code (U.S.C.). While you should cite to the official code, unofficial codes are often better research tools, as they provide additional research material in the form of annotations. Two unofficial versions of the United States Code exist. The first, United States Code Service (U.S.C.S.), is published by Lexis and available in print and on Lexis. The second, United States Code Annotated (U.S.C.A.), is published by West, and is available in print and on Westlaw.

HELPFUL RESEARCH MATERIALS IN ANNOTATED U.S. CODE

Statutory History
The history includes when the initial law was passed,
when it went into effect, and whether it has been amended; it lists
both public law numbers and session law citations.

Related Statutes, Laws, and Regulations

Notes of Decisions
Short summaries of both cases and agency decisions interpreting
the statute are organized topically (with an internal index of topics within the
annotations themselves).

Related Secondary Sources
Citations are also included to law reviews, practice guides, treatises,
and other materials discussing the relevant statute.

---

[31] A law (whether published as a slip law, a session law, or a code section) should read the same regardless of the publication format. This is why it makes the most sense to research using a topically organized set of statutes. However, if for some reason the versions differ in any way, be aware that the law provides that the "United States Statutes at Large shall be legal evidence of laws, concurrent resolutions, treaties, international agreements other than treaties, proclamations by the President, and proposed or ratified amendments to the Constitution of the United States therein contained, in all the courts of the United States, the several States, and the Territories and insular possessions of the United States." 1 U.S.C. § 112.

2. Researching Statutes

Whenever you get a research assignment, you should first determine whether the area of law is governed by a statute. Sometimes, you may know this without having to do any research. After all, if your assignment is something like "Describe the operative provisions of the Genetic Information Nondiscrimination Act," you certainly do not have to guess whether a statute is involved.

If you are unsure whether the issue is governed by a statute, do not be afraid to ask the assigning attorney (unless you are a solo practitioner, in which case, you are on your own) whether he or she knows what the governing statute is. If the attorney does not know, start with a topical search for background information in secondary sources. You will probably discover the relevant statute there. If not, you can always look at the subject matter index or table of contents in the relevant jurisdiction's code or search the statutory databases in Westlaw or Lexis.

If you know the popular name of a statute (The Americans with Disabilities Act, The Civil Rights Act of 1991, etc.), both Westlaw and Lexis link to popular name tables that will lead you to the full-text annotated version of the relevant statute. (The print versions of the annotated codes also contain Popular Name Tables, usually shelved at the end of the set of code volumes.) Of course, if you know the name of the statute, you might first just try running a simple (and free) Google search to find the statutory citation. Then, of course, you should go to a more authoritative source to make sure the information you have found is correct.

PATH TO POPULAR NAME TABLE ON MAJOR COMMERCIAL DATABASES

LEXIS.COM[32]

Option One: Legal > Federal Legal - U.S. > Find Statutes, Regulations, Administrative Materials & Court Rules > United States Code Service (USCS) Materials > USCS Popular Names Table

Option Two: Click on the "Search by Source" tab. Under "Option Two," click on "Find a Source." In the search box, enter "Popular Names Table."

WESTLAW CLASSIC

Option One: Click on the "Search for a Database" box on the left side of the screen. Then type in the database identifier for the United States Code Annotated, which is

---

[32] As of August 2013, the Popular Name Table was not yet available on Lexis Advance. To check on its availability in the future, select "Help" under the "Help" drop-down menu at the top of the screen, then select "Content Listing." This will open a PDF document, which can be searched for "Popular Name Table." Once the Popular Name Table is available on Lexis Advance, this path should work: Enter "Popular Name" in the search box, and select "Browse Sources." On the left side of the screen, under "Content Type," select "More," then "Statutes and Legislation."

"USCA." Once you click on "Go," a link to the Popular Names Table will appear in the upper right corner of the USCA search page.

Option Two: Statutes > All Federal >United States Code Annotated > Popular Names Table (upper right hand corner of the screen)

WESTLAW NEXT

Option One: Enter "Popular" in the search box, and select "USCA Popular Name Table" from the drop-down menu that appears.

Option Two: Click on the "Federal Materials" tab, and select "United States Code Annotated (USCA)." A link to "USCA Popular Name Table" will appear on the right side of the screen under "Tools and Resources."

EXERCISES

For all exercises, note how long it took you to find the information as well as any difficulty you had finding the relevant information.

1) Look up the Americans with Disabilities Act using the USCA Popular Name Table online. Once you have located the statute using the Popular Name Table, provide the citation and text of the prohibition on discrimination against a qualified individual with a disability. *Hint*: When you find the Act in the Popular Name Table, it will likely lead you to the first relevant section of the Act (findings and purpose). You can browse surrounding sections by looking at the top of your screen and clicking on the "Book Browse" option.

2) Go to the law library and look up the Americans with Disabilities Act using the United Sates Code Annotated Popular Name Table. Provide the citation and text of the prohibition on discrimination against a qualified individual with a disability.

3) Look up the Americans with Disabilities Act using a free search engine like Google. Find an accurate and authoritative source for the statute, and provide the citation and text of the prohibition on discrimination against a qualified individual with a disability.

4) Look up the Genetic Information Nondiscrimination Act of 2008 using the method you found most efficient and effective in the preceding three exercises. Then:

   a) Explain why you chose the search method you did.

   b) Provide the relevant citation and operative text that answers the following question: When can an employer "request, require, or purchase genetic information with respect to an employee or a family member of the employee"?

You should almost always do your research in an annotated code. Once you have found a section of the U.S.C. (or relevant state code), make sure to review sections around the one you have found to make sure that no additional sections are relevant. Also check the index or table of contents to make sure your topic is not governed by additional statutes.[33]

Always update your research. If you are using a print version of a statute, you should check pocket parts and supplements to make sure no new legislation has modified or superseded your statute. You can also look for recently-passed legislation using an advance legislative service. Advance legislative services contain only copies of new laws that have not been codified, and they are organized chronologically rather than topically. Both annotated versions of the United States Code have advance legislative services. Moreover, Lexis provides access to advance legislative services for state statutes.

The online versions of statutes are updated more frequently than the paper versions. Even so, you should always use one of the commercial citators (Shepard's or Keycite) to find the most updated information about the statute. There, you can find information regarding whether your statute has been repealed or altered by recent legislation or found unconstitutional by a recent case. A citator will also provide the most recent cases citing your statute, even those not yet listed in the annotated code.

Another important thing to keep in mind is that the statutory language governing your client's problem is the language that was in effect at the time the legal issue arose, not at the time of trial.[34] This is another reason why the editorial notes at the end of the statute are so helpful, as they list the original date of enactment as well as any amendments to the statute.

If you need quick, free access to the United States Code, you can view a copy of the U.S.C. on THOMAS, the legislative database maintained by the Library of Congress. While it is more difficult to use than the commercial databases (and, more importantly, it does not contain annotations), it is a free resource of which you should be aware.

3. When to Research Session Laws

Because session laws are organized chronologically rather than by subject matter and because they do not contain additional research references, they are not as useful as a code, which is organized by subject matter. However, you may

---

[33] You should also check to see whether an agency has published administrative regulations implementing the statute. If you have found the statute by going to the relevant government agency charged with administering the statute, you will find links to relevant regulations on the agency website. If you have found the statute on Westlaw or Lexis or in print versions of the annotated statutes, relevant regulations and related statutes will be included in a box of related references on the computer screen or in the annotations at the end of the statute.

[34] An exception to this rule is when the legislature has specifically stated that amendments to a statute apply retroactively.

still occasionally have to research session laws. Why? Because print versions of codes are updated less frequently than online versions, and there may be some lag even with Westlaw or Lexis versions of annotated statutes. If you believe your law is too new to be included in the code, or if you want to make sure an existing statute has not been affected by extremely new legislation, you can check the session laws by looking at *Statutes at Large*.

You can find *Statutes at Large* in several locations.[35] First, you may have access to a print version. Second, *Statutes at Large* is available in several places online, including (1) www.fdsys.gov (the U.S. Government Printing Office website);[36] (2) HeinOnline (which also includes easy access to state session laws); and (3) Westlaw or Lexis. Finally, another print resource, the *United States Code Congressional and Administrative News*, provides the status of legislation and the full text of public laws signed during a given period.

B. RESEARCHING PENDING LEGISLATION AND TRACKING THE LEGISLATIVE IMPACT OF NEW LEGISLATION ON EXISTING LEGISLATION

Much of employment discrimination law is governed by statutes. You will, therefore, become very familiar both with the language of the operative sections of state and federal antidiscrimination statutes and the key issues arising under those statutes. However, statutory law is not static. New laws are often passed that either supersede or alter all or part of an existing statute. You will need to track any possible changes to key state and federal statutes affecting your clients.

1. Researching Pending Legislation using Government Websites

a. Federal Legislation

Three online government websites provide databases of House and Senate Bills and Resolutions. The first is FDSys, a service provided by the Government Printing Office (www.fdsys.gov). Using the Congressional Bill search form, you can search legislation in the current Congress as well as bills going back to the 103rd Congress (1993-1994). The database is updated daily at six a.m. If you run a search for bills on a particular topic, you will get a list of all bills matching your search parameters. Each entry will provide a link to the full text of the relevant bill and a summary of the legislation. The entry also lists the status of the legislation. A sample entry might look something like this: "S. 2189 (is)." The "S" stands for senate bill. The "(is)" abbreviation after the bill number indicates the status of the bill—introduced in the Senate. If you cannot translate one of the abbreviations in the results list, a glossary can be found by selecting "About the Congressional Bills" from the main "Congressional Bills" page.

---

[35] Because session laws are organized chronologically, you will have to either know the citation in *Statutes at Large* or use the index to find material in *Statutes at Large*.
[36] FDSys replaced the U.S. Government Printing Office's previous website, GPO Access, on March 16, 2012.

The second online source for researching Congressional Bills and Resolutions is THOMAS, a repository for federal legislative information maintained by the Library of Congress.[37] THOMAS provides a searchable database of all Bills and Resolutions in the House and Senate from the 93rd Congress (1973) to the current Congress. You can search one session of Congress or multiple sessions concurrently. Although THOMAS has bills going back several years earlier than the database provided by the Government Printing Office (FDSys), you might still sometimes need to check FDSys. According to the Library of Congress, "[m]ost of the documents in THOMAS originate in the House and Senate, which in turn transmit them to the Government Printing Office (GPO) for printing and further electronic processing. GPO then transmits them to the Library of Congress, which performs some further processing before making them available on THOMAS."[38] Thus, documents will appear on the House and Senate web pages as well as on FDSys a short time before they appear on THOMAS. Moreover, if you are not familiar with all the terms used to describe the status of legislation, the FDSys site has a very thorough glossary of terms.

On the other hand, THOMAS provides a number of daily e-mail updates and RSS Feeds if you want to track the actions of the current Congress or its committees. From the THOMAS home page, you can subscribe to e-mail or RSS updates for material "On the House Floor Today," Senate Floor Today," or "Bills Presented to the President." You can also subscribe to the Congressional Record Daily Digest.

Finally, Congress.gov was introduced by the Library of Congress in September 2012 as an eventual replacement for THOMAS.[39] Beginning in November 2013, THOMAS.gov will automatically redirect to Congress.gov,[40] which gov contains legislation from the 103rd Congress (1993) to the present. You can search multiple sessions concurrently, then narrow your results to particular Congress. You can get guidance for conducting searches on Congress.gov by selecting "Search Tips," a link located next to the search bar on the main page. As of August 2013, other resources on Congress.gov include selected profiles of Members of Congress from the 71st Congress (1929) to the present, the Congressional Record from the 104th Congress (1995) to the present, and Committee Reports from the 104th Congress (1995) to the present.

You can also do research on current and pending legislation on the websites for the United States House and Senate. However, if you try to search a bill on the Senate or House website, you are actually just linking in to the THOMAS

---

[37] THOMAS will eventually be replaced by Congress.gov, which was launched in September 2012. http://blogs.loc.gov/law/2012/09/introducing-congress-gov/ (last accessed August 5, 2013). Because not all content from THOMAS has been migrated to Congress.gov and because Congress.gov is still in beta testing, an overview of both THOMAS and Congress.gov is included here.
[38] http://thomas.loc.gov/home/faqlist.html#16 (last accessed August 5, 2013).
[39] See http://beta.congress.gov/about (last accessed August 5, 2013) for information about the latest updates and a timeline for Congress.gov.
[40] See http://blogs.loc.gov/law/2013/07/congress-gov-continues-to-grow-committee-pages-reports-more-added/ (last accessed August 5, 2013).

database. You may still find useful information on the Senate and House websites, however, so we encourage you to get to know the content on those sites as well.

b. State Legislation

You can also research bills and resolutions being considered by state legislatures. Lexis offers the Legislative Impact service for state statutes as well as federal statutes. Moreover, state legislatures often maintain their own websites with searchable legislative databases. For example, Michigan has one unified website for accessing legislation in either the state house or senate, located at http://legislature.mi.gov. From the home page, you can search for a bill in the current session of the House or Senate using a bill number or a key word search. You can also search for statutory sections by section number in the Michigan Compiled Laws (the official version of the Michigan state statutory code). There is also a link to subscribe to Bill Updates. This service allows you to track when the status of a particular bill changes or to get e-mail updates on all legislation on selected subjects. If you want to search for bills from prior sessions, click on the link on the home page to "bills" in the left-hand column. Clicking on that link leads you to a new search page.

■ **PRACTICE NOTE:** Create bookmarks for websites you plan to visit frequently. You will save yourself time (and your client money) if you have a readily-available list of key free web resources.

EXERCISES

1) Using the Definitions section from "About Congressional Bills" on FDSys to help guide you, answer the following questions:

   a) What is a simple resolution? Would statutory employment discrimination law ever be the subject of a simple resolution? If so, when? If not, why not?

   b) What does it mean for a bill to be "Engrossed in Senate"?

   c) What does it mean if a bill has been "Placed on Calendar House"?

2) Go on the THOMAS Website or the Library of Congress website and subscribe to the "House Floor Today" and "Senate Floor Today" e-mail updates. For the amount of time determined by your professor, keep track of all material relevant to employment discrimination law that you find in the e-mail updates.

3) Search the current Congress on the FDSys site to see if any current or pending legislation will affect the Family and Medical Leave Act. Print and turn in a copy of the report you receive, and provide a short paragraph summarizing

what you found that you feel you would need to bring to the attention of your co-workers if you worked in a large law firm office representing defendants in employment discrimination cases.

4) Go to the Michigan Legislature website. Research how to subscribe to bill update notifications. Locate the place where you can subscribe to bill notification by category. Select the categories you think might be relevant to employment discrimination, and set up notifications for those categories. Then search the current house and senate session for any bills related to employment discrimination issues. Sign up for the bill update service for one of those laws. E-mail your professor a list of the categories you chose as well as the specific bill you selected to track.

5) Choose the state you hope to practice in when you graduate. Search for the official government website offering legislative information for that state. Provide the web address and a short summary of what information you can get access to on the site. If the state you choose has more than one website with information, determine whether one or more are official, and explain which one is the best for research (and why).

2. Researching Pending Legislation using Commercial Databases

Both Westlaw and Lexis offer services to help keep you up-to-date regarding new legislation that might affect current statutes. This section offers a brief discussion of some of the most useful services offered by Westlaw and Lexis.

Lexis Advance

When you look up a statute on Lexis Advance, you will see a *"Pending Legislation"* link to any proposed legislation that might affect your statute. Clicking on a link for the pending legislation will take you to the full text of the proposed bill.

Lexis.com

When you look up a statute on Lexis.com, the page with the operative section does not include any indication of whether there is any proposed legislation. To obtain this information, you must Shepardize the statute. If there is any pending legislation related to your statute, you will see a link to *"Pending Legislation"* on the right side of the screen. Like in Lexis Advance, if you click on the link, you will see a list of the current bills and can click on the links to access the full text of the bills.

WestlawNext and Westlaw Classic

WestlawNext and Westlaw Classic contain identical legislative history information, though the interfaces are slightly different. When you look up a statute on Westlaw Classic, you will see a *"Proposed Legislation"* flag at the top of the screen if there is any proposed legislation affecting that statute. If you click on the link, you will see links to the full text of current bills that might affect the statute you are researching.

WestlawNext allows you to view past amendments to a statute as well as pending legislation regarding a statute using the "Graphical Statutes" function. From the statute, select "Graphical Statute" from the dropdown menu under "History."

EXERCISES

1) Sign on to Lexis Advance. Retrieve the Fair Labor Standards Act of 1938 and review any proposed legislation affecting the statute. Be prepared to provide a short oral summary of your findings (no longer than 10 minutes). In performing this task, take on one of the following roles (assigned by your professor):

    a) A young associate in a large law firm advising a senior attorney regarding the status of the law.

    b) A mid-level associate discussing compliance issues with the human resources manager for one of your corporate clients.

    c) A disability rights advocate speaking to a colleague about what to include in an alert on a public website about recent and upcoming changes to disability discrimination law in the workplace.

2) Sign on to Lexis Advance. Retrieve the Age Discrimination in Employment Act of 1967 and review any pending legislation affecting the statute. Draft a one-page informal memorandum summarizing the material you found there.

3) Sign on to WestlawNext. Link to the Graphical Statutes version of the Family and Medical Leave Act. Browse the features, and explain the material you find there. How might the material be useful to you in your day-to-day work as a practicing employment lawyer?

ADDITIONAL CUMULATIVE EXERCISES FOR CHAPTERS 5–6

1) Identify the type of problem presented by each of the following questions (pure legal question, remedies question, procedural question, etc.). Write a short memorandum to the partner answering the question, using the format that makes the most sense given the type of question you have been asked.

□ Does a plaintiff alleging national origin discrimination in violation of Title VII have to file an administrative complaint with the EEOC prior to filing a complaint in federal court? If so, what are the deadlines for doing so?

□ Can a court order reinstatement of a terminated employee if the employee wins a retaliation lawsuit filed under Title VII? *For this question only,* prepare your response in the form of an e-mail to your professor. Write the e-mail as if you were writing to Sarah Smith, the human resources manager for one of your clients. Assume this is one of your early communications with this individual. At the end of your e-mail, note whether you would change anything about your e-mail if you regularly corresponded with Sarah Smith.

□ In what state is Best Buy incorporated? How many employees are employed by Best Buy? How many race discrimination lawsuits have been filed against Best Buy in the past 5 years?

□ Research and provide a list of states with a state whistle blowing statute that applies directly to private employers. List the state statute, and summarize key cases in each jurisdiction.

□ Research which states recognize the tort of wrongful discharge in violation of public policy. Summarize key cases on the issue.

2) Research the following questions. Come prepared to present your results orally in class.

□ Summarize the provisions of the ADA Amendments Act. How does it change the ADA? Which Supreme Court cases interpreting the ADA are no longer good law after the passage of the ADA Amendments Act?

□ Has the EEOC published guidance on the ADA Amendments Act? If so, bring a copy of the EEOC's most recent guidance, state whether it is in proposed or final form, and summarize that material.

3) Create a short article to educate clients on the following topics. Before you do so, review client alerts/updates on labor and employment law issues on the websites of several law firms. Note the length, tone, number of footnotes, etc., and try to create an alert similar to those you found effective on the firm websites you reviewed. Review the websites of at least three of the following firms:

Drinker Biddle & Reath LLP
Duane Morris LLP
Fisher & Phillips LLP
Ford & Harrison LLP
Greenberg Traurig
Hinshaw & Culbertson
Jackson Lewis LLP
Littler Mendelson P.C.
McGuire Woods LLP
Ogletree, Deakins, Nash, Smoak & Stewart
Winston & Strawn LLP

- ☐ Choose an employment discrimination case decided by a state supreme court in the past year. Create a report educating corporate clients regarding how the decision will affect them.
- ☐ What are the key provisions of the Genetic Information Non-Discrimination Act of 2008, and how will the statute affect employees?
- ☐ In what ways (if any) does California's discrimination statute differ from Title VII on the following issues:

  a) What groups are protected?

  b) What is the statute of limitations?

  c) Is there an exhaustion requirement?

  d) What conduct is prohibited?

  e) How is the term "employer" defined?

RESEARCHING EMPLOYMENT DISCRIMINATION ISSUES SPECIFICALLY

I. INTRODUCTION

Good researchers can adapt when researching different areas of law fairly easily, as basic legal research strategy does not change depending upon the topic researched. However, every area of the law presents its own unique set of issues and questions, and this section provides some specialized guidance for those researching employment discrimination law.

II. BASIC LEGAL RESEARCH STRATEGY TEMPLATE—A REVIEW

Chapter 5 of this section of the book addressed a basic template for conducting effective, efficient legal research. These steps are the foundation upon which you will build more sophisticated and topic-specific research skills, so you should take some time to review the steps now before moving on. The steps are as follows:

Step One: Know the issue(s) you have been asked to research.

Step Two: Make sure you have all relevant background material, and read it carefully.

Step Three: If you are relatively unfamiliar with the subject matter you are researching, consult a relevant secondary source to get background information and additional research references.

Step Four: Incorporate what you have learned from the secondary source(s) (terms of art, for example) into a more refined statement of the issue or issues you have been asked to research. If possible, begin to develop an outline of relevant issues or sub-issues.

Step Five: Research primary authority, starting with constitutions, statutes, and regulations, and then moving to cases (binding before persuasive).

Step Six: Fill in your outline of issues and sub-issues with relevant primary authority. Find 1-2 cases for general propositions of law. Once you have supported the basic propositions of law with binding authority, look for factually analogous cases for each issue and sub-issue (unless you're researching an issue of pure law).

Step Seven: Make sure all cases are still good law for the points for which you are using them.

If you need a more detailed refresher on these steps, refer back to Chapter 5 of this section of the book. Do not continue until you are comfortable with the basic process of legal research.

III. ADAPTING LEGAL RESEARCH STRATEGIES FOR EMPLOYMENT DISCRIMINATION ISSUES

When researching employment law issues, an attorney should begin with some very basic questions. The answer to these questions will determine key issues, such as what law applies, whether the employee must file an administrative complaint before filing in court, whether the employee should file in state or federal court, and whether the employee has claims under more than one law (and, if so, whether the employee can or must file suit under only one or both laws). Once an attorney has been practicing in the area for a while, many of the answers to these threshold questions will be apparent without research. In the beginning, though, the novice attorney should address these key questions.

First, the attorney should determine whether the employer is private or public, as different rights and responsibilities accrue depending upon the category in which the involved employer falls. Second, the attorney should determine whether the client's problem is governed by federal, state, or local law (or some combination of these). Third, the attorney should determine whether the problem is governed by the constitution, by statute, or by the common law. Fourth, if the problem is governed by statutory law, the attorney should determine whether there are regulations interpreting the statute and whether the client must exhaust administrative remedies prior to filing suit. Finally, the attorney should address questions of preemption and exclusivity of remedies.

1. Is the employer private or public?[41]

Some laws apply equally to both private and public employers (though requirements under those laws may differ depending upon the type of employer), while other laws apply solely to public employers. For example, Title VII, the ADA, the ADEA, Genetic Information Nondiscrimination Act (GINA), and the Equal Pay Act (EPA) all apply to both private employers and federal, state, and local governments. The federal government is subject to additional laws. Sections 501 and 504 of the Rehabilitation Act cover the federal government and incorporate the provisions of the ADA. The Civil Service Reform Act governs most employees of federal agencies, though there are exceptions.

QUESTIONS

What is the Civil Service Reform Act? What federal government agencies are not covered by the Civil Service Reform Act? What is the rationale for limiting coverage to only a subset of federal agencies?

2. Is the problem governed by federal, state, or local law?

Realize that the problem your client faces may be governed by some combination of two or more of these categories. Furthermore, the types of claims available under federal, state, or local law may differ. For example, Title VII governs sexual harassment in the workplace. Decisions under Title VII have made clear that Title VII covers same-sex sexual harassment claims. On the other hand, Title VII only applies to employers with 15 or more employees.[42] States and municipalities have also enacted statutes prohibiting sexual harassment in the workplace. Only some of these state and local laws cover same-sex harassment. However, state and local laws may cover employers with fewer employees than Title VII or offer a broader range of remedies than those offered by Title VII. Thus, if your client is a man claiming sexual harassment by another man, the state statute where he lives might not provide relief. Title VII would provide relief, though only if your client works for an employer with at least 15 employees.

---

[41] Examples of public employers include federal, state, and local governments. School districts are also included in the list of entities considered public employers.

[42] More specifically, Title VII defines "Employer" as "a person engaged in an industry affecting commerce who has fifteen or more employees for each working day in each of twenty or more calendar weeks in the current or preceding calendar year, and any agent of such a person." 42 U.S.C. § 2000e(b). The term excludes "the United States, a corporation wholly owned by the Government of the United States, an Indian tribe, or any department or agency of the District of Columbia subject by statute to procedures of the competitive service . . . [and] a bona fide private membership club (other than a labor organization) which is exempt from taxation under [certain provisions of the Internal Revenue Code." *Id.*

■ **EXAMPLE:** Your client is a female working for an employer in Manhattan. The employer has 10 full-time employees. She wishes to sue her employer based on alleged sexual discrimination (not harassment) based on her sexual orientation. Specifically, she believes she has been repeatedly passed over for promotions because her supervisor does not like gay people. What law applies?

Analysis:

Federal Discrimination Law. Your client cannot seek relief under Title VII. While Title VII provides relief for same-sex harassment, your client works for an employer who has too few employees to qualify as an "Employer" under Title VII. Moreover, Title VII does not count sexual orientation as one of the protected classes under its purview.

State Discrimination Law. Your client may seek relief under the New York State Human Rights Law. The law applies to employers with at least four employees. Section 292(5). Furthermore, according to section 296(1)(a) of New York State Executive Law Article 15, "It shall be an unlawful discriminatory practice: (a) For an employer or licensing agency, because of an individual's age, race, creed, color, national origin, sexual orientation, military status, sex, disability, predisposing genetic characteristics, marital status, or domestic violence victim status, to refuse to hire or employ or to bar or to discharge from employment such individual or to discriminate against such individual in compensation or in terms, conditions or privileges of employment."[43]

Local Discrimination Law. Your client may also be able to sue under Title 8 of the Administrative Code of the City of New York. Section 8-102(5) of the New York Human Rights Law states that its use of the term "'[E]mployer' does not include any employer with fewer than four persons in his or her employ" and that "natural persons employed as independent contractors to carry out work in furtherance of an employer's business enterprise who are not themselves employers shall be counted as persons in the employ of such employer." This definition of employer is much broader than the definition provided under Title VII.

Furthermore, the list of unlawful discriminatory practices under the New York Human Rights Law is broader than the one provided under Title VII. Section 8-107(1)(a) provides that

---

[43] In fact, Section 291(1) of the New York State Human Rights Law provides that "[t]he opportunity to obtain employment without discrimination because of age, race, creed, color, national origin, sexual orientation, military status, sex, marital status, or disability is . . . a civil right."

> [i]t shall be an unlawful discriminatory practice: (a) For an employer . . . because of the actual or perceived age, race, creed, color, national origin, gender, disability, marital status, partnership status, sexual orientation or alienage or citizenship status of any person, to refuse to hire or employ or to bar or to discharge from employment such person or to discriminate against such person in compensation or in terms, conditions or privileges of employment.
>
> Before deciding how to proceed, of course, you would also want to research the remedies available to your client under each relevant statute as well as any available common law claims. You would also need to ensure that none of the relevant laws have exclusive remedies provisions (discussed below).

3. Is the problem governed by a statute or ordinance, or is the problem governed by the common law?

Much of employment discrimination law is statutory, though there are some available state common law claims as well. For example, some states provide a common law remedy for wrongful discharge in violation of public policy. Moreover, a plaintiff in a sexual harassment or other discrimination lawsuit may also consider bringing a claim for intentional infliction of emotional distress. Some other common law claims that may arise in the employment law context include claims for (1) negligent infliction of emotional distress; (2) defamation or self-publication defamation; (3) intentional interference with contract or business relations; (4) assault; (5) battery; (6) false imprisonment; and (7) negligent hiring, retention, and supervision.

Importantly, some tort claims may be available against a manager or supervisor in his or her individual capacity, even if the underlying statutory scheme would not allow such relief.

Example: You represent a terminated employee who would like to sue her former employer under Title VII after her manager coerced her into engaging in unwelcome sexual relations during a performance review. The manager locked the door and said, "If you want to keep your job, do what I say. We can do this the easy way or the hard way." The employee strongly wishes to sue her manager as well, but Title VII does not provide for claims against individual managers. You might want to explore the possibility of bringing claims against the individual supervisor for assault, battery, and false imprisonment.

Not all common law claims are available to employees or employers in every state. Moreover, as discussed below, some claims may be preempted by various statutory schemes.

EXERCISE

You represent an employee who worked as a cocktail waitress at a large New York nightclub that employs 30 people. She believes she was fired because she refused to tolerate what she referred to as the "fraternity boy" culture at work. She claims that the manager's back office was "littered with pornography," that the manager made sexually suggestive comments every day she came to work, and that the manager once told her in front of a group of male bartenders that if she really wanted to earn good tips, she needed to stop coming to work in "grandma" clothes and instead show everyone more of her "stuff."

Furthermore, she applied for a job as bartender several times, each time being rejected in favor of a male candidate with less experience. When she confronted the manager, he said he was doing her a favor, because she'd make more money out in the crowd where men could see her "strut her stuff." He then slapped her bottom and told her to "get to work entertaining the crowd."

Two days later, after her shift, she went to her manager's office to get her paycheck. The manager was in the office with two of her male co-workers looking at pornography. When she asked for her paycheck, the manager said, "it's not much, but I know how you could earn more." He then pointed to one of the centerfolds on his wall and said, "That's what you should wear to work." Everyone in the room laughed. She told the manager that she was tired of being treated like a second-class citizen at work and that she was offended by all the pornography. He told her to "get over it, or get out."

She called in sick the next day, but she decided to return to work after that because she really needed the money to pay her rent. When she arrived at work, the manager fired her. He called everyone who was at work over to hear him fire her. The manager said that he knew she was lying when she called in sick, and he also accused her of stealing from the business by selling drinks, tearing up the receipts, and keeping the money. When she denied it, he said, "Maybe next time you'll learn to play by the rules."

She wants to sue her employer because her supervisor harassed her, refused to promote her, embarrassed her in front of her coworkers, lied about her in front of others, and terminated her unfairly. Putting aside any statutory claims that might be available to your client, what common law claims might she consider bringing?

4. **If the problem is governed by a statute, are there regulations interpreting the statute? Must a plaintiff comply with certain prerequisites prior to filing suit (known as "exhausting administrative remedies")?**

a. Regulations and their Authority as Law

Regulations are rules drafted by state or federal agencies to provide guidance in interpreting statutes. Courts will generally follow regulations if they do not conflict with the court's interpretation of the relevant statutory language. Federal regulations are collected in the Code of Federal Regulations. For more guidance on researching regulations, see the preceding section of this book.

b. Exhaustion of Administrative Remedies

So what does it mean to require a plaintiff to "exhaust administrative remedies" as a prerequisite to filing suit? If a statutory scheme requires a plaintiff to "exhaust administrative remedies," the plaintiff must first file a charge with the relevant administrative agency prior to filing suit in court.[44] For example, a number of laws are enforced by the Equal Employment Opportunity Commission (EEOC), including Title VII, the ADA, the ADEA, the EPA, and the GINA.

EXERCISE

1) Go to the EEOC's website. What law enforced by the EEOC does not require complainants to file a charge with the EEOC prior to filing suit in court?

2) Are the exhaustion requirements of Title VII and the ADA the same? If not, describe the key difference(s).

3) How many days does an employee have to file a claim under Title VII?

4) Do the same exhaustion rules apply to federal employees? If not, what are the rules for federal employees?

5) Is there ever a time when you can file a lawsuit prior to the completion of an EEOC investigation? If so, how?

6) If a state has laws prohibiting the same conduct as is prohibited by Title VII, does the exhaustion requirement change at all? If so, how?

■ **PRACTICE NOTE:** If you are helping a complainant file a charge with the EEOC, make sure the charge encompasses all possible claims you might want to bring later in court. For example, if you have an African American client who claims she was consistently denied promotions when similarly situated white employees were promoted, alleging as much would exhaust your administrative remedies for a disparate treatment case. However, if your client believes that the discriminatory treatment was caused by the use of a facially neutral test or the application of a facially neutral policy that disproportionately affected African-Americans, you would need to include these facts in the complaint filed with the EEOC. Otherwise, a court could later find that your client exhausted administrative remedies as to the disparate treatment claim, but not as to the disparate impact claim.

---

[44] *See* www.eeoc.gov/employees/charge.cfm (last accessed Mar. 6, 2013).

5. **If the problem is governed by more than one body of law, does one preempt the other? Do any of the relevant laws have exclusivity of remedies provisions?**

a. Preemption

In some situations, a federal law may preempt the application of a state or local law. The most obvious area for preemption is in employee benefits law. The Employment Retirement Income Securities Act (ERISA),[45] for example, provides that it "shall supersede any and all State laws" inasmuch as they "relate to any employee benefit plan" as described under ERISA.[46] According to the terms of ERISA, "'State law' includes all laws, decisions, rules, regulations, or other State action having the effect of law, of any State."[47] Furthermore, a "State" includes "a State, any political subdivisions thereof, or any agency or instrumentality of either, which purports to regulate, directly or indirectly, the terms and conditions of employee benefit plans [covered under ERISA]."[48] ERISA preemption is a complex area of the law,[49] but one in which lawyers should be familiar when practicing employment law.[50]

b. Exclusivity of remedies

Another key aspect of employment discrimination law is whether, by bringing a claim under one statutory scheme, an employee has waived the right to proceed with a claim under another statute. For example, in 2008, the Texas Supreme Court addressed a case in which an employee sued his employer, the City of Waco, for retaliatory discharge under the Texas Whistleblower Act. However, the Texas Supreme Court found that the Texas Commission on Human Rights Act was the exclusive remedy for the city employee's claim of retaliation. *City of Waco v. Lopez*, 259 S.W. 3d 147 (Tex. 2008). Similarly, the Ninth Circuit recently concluded that the ADEA was the exclusive remedy for a claim of age discrimination,

---

[45] ERISA is codified at 29 U.S.C. § 1144 (also referred to as ERISA § 514).
[46] ERISA § 514(a). As with most laws, this broad statement is subject to exceptions. ERISA § 514(b).
[47] ERISA § 514(c)(1).
[48] ERISA § 514(c)(2).
[49] Examples of the types of complexities arising in ERISA law abound. What does it mean to "relate to" an employee benefit plan? Does the plan at issue qualify under ERISA as an employee benefit plan? Are there statutory exceptions to preemption? For example, ERISA provides that nothing in its terms "shall be construed to alter, amend, modify, invalidate, impair, or supersede any law of the United States." ERISA § 514(d). Likewise, in a section of ERISA known as the "savings clause," ERISA provides that its terms shall not "be construed to exempt or relieve any person from any law of any State which regulates insurance, banking, or securities." ERISA § 514(b)(2)(A). On the other hand, the "deemer clause" then provides that no employee benefit plan "shall be deemed to be an insurance company or other insurer, bank, trust company, or investment company or to be engaged in the business of insurance or banking for purposes of any law of any State purporting to regulate insurance companies, insurance contracts, banks, trust companies, or investment companies." ERISA § 514(b)(2)(B). The "savings" and "deemer" clauses have been the subject of much interpretation and litigation. Finally, one other example of an exception to the provisions of ERISA is that it does "not apply to any generally applicable criminal law of a State." ERISA § 514(b)(4).
[50] In many large firms, the Employment and Labor Law practice group is separate from the Employee Benefits group. Nevertheless, employment law attorneys should be familiar enough with the basics of employee benefits law to at least recognize key issues and know when to bring in experts in that field.

concluding that the ADEA precluded even constitutional equal protection claims under Section 1983.[51]

Another hotly contested issue is the relationship between workers' compensation statutes and discrimination claims. Almost every state workers' compensation statute provides that it is the exclusive remedy for workplace injuries. One tactic routinely taken by employers is to raise these exclusive remedies provisions as an affirmative defense in employment discrimination cases. For example, in a sexual harassment lawsuit, an employee might assert numerous tort claims in addition to statutory sexual harassment claims. These tort claims could include wrongful termination in violation of public policy, invasion of privacy, intentional or negligent infliction of emotional distress, assault and battery, and others. Depending upon the courts' interpretation of the language of the workers' compensation law in the state in which you practice and the specific claims brought by an employee, a court may or may not find some of the claims barred by the exclusive remedies provisions of the state workers' compensation law.

EXERCISE

Some courts have concluded that section 501 of the Rehabilitation Act is the exclusive remedy for alleging disability discrimination against a federal employee by a federal employer. Other courts have found that employees may also bring a cause of action against a federal employer under section 504 of the Rehabilitation Act. Review the relevant statutory language as well as the discussion of this issue in *Rivera v. Heyman*, 157 F.3d 101 (2d Cir. 1998). Are you persuaded by the reasoning in *Rivera*? What are your best arguments against the position in *Rivera*?

IV. CREATING AN IMPORTANT REFERENCE/ CONTACT LIST

One of the most useful things you can do for yourself in the early years of practice is to create a comprehensive list of web-based and print resources for various topics along with a list of important contact phone numbers. For example, consider the following excerpt from a contact and reference list prepared by a labor and employment law attorney in Chicago, Illinois:

---

[51] *Ahlmeyer v. Nevada Sys. of Higher Educ.*, 555 F.3d 1051 (9th Cir. 2009). The Seventh Circuit, however, declined to follow the Ninth Circuit's decision in *Ahlmeyer*, and concluded that the ADEA does not preclude a section 1983 claim. *Levin v. Madigan*, 692 F.3d 607 (7th Cir. 2012). On March 18, 2013, the Supreme Court granted certiorari to resolve the split among the circuits. When the Supreme Court decides the issue, the authors will add an update to the companion website to this book.

PUBLIC RECORDS AND OTHER DOCUMENTS

Northern District of Illinois Complaints and Docket Sheets—You can access complaints, docket sheets, and other court documents using Pacer on the Northern District of Illinois website.

Specific Rules for Judges—All judges vary somewhat on the rules in their courtrooms—i.e. days and times that they hear motions, courtesy copy requirements, filing requirements, etc. Each judge will likely have a standing order governing these topics. You may find these on the court's website or by calling the clerk's office.

■ **PRACTICE NOTE:** When you create a chart for yourself, actually include key phone numbers like the clerk's office phone number.

USEFUL WEBSITES

State of Illinois—www.illinois.gov

The State of Illinois website includes a list of state agencies, state officials, and contact phone numbers. Furthermore, the website includes the full text of Public Acts, the Illinois Compiled Statutes, the Illinois Constitution, and the Illinois Handbook of Government. Website has Bill and Resolution search capabilities.

Illinois Department of Labor—www.state.il.us/agency/idol

The Illinois Department of Labor website provides information on the following topics (including text of relevant laws, regulations, and agency guidance):

1. Child Labor Law
2. Day and Temporary Labor Services Act
3. Minimum Wage Law
4. One Day Rest in Seven Act
5. Illinois Wage Payment and Collection Act
6. Employee Classification Act
7. Prevailing Wage Act
8. Worker Adjustment and Retraining Notification (WARN) Act
9. Personnel Records Review Act
10. Right to Privacy in the Workplace Act
11. Equal Pay Act of 2003
12. Victims' Economic Security Act
13. Labor Arbitration Services Act

Illinois Human Rights Commission—www.state.il.us/ihrc

The Illinois Human Rights Commission website provides the following materials:

1. Full text of the Illinois Human Rights Act
2. Human Rights Commission Decisions
3. Other agency guidance on the Illinois Human Rights Act

Illinois Department of Human Rights—www.state.il.us/dhr

1. Illinois Human Rights Act
2. Regulations and other guidance materials regarding the Illinois Human Rights Act

Illinois Department of Employment Security (Unemployment)—www.ides.state.il.us

The Illinois Department of Employment Security website includes information for employees and employers regarding the Unemployment Insurance Act. In the employer section, the following materials are available:

1. The full text of the Unemployment Insurance Act
2. A guide to the Unemployment Insurance Act
3. Links to Illinois Department of Employment Security Rules
4. A Digest of Adjudication Precedents
5. Forms

Illinois Secretary of State—www.cyberdriveillinois.com/departments/business_services/corp.html

This website contains a searchable database of Illinois corporations and LLCs. You can obtain reports on companies and LLCs, as well as Certificates of Good Standing for existing entities. You can also search to see if a new company name is available. The database is updated in real time.

Cook County Circuit Court—www.cookcountycourt.org

The Cook County Circuit Court website includes the Rules and General Orders of the court. Also included are selected General Administrative Rules and Orders issued by the Chief Judge.

EXERCISE

Complete the contact/reference list above by adding your own entries for the following websites. Provide the web address as well as a summary of key information available at the relevant website.

1) Website for the Cook County Circuit Court Clerk

2) Website for the Northern District of Illinois

3) Website for the Seventh Circuit Court of Appeals

4) Website for the American Arbitration Association

5) Website for Federal Mediation and Conciliation Services

6) Website for the Chicago Commission on Human Relations

7) Website for the Cook County Commission on Human Rights

CHAPTER
8

USEFUL RESOURCES FOR LAWYERS PRACTICING EMPLOYMENT DISCRIMINATION LAW

One area in which experienced lawyers have a distinct advantage over new lawyers is simply exposure to (and familiarity with) the body of relevant resources for researching specific topics. A lawyer who has practiced employment law for many years will have already used multiple secondary sources for researching employment law issues and will likely have identified a list of reliable go-to resources for various topics and subtopics.

Another advantage experienced lawyers have is that they are aware of many of the seminal cases and statutes on various employment discrimination law topics, so experienced lawyers rarely begin a research project with a completely blank slate.

Chapter 8 is designed to shorten the learning curve for new lawyers by providing lists of available resources for conducting employment discrimination research in subject matter-specific secondary sources; jumpstarting employment discrimination research online via free government agency websites; and staying abreast of new statutory and case developments in employment discrimination law. The Chapter concludes with charts of selected federal statutes and United States Supreme Court cases on employment discrimination issues.

I. LIST OF USEFUL SECONDARY SOURCES RELATED TO EMPLOYMENT DISCRIMINATION LAW

A. FEDERAL LAW

Secondary sources are a necessary first-step in a research project if you are unfamiliar with the particular subject matter you have been asked to research.[52] Numerous secondary sources exist for researching employment law issues at the federal level. The following list is not exhaustive, though it does provide the most often-used resources. Materials are divided into four categories: (1) General Treatises, Hornbooks, and Loose-leaf Services on Employment Law; (2) General Employment Discrimination Law Resources; (3) Secondary Sources on Specific Employment Discrimination Law Topics; and (4) Employment Law Journals and Law Reviews.

An important thing to realize is that many treatises and loose-leaf services are not available online. Where a resource on this list is available online via Lexis or Westlaw, we have indicated that fact (if information was available at the time of printing).

I. *General Treatises, Hornbooks, and Loose-Leaf Services on Employment Law (and a Few Labor Law Resources)*

    a. N. Peter Lareau et al., *Labor and Employment Law* (2013). This is a comprehensive treatise covering both labor law and employment law. It also covers both state and federal topics. It is available in print and on Lexis. It is updated quarterly.

    b. Karen E. Ford, et al., *Fundamentals of Employment Law* (2d ed. 2000). This book provides an overview of employment law, including statutes, regulations, and guidance for bringing and defending against employment discrimination lawsuits. It is written by attorneys at a major employment law firm, Littler Mendelson P.C. It is not updated regularly, so it is only current through its publication date.

    c. Mark W. Bennett, et al., *Employment Relationships: Law & Practice* (2009). This resource analyzes and discusses state and federal employment laws as well as recent trends in the law. Practice pointers are included throughout the text. While employment discrimination is only one topic covered (others include formation of the employment relationship, rights and obligations of employers and employees, privacy and technology issues, and alternative dispute resolution), the book does cover

---

[52] Another incredibly valuable resource for researching state law in particular is a state law encyclopedia. Almost every state publishes a legal encyclopedia, but these encyclopedias cover a range of topics (rather than simply employment law). For that reason, state encyclopedias are not included in this text. However, they are often a good resource for finding general information about various state employment discrimination law issues.

all aspects of federal employment discrimination law, including sexual harassment, Title VII, the ADA, the ADEA, the EPA, and the FMLA. The treatise also addresses employment contracts. It is updated annually.

d. Donald H. Weiss, *Fair, Square & Legal: Safe Hiring, Managing & Firing Practices to Keep You & Your Company Out of Court* (4th ed. 2004). Preventative lawyering is a topic discussed too infrequently in law school. This relatively short book is directed to business managers and human resources personnel dealing with personnel issues. However, it is a good resource for lawyers as well. It covers information on how to avoid lawsuits by staying within the law in all aspects of a company's relationship with a prospective or new employee, including recruitment and hiring, sexual harassment, evaluation and promotions, discipline and firing, affirmative action issues, and the like. The book summarizes EEOC guidelines and major statutes and cases on employment law, and it also raises issues related to technology and employment law.

e. Am. Bar Ass'n, *Model Jury Instructions: Employment Litigation* (2d ed. 2005). This book is published by the ABA Section on Litigation, and it includes over 200 model jury instructions. Each topic begins with an overview of the law on the subject of the instruction, commentary regarding relevant cases used in creating the model jury instruction, and how to adapt a model for a particular purpose. Employment discrimination topics are covered in addition to other employment litigation topics. Citations to authority provide a starting point for additional research on a given topic. While the book has not been updated since 2005, it does include the jury instructions on CD-Rom, so you can edit them to make them consistent with current law. This resource is also available on Lexis for some subscribers.

f. Bureau of National Affairs, Inc., *Employment Guide* (2013). This treatise is available in paper form and as an online subscription service through Bloomberg Law. The print resource is updated monthly, though it is supplemented by a weekly *Bulletin to Management* (indexed quarterly). The online resource is updated more frequently. This service is a resource for in-house counsel, human resources personnel, and managers in small and mid-sized organizations. Resources include model forms and policies, charts and checklists (including state comparison charts), and updates on recent developments in the law.

g. Mark A. Rothstein et al., *Employment Law* (4th ed. 2009). Part of West Group's Practitioner Treatise Series, this two-volume treatise covers basic rules, cases, and statutes related to employment law. Volume One has extensive coverage of employment discrimination law, including extensive references to other primary and secondary authorities to enhance your research efficiency. Volume Two includes an appendix with guidance on how to research various employment law issues.

h. Orrick, Herrington & Sutcliffe LLP, *Employment Law Yearbook 2012.* This publication of the Practicing Law Institute covers the entire range of employment law issues, and it is written by practitioners who specialize in employment law. Included among the topics are employment discrimination topics. The book is revised annually. When last checked, this resource was available on both Lexis and Westlaw.

    i. *Employment Litigation Handbook* (Jon W. Green & John W. Robinson IV, eds., 1998).

    j. Gordon Jackson, *Labor and Employment Law Handbook* (3d ed. 2009).

    k. Mark R. Filipp, *The Practical Guide to Employment Law* (2012).

    l. CCH, Inc., *Labor Relations Reporter* (2012). When last checked, this resource was available on both Lexis and Westlaw.

    m. Bureau of Nat'l Affairs, Inc., *Labor Relations Reporter* (2012). When last checked, this resource was available on both Lexis and Westlaw.

2. General Employment Discrimination Resources

    a. Barbara Lindemann & Paul Grossman, *Employment Discrimination Law* (4th ed. 2007 & Supp. 2010).

    b. Donald R. Livingston, *EEOC Litigation and Charge Resolution* (2005).[53]

    c. Lex K. Larson, *Employment Discrimination* (2d ed. 1994 & Supp. 2013). This is a highly-regarded 11-volume treatise that extensively covers the entire range of employment discrimination issues from both a compliance and litigation perspective. The book provides thorough analysis of all areas of employment discrimination law, and includes numerous references to authority and digests of cases. It covers issues related to public and private employers, voluntary affirmative action, and numerous cutting edge issues. The resource also provides numerous forms and sample documents, including those related to EEOC filings and court filings. In addition to being available in book form, it is available on Lexis and in e-book formats.

    d. Mack A. Player, *Federal Law of Employment Discrimination in a Nutshell* (6th ed. 2009). More useful as a student resource than as a practitioner resource, this short book covers federal employment discrimination law, including labor relations, statutory prohibitions against discrimination,

---

[53] According to the BNA Books website, the book explains how the EEOC is organized; how the charge-filing process works; and how investigations are prioritized and conducted, including investigations under EEOC commissioner charges. The treatise also explains the EEOC's conciliation and litigation processes and provides extensive sample language from actual EEOC conciliation and settlement agreements.

    For plaintiff attorneys, this reference details the EEOC's multiple-component charge-filing practices and suggests steps practitioners can take to improve the charging party's chances of receiving a mediation settlement, or a thorough investigation and a finding of reasonable cause. *EEOC Litigation and Charge Resolution* also provides suggestions for working with the EEOC as co-plaintiff in class cases, and explains how to obtain access to the EEOC's internal files.

    For defense attorneys, this treatise explains how to effectively interact with the EEOC during investigations and how to write better position statements. It also provides information on the EEOC's litigation and settlement practices and clarifies when and how the EEOC uses investigative subpoenas and when it litigates to enforce them. The treatise also discusses the EEOC's litigation practices and the special rules that apply to EEOC litigation, and explains how and when the EEOC and defendants rely on expert testimony. *EEOC Litigation and Charge Resolution* also gives information on how the EEOC exercises its authority to seek temporary injunctions, and how the EEOC conducts its appellate litigation and amicus participation.

    http://www.bna.com/eeoc-litigation-charge-p11761/ (last visited May 9, 2013).

the role of the EEOC, remedies, and theories of recovery. Available in book format and on Westlaw.

e. *Employment Discrimination Litigation: Developments and Strategies* (David L. Leitner, ed., 1999). This book is designed as a reference for both experienced and new litigators. It provides information and perspectives on employment discrimination litigation for plaintiff and defense counsel, judges, in-house counsel, and human resource personnel. Articles in the book are written by experienced employment discrimination litigators, and topics include litigation under the ADA, the ADEA, Title VII, and EEOC cases. Additional coverage includes details on discovery issues as well as alternative dispute resolution issues (mediating, arbitrating, and settling employment discrimination lawsuits). Also discussed are software programs to organize a case and employment practices liability insurance issues. It is not updated regularly, so it is only current through its publication date.

f. Thomson West, *Employment Discrimination Coordinator* (2013). This multivolume loose-leaf service is regularly updated, and it covers both state and federal discrimination laws (public and private sector employment). It offers state-by-state analysis as well as a comparison of key differences between state and federal law. It discusses wrongful discharge and remedies and provides citation to key controlling authorities (both state and federal). This is a particularly useful resource for in-house counsel and human resources personnel. It is also available on Westlaw.

g. Bureau of Nat'l Affairs, Inc., *Employment Discrimination Report*. This publication is issued in print and on the internet through Bloomberg Law on a weekly basis. The print version is archived quarterly. The report covers all areas of equal employment opportunity (EEO) law (cases, statutes, and regulations). Practitioners can use the weekly report to track key circuit splits, review summaries of briefs filed by the EEOC, and stay abreast of hot topics and trends in EEO law.

h. Henry H. Perritt, Jr., *Civil Rights in the Workplace* (3d ed. 2009 & Supp. 2012).

3. Secondary Sources on Specific Employment Discrimination Law Topics

In addition to books on general employment law and employment discrimination law topics, numerous secondary sources exist that focus on specific topics within employment discrimination law. This section lists some of those subject matter-specific resources, and it concludes with a short listing of resources targeting specific audiences (plaintiff's counsel, defense counsel, in-house counsel, and employees).

<u>Age Discrimination</u>

a. Barbara T. Lindemann & David D. Kadue, *Age Discrimination in Employment Law* (2003 & Supp. 2011). This treatise is designed for both counseling clients regarding compliance with the ADEA, bringing lawsuits under the ADEA, and defending claims brought under the ADEA. Covers all aspects of the ADEA, including issues pertaining to hiring, firing, mandatory retirement, reductions in force, and constructive discharge. Addresses who is protected under the Act, who can be sued, and what special issues arise in the labor union context. Fully discusses legislative, regulatory, and case developments.

b. Louis A. Jacobs & Andrew Ruzicho, *Litigating Age Discrimination Cases* (2003 & Supp. 2012). This treatise covers all aspects of the ADEA, including how to investigate age discrimination claims and evaluate a case. It also provides samples of pleadings, motions, and jury instructions. This treatise is available on Westlaw.

Disability Discrimination

Important Note: The ADA Amendments Act made some significant changes to disability discrimination law. Do not rely on any treatise that has not been updated since the enactment of the ADA Amendments Act.

a. Henry H. Perritt, Jr., *Americans with Disabilities Act Handbook* (4th ed. 2003 & Supp. 2012). This two-volume loose-leaf set covers the full range of ADA issues, including employment issues. Statutory and regulatory requirements are addressed for both public and private employers. The text also includes extensive forms and citations to relevant case law and an analysis of the ADA Amendments Act. Case law is organized both by frequently-litigated topics and by type of physical or mental impairment and accommodation, among other things.

b. Peter A. Susser, *Disability Discrimination and the Workplace* (2d ed. 2011). This relatively short treatise covers all aspects of disability discrimination. It also addresses the interaction of the ADA with other federal and state statutes, such as ERISA, the FMLA, and the NLRA. Available on Bloomberg Law.

c. Jonathan R. Mook, *Americans with Disabilities Act: Employee Rights and Employer Obligations* (published 1992, but revised annually). This practice guide provides guidance on creating compliant hiring, discipline, and termination policies, and it also touches on issues surrounding employee evaluations and promotion. The guide also provides checklists and forms, common factual scenarios and suggested solutions, practice pointers, and text of the ADA and EEOC regulations on disability discrimination. The book has been revised to reflect changes brought about by the enactment of the ADA Amendments Act of 2008.

d. Thomas R. Trenkner, *Americans with Disabilities: Practice and Compliance Manual* (2009). Available on Westlaw.

e. Michael A. Faillace, *Disability Law Deskbook: The Americans with Disabilities Act in the Workplace* (2009). This deskbook is published by the Practicing Law Institute and is targeted to employers, attorneys, and human resources personnel. The book contains detailed compliance information as well as information for defense attorneys when defending a client in a disability discrimination lawsuit. Available on Lexis and on Westlaw.

f. Peter Blanck et al., *Disability Civil Rights Law and Policy* (2004). This is a single-volume hornbook covering all aspects of disability law, including disability discrimination in employment. Probably more useful as a student resource than a practitioner's resource. It is available on Westlaw.

g. Bonnie Poitras Tucker & Adam A. Milani, *Federal Disability Law in a Nutshell* (3d ed. 2004). This may be a useful student resource, though other more comprehensive treatises should be consulted by practitioners. Includes an overview of federal laws on disability, including employment discrimination under the ADA. Updated periodically, though not regularly. It is available on Westlaw.

Sex Discrimination

a. Susan M. Omilian & Jean P. Kamp, *Sex-Based Employment Discrimination* (1990-present). Available on Westlaw.

Sexual Harassment

a. Barbara Lindemann & David D. Kadue, *Sexual Harassment in Employment Law* (1992–present).

b. William Petrocelli & Barbara Kate Repa, *Sexual Harassment on the Job: What It Is and How to Stop It* (4th ed. 1999).

c. Barbara Lindemann & David D. Kadue, *Primer on Sexual Harassment* (1992).

d. Alba Conte, *Sexual Harassment in the Workplace: Law & Practice* (4th ed. 2012).

Wrongful Termination and Retaliation

a. Adolph M. Koven, Susan L. Smith, Kenneth May & Donald F. Farwell, *Just Cause: The Seven Tests* (3d ed. 2006).

b. Daniel P. Westman & Nancy M. Modesitt, *Whistleblowing: The Law of Retaliatory Discharge* (2d ed. 2004 & Supp. 2012).

c. Henry H. Perritt, Jr., *Employee Dismissal: Law and Practice* (5th ed. 2006 & Supp. 2012).

d. Lex K. Larson, *Unjust Dismissal* (2013). This is a three-volume loose-leaf service providing an overview of laws implicated by wrongful termination. Topics include issues surrounding employee handbooks and personnel manuals, whistleblowing cases, free speech and privacy, and the like. The book covers contractual, tort, and statutory theories of unjust dismissal. Importantly, the book provides an "Employee Relations Guide" that details key preventative practices employers can use to avoid claims in the first place. Appendix includes model forms, interrogatories and motions, jury instructions, and the like. This treatise is updated regularly and is available on Lexis.

Wages and Hours

a. *The Fair Labor Standards Act* (Ellen C. Kearns ed., 2d ed. 2010 & Supp. 2012). Available on Bloomberg Law.

b. Laurie Leader, *Wages and Hours: Law and Practice* (LexisNexis-Matthew Bender 1990 & Supp. 2012). Available on Lexis.

c. *Wage and Hour Laws: A State-by-State Survey* (Gregory K. McGillivary ed., 2d ed. 2011). Available on Bloomberg Law.

Family & Medical Leave

a. *The Family and Medical Leave Act* (Michael J. Ossip & Robert M. Hale eds., 2006 & Supp. 2013). Available on Bloomberg Law.

b. Peter A. Susser & David B. Berry, *The Family and Medical Leave Handbook* (2008 & Supp. 2012). This text and the related *Family and Medical Leave Handbook Newsletter* are available on Westlaw.

c. CCH, Inc., *Family and Medical Leave Act, Military Family Leave Final Regulations 2008.*

d. CCH, Inc., *Family and Medical Leave Guide* (Aspen Publishers 2012).

Section 1983 Litigation

a. David W. Lee, *Handbook of Section 1983 Litigation* (2011 ed.).

b. Martin A. Schwartz et al., *Section 1983 Litigation Law* (2012).

Employment Arbitration

a. Frank Elkouri & Edna Asper Elkouri, *How Arbitration Works* (Marlin M. Volz & Edward P. Goggin, eds., 7th ed. 2012).

b. Dennis R. Nolan, *Labor and Employment Arbitration in a Nutshell* (2d ed. 2007). Available on Westlaw.

c. Daniel O'Meara, *Employment Arbitration* (2009). Available on Lexis.

d. Littler Mendelson, P.C., *Employment Arbitration Agreements: A Practical Guide* (Aspen Publishers 2009).

Books designed to Educate Employees about their Rights

a. Barbara Kate Repa, *Your Rights in the Workplace* (NOLO ed., 9th ed. 2010).

Books for HR Professionals and/or In-House Counsel

a. Dana Shilling, *Complete Guide to Human Resources and the Law* (Aspen Publishers 2013 ed.).

b. John F. Buckley & Ronald M. Green, *State by State Guide to Human Resources Law* (Aspen Publishers 2013 ed.).

c. *U.S. Employer's Guide* (Aspen Publishers 2010).

Books Focused on Litigation from the Defense Perspective

a. Gerald S. Hartman & Gregory W. Homer, *Defending & Preventing Employment Litigation* (Aspen Publishers 2013 ed.).

Books Focused on Litigation from the Plaintiff's Perspective

a. Robert E. McKnight, Representing *Plaintiffs in Title VII Actions* (3d ed. 2012).

Agency Guidance

Note that probably the best place to find agency guidance is directly on the relevant agency's website. Nonetheless, here are a few other sources and locations of agency guidance.

a. Equal Employment Opportunity Comm'n, *EEOC Compliance Manual*. Available on Westlaw, Lexis, and Bloomberg Law.

b. Equal Employment Opportunity Comm'n, *Technical Assistance Program: Resource Manual: Laws, Regulations and Relevant Policy Statements* (1993).

c. *Americans with Disabilities Act Technical Assistance Manuals* (multiple titles).

4. Selected List of Employment Law Journals

Some law journals and periodicals focus specifically on employment law topics, and these can be useful for an in-depth analysis or critique of various issues. Remember that academic law reviews have a different focus and purpose than practitioner resources (both types of journals are included below). While the analysis in academic journals can be quite sophisticated, the articles are static, meaning they are not updated as the law changes. Nevertheless, academic journals are a good place to look for analysis of circuit splits, policy arguments, and arguments for change to the law. Here are just a few of the well-known journals focusing on employment and/or labor law:

a. **Berkeley Journal of Employment and Labor Law:** Both Westlaw and Lexis offer this journal, though neither service provides coverage from the inception of the journal. Lexis has issues starting with volume 14 (1993), while Westlaw has limited coverage from 1984 and full coverage beginning with volume 15 (1994). For full coverage from the first volume in 1976, you can access Hein Online.

b. **Employee Relations Law Journal:** This journal has been published for over 25 years by Aspen Publishers. Authors of articles in the journal are practitioners, and topics range from issues under the ADA, the FMLA, the ADEA, and Title VII. You can find guidance on terminations and

Reductions in Force (RIFs), alternative dispute resolution, and recent trends in the law.

   c. **Employee Rights and Employment Policy Journal:** This journal is available on both Westlaw and Lexis. The first volume of this Journal was published in 1997.

   d. **Hofstra Labor & Employment Law Journal (previously the Hofstra Labor Law Journal):** Lexis (database identifier HLABLJ) offers coverage from volume 11 in 1993, while Westlaw offers coverage from volume 15. Hein Online offers full coverage from volume 2.

B. SELECTED TREATISES ON STATE LAW

State materials on employment law also exist in nearly every state. In addition to 50-state surveys on various topics, you can find practice guides and deskbooks on employment law generally. Some are published by commercial publishers. For example, Matthew Bender publishes (through Lexis) a series called "*Employment in [State]: A Guide to Employment Laws, Regulations and Practices.*"

The state bar associations of many states also publish subject matter-specific guides, usually through their continuing legal education departments. For example, one of the most well-developed state bar association websites providing secondary source materials is Michigan's Institute for Continuing Legal Education (ICLE). When you begin to practice, make sure you know the materials available in your state through the bar association.

Most states also have a deskbook of laws and regulations governing employment law. These deskbooks are updated annually, and they do not contain analysis of the law. Rather, they simply collect all the relevant laws, regulations, and constitutional provisions related to employment law. For example, attorneys practicing in California have access to a deskbook published by West Publishing, entitled *California Employment Laws* (California Desktop Codes 2013 ed.).

One of the best things you can do when you start out in practice is to develop your own list of go-to resources for state-specific employment law topics. To find what to put on that list, take the following steps (probably best in this order): (1) ask a senior attorney and the firm librarian (if you have one) what books are available in your area; (2) peruse the shelves in the firm library (if it has one) to familiarize yourself with the resources available; (3) check what materials are published by your state bar association; and (4) search the databases in Westlaw and Lexis for relevant material.

For example, if you practice in California, you will quickly discover at least the following materials (not an exclusive list):

California

Ming W. Chin et al., *The Rutter Group California Practice Guide: Employment Litigation* (2013). This loose-leaf resource is an extremely well-respected source for employment law in California. Aimed at practitioners, the book covers all aspects of employment law, including discrimination and harassment. It collects recent cases, statutes, and court rules, and provides multiple illustrations. The book also includes forms with suggestions for how to use them, practice tips and strategies (including time-saving suggestions), and "matrix charts [to] compare possible employee claims, remedies, and employer responses." west.thomson.com/productdetail/13775/40030744/productdetail. aspx (last accessed May 13, 2013). Rutter Group materials are available on Westlaw.

California Employment Law (Matthew Bender 2004 & Supp. 2012). Available on Lexis.

West Publishers, *Employment Litigation (California Civil Practice)*(2001-2012) (updated regularly).

Note: Witkin's *Summary of California Law* also has extensive information on employment law, though it is not devoted exclusively to the subject.

In contrast, if you practice in Ohio, you might turn to these materials (among others):

Ohio

Bradd N. Siegel & John M. Stephen, *Ohio Employment Practices Law* (Baldwin's Ohio Handbook Series 2013 ed.). This book is written by practicing attorneys, and it provides coverage of Ohio's at-will employment rules, along with "substantive law and procedural aspects of defending wrongful discharge actions and similar claims. [The book includes] a Table of Lawful/Unlawful Interview Questions; an extensive glossary; and articles on the implications of federal laws, such as the Americans with Disabilities Act." http://west.thomson. com/productdetail/159426/13780554/productdetail.aspx (last accessed May 13, 2013). Available on Westlaw.

Maynard G. Sautter, *Employment in Ohio: A Guide to Employment Laws, Regulations, and Practices* (Matthew Bender 3d ed. 1997 & Supp. 2013). This single-volume loose-leaf service provides information concerning Ohio labor and employment laws and regulations. Available on Lexis.

EXERCISES

1) Choose one of the states above (California or Ohio). Take the four steps suggested above for locating state-specific materials. If you are still in school, ask a law librarian rather than a practicing attorney. Add to the list of go-to resources provided above. For each resource on your list, briefly summarize the type of material available in that resource so you can remember later.

2) Choose the state in which you plan to practice. Develop a list of state-specific resources for that state using the steps suggested above. If your state is Ohio or California and you already completed it in the first exercise, choose a different state for this problem.

II. JUMPSTARTING EMPLOYMENT DISCRIMINATION RESEARCH ONLINE VIA FREE GOVERNMENT AGENCY WEBSITES AND COURT WEB PAGES

A. RESEARCHING USING GOVERNMENT WEBSITES

One of the best places to find simple answers to many employment discrimination questions is the website of the government agency charged with administering the relevant law. Government agency websites collect a treasure-trove of basic legal information, including the full text of relevant statutes, regulations, and other agency guidance; information about requirements for exhausting administrative remedies before filing suit; and information regarding whether another agency might also have responsibility for some or all of legal issues you are researching.

The most important federal government websites for attorneys practicing employment discrimination law are the websites for the Department of Justice (DOJ), the Department of Labor (DOL), and the Equal Employment Opportunity Commission (EEOC).

EXERCISE

Access the websites for the DOL, the DOJ, and the EEOC. Create a chart that lists the laws related to employment discrimination and what agency administers those laws. List employment laws governing both private and public sector employers. In paragraph form, list the kinds of information you were able to find on these websites.

Most states also have agencies that administer rules and regulations governing employment discrimination issues. These state government websites can be invaluable research tools. The following chart lists the relevant government agency and its website for several major states:

State	Relevant Government Agency and Website
Texas	**Texas Workforce Commission (TWC)** www.twc.state.tx.us/ The TWC website provides information regarding employment discrimination under both federal and Texas state law. From this page, you can link to federal and state laws and regulations on employment discrimination issues. The TWC Civil Rights Division has the responsibility of enforcing the Texas Commission on Human Rights Act. This Act is codified in Chapter 21 of the Texas Labor Code ("Employment Discrimination"). As of August 5, 2013, the link for information specifically about the laws enforced by the TWC was www.twc.state.tx.us/customers/bemp/employment-law.html. This link also provides additional links to federal and state laws and regulations on civil rights and employment discrimination issues.
Florida	**Florida Commission on Human Relations (FCHR)** http://fchr.state.fl.us/fchr/complaints__1/employment This is the link within the FCHR website that provides information regarding filing an administrative complaint under the state law on employment discrimination, Chapter 760 of the Florida Statutes. By following the "Resources" link on that page, you can access the full text of Chapter 760 as well as links to federal employment discrimination statutes.
California	In 2012, California's key civil rights law, the Fair Employment and Housing Act (FEHA), underwent several major changes. Prior to these changes, the Department of Fair Employment and Housing (DFEH) served as the prosecutorial agency under FEHA. The DFEH can be accessed online at www.dfeh.ca.gov. From this location, you can link to information regarding the administrative complaint process under FEHA. Prior to January 1, 2013, the California Fair Employment and Housing Commission (FEHC) was charged with actually enforcing California's civil rights laws. Although discrimination complaints were filed with the DFEH, the FEHC was responsible for administrative adjudication; mediations; regulations; legislation; and public information and training. However, on June 27, 2012, Governor Brown signed SB 1038 into law. One of the key changes SB 1038 made was that it "amend[ed] the Fair Employment and Housing Act (FEHA) to: eliminate the Fair Employment and Housing Commission and replace it with a Fair Employment and Housing Council within the Department; (2) transfer the Commission's regulatory function to the Department's Council; and (3) end administrative adjudication of FEHA claims." www.dfeh.ca.gov/FairEmploymentAndHousingCouncil.htm (last accessed May 10, 2013). To learn more about the changes to California law, you can read an article written by the current director of the DFEH, Phyllis W. Cheng. The article is currently found at www.dfeh.ca.gov/res/docs/Publications/Articles/Transformative%20year%20for%20civil%20rights%20in%20CA%20PCheng%20DJ%208-2-12.pdf.

State	Relevant Government Agency and Website
New York	**New York State Division of Human Rights (NY DHR)** http://www.dhr.ny.gov/ This is the NY DHR home page. From this location, you can link to information regarding filing an administrative complaint under the state law on civil rights and employment discrimination, New York State Executive Law, Article 15, the Human Rights Law. You can also link to the text of state laws and regulations on civil rights and employment discrimination issues.
Illinois	**Illinois Department of Human Rights (IDHR)** www.state.il.us/dhr This is the IDHR home page. From this location, you can link to information regarding filing an administrative complaint of discrimination under the Illinois Human Rights Act. You can also find links to information regarding the scope of coverage of the employment discrimination provisions of the Illinois Human Rights Act.

EXERCISES

For all questions, only use material you find by searching the relevant state administrative agency websites. If you find the answer in a fact sheet published by the agency (secondary authority), also check to find the answer in the text of the statute itself. Provide the relevant language of the statute as well as the statutory citation. Provide the amount of time it took you to find the answer to the question.

1) Texas Labor Code Section 22 also deals with a specific employment discrimination issue. What is it? Can an employee file a claim with the Civil Rights Division of the Texas Workforce Commission under Section 22?

2) Provide the definition of "employer" under the following laws: Chapter 21 of the Texas Labor Code, the Illinois Human Rights Act, and the New York State Executive Law, Article 15 (the "Human Rights Law").

3) How many days after an alleged act of discrimination does one have to file a claim with the California Department of Fair Employment and Housing? The Florida Commission on Human Relations?

4) What categories are protected under the New York Human Rights Law? The Illinois Human Rights Act? The California Department of Fair Employment and Housing?

5) Does the Texas Labor Code prohibit pregnancy discrimination? Genetic discrimination?

B. RESEARCHING LOCAL RULES REQUIREMENTS

If you are simply trying to locate basic formatting requirements specific to the court you are filing in, the best resource is the web page for the court itself. There, you can find full-text versions of the local rules requirements for filing. Also look to see if the specific judge has additional rules. If so, these will be located on the relevant court's web page as well. If you cannot find the local rules online, call the court clerk to get this information.

III. STAYING ABREAST OF NEW STATUTORY AND CASE DEVELOPMENTS IN EMPLOYMENT DISCRIMINATION LAW

It would be so much easier to be a lawyer if the law remained static. However, the law is constantly changing. Statutes may be repealed, amended, or added. New cases may appear that interpret the law in new ways. Consequently, the best lawyers develop systems to keep abreast of new developments in the law.

There are several ways to ensure that you are keeping up with relevant changes and trends in your field of law. First, state bar associations and other organizations offer continuing legal education (CLE) courses specifically focused on new developments in specific areas of employment discrimination law. Second, the American Bar Association (ABA) offers its members the opportunity to join specialized sections. The ABA's Section on Labor and Employment Law publishes a quarterly newsletter with discussion of hot topics in the area. The Section also publishes "The Flash," a monthly e-mail from the Section that keeps members informed of upcoming CLE offerings and hot topics in the field. The ABA also publishes the ABA Journal of Labor and Employment Law, a quarterly newsletter, and various e-alerts. Most state bar associations offer the opportunity to join similar specialized sections.

A third way to stay informed about developments in employment discrimination law is by tracking those developments on a blog. Remember, though, that you should always evaluate internet sources for authoritativeness. Verify the substance of the primary authorities mentioned in the blog for yourself, and choose a blog that is well-respected by members of your field. Here are a few blogs on labor and employment law topics:

- Workplace Prof Blog: http://lawprofessors.typepad.com/laborprof_blog/
- Law Memo: First In Employment Law Blog: www.lawmemo.com/blog/
- Nolo's Employment Law Blog: www.employmentlegalblawg.com/
- Employment Law Information Network Blog on Employment Law: www.elinfonet.com/blog/index
- Wolters Kluwer Law & Business WorkDay Blog: www.employmentlawdaily.com/index.php/blog

EXERCISE

Look up two of the blogs listed above. Describe the content of the blogs. Can you tell who authors them? Do they look like authoritative sources and, if so, why? What features do you like or dislike about the blogs you have reviewed?

A fourth way to keep track of new case law or statutory developments is to set up alerts for cases and laws you use regularly. Both Lexis and Westlaw offer the opportunity to set up alerts, as do some government websites. A fifth thing you should do to keep abreast of developments in the area is to subscribe to relevant daily or weekly newsletters. For example, you can subscribe to BNA's Daily Labor Report through Bloomberg Law. You can also subscribe to other BNA publications related to employment law through Bloomberg Law. Finally, make sure you bookmark key government web pages. You can always check for new regulatory developments by visiting the web page of the EEOC, for example.

EXERCISE

This short section described a number of ways to keep abreast of developments in the law of employment discrimination. However, the list is not organized in order of importance or relevance. Answer the following two questions:

- ☐ Should you take all of the steps listed above to make sure you're staying up-to-date on relevant law? If not, why not?
- ☐ In what order would you most likely want to check the resources discussed above? Explain your reasoning.

IV. DEVELOPING CHARTS OF KEY FEDERAL STATUTES AND UNITED STATES SUPREME COURT CASES ON EMPLOYMENT DISCRIMINATION ISSUES

If you follow the strategies in this book for designing and implementing an effective research strategy, you will be able to find relevant cases on your own. However, one thing that distinguishes seasoned employment lawyers from beginning lawyers or law students is that experienced lawyers already have a database of basic knowledge from which they can draw when they are faced with a new legal issue. This book aims to provide students with some of that foundational knowledge now, so that entry into practice is smoother.

Research is always easier if you can start with a seminal case on your topic. What follows is a chart of some key foundational Supreme Court decisions on employment discrimination topics. While you will obviously need to find recent cases in your jurisdiction when researching an employment discrimination topic, you will likely find that task less daunting if you start with a seminal case. Some of those major cases are included in the list below, though you should continue to add to the list as you come across relevant cases in your research.

Selected United States Supreme Court Cases by Topic

Class Action Requirements

Arbaugh v. Y&H Corp., 546 U.S. 500 (2006).

Wal-Mart Stores, Inc. v. Dukes, 131 S. Ct. 2541 (2011).

Circumstantial Evidence

McDonnell Douglas Corp. v. Green, 411 U.S. 792 (1973).

Reeves v. Sanderson Plumbing Products, Inc., 530 U.S. 133 (2000).

St. Mary's Honor Ctr. v. Hicks, 509 U.S. 502 (1993).

Texas Dept. of Community Affairs v. Burdine, 450 U. S. 248 (1981).

Mixed Motive

Desert Palace, Inc. v. Costa, 539 U.S. 90 (2003).

Price Waterhouse v. Hopkins, 490 U.S. 228 (1989).

Disparate Impact

Griggs v. Duke Power Co., 401 U.S. 424 (1971).

Int'l Bhd. of Teamsters v. United States, 431 U.S. 324 (1977).

Lewis v. City of Chicago, 560 U.S. 205 (2010).

Meacham v. Knolls Atomic Power Lab., 554 U.S. 84 (2008).

Ricci v. DeStefano, 557 U.S. 557 (2009).

Smith v. City of Jackson, 544 U.S. 228 (2005).

Pattern and Practice, Class-Wide Discrimination, Etc.

Int'l Bhd. of Teamsters v. United States, 431 U.S. 324 (1977).

Use of Statistical Evidence in Employment Cases

Griggs v. Duke Power Co., 401 U.S. 424 (1971).

The Intersection between Disparate Treatment and Disparate Impact

Ricci v. DeStefano, 557 U.S. 557 (2009).

Definition of "Supervisor" for Purposes of Title VII Liability

Vance v. Ball State Univ., 133 S. Ct. 2434 (2013).

Sex Discrimination

Johnson v. Transportation Agency, 480 U.S. 616 (1987).

Sexual Harassment

Burlington Industries, Inc. Ellerth, 524 U.S. 742 (1998).

Faragher v. City of Boca Raton, 524 U.S. 775 (1998).

Harris v. Forklift, 510 U.S. 17 (1993).

Meritor Savings Bank v. Vinson, 477 U.S. 57(1986).

Oncale v. Sundowner Offshore Serv., Inc., 523 U.S. 75 (1998).

Pennsylvania State Police v. Suders, 542 U.S. 129 (2004) (and retaliation).

Vance v. Ball State Univ., 133 S. Ct. 2434 (2013).

Pregnancy Discrimination or Bias

AT&T Corp. v. Hulteen, 556 U.S. 701 (2009).

Cleveland Bd. of Ed. v. LaFleur, 414 U.S. 632 (1974).

Race Discrimination and Reverse-Race Discrimination

Ash v. Tyson Foods, Inc., 546 U.S. 454 (2006).

Ricci v. DeStefano, 557 U.S. 557 (2009).

Religious Discrimination

Hosanna-Tabor Evangelical Lutheran Church & Sch. v. E.E.O.C., 132 S. Ct. 694 (2012) (ministerial exception).

Americans with Disabilities Act, the Rehabilitation Act, and the ADA Amendments Act

Barnes v. Gorman, 536 U.S. 181 (2002).

Bragdon v. Abbott, 524 U.S. 624 (1998).

Chevron U.S.A. Inc. v. Echazabal, 536 U.S. 73 (2002).

Equal Employment Opportunity Commission v. Waffle House, Inc., 534 U.S. 279 (2002) (and arbitration).

Murphy v. United Parcel Service, Inc., 527 U.S. 516 (1999).

PGA Tour, Inc. v. Martin, 532 U.S. 661 (2001).

School Board of Nassau County v. Arline, 480 U.S. 273 (1987).

Sutton v. United Airlines, Inc., 527 U.S. 471 (1999).

Toyota Motor Manufacturing, Kentucky, Inc. v. Williams, 534 U.S. 184 (2002).

U.S. Airways, Inc. v. Barnett, 535 U.S. 391 (2002).

EXERCISE

Of the cases on this list, which cases have been affected by the ADA Amendments Act of 2008? For affected cases, how have they been affected? Completely overruled? Distinguished? Clarified?

Equal Pay Act

Ledbetter v. Goodyear Tire & Rubber Co., 127 S. Ct. 2162 (2007) (overturned by the Lilly Ledbetter Fair Pay Act).

Age Discrimination in Employment Act

Federal Express Corp. v. Holowecki, 552 U.S. 389 (2008).

Gomez-Perez v. Potter, 553 U.S. 474 (2008).

General Dynamics Land Systems, Inc. v. Cline, 540 U.S. 581 (2004).

Gross v. FBL Financial Services, Inc., 557 U.S. 167 (2009).

Kentucky Retirement Systems v. EEOC, 554 U.S. 135 (2008).

Meacham v. Knolls Atomic Power Laboratory, 554 U.S. 84 (2008).

Smith v. City of Jackson, Mississippi, 544 U.S. 228 (2005).

Kimel v. Florida Bd. of Regents, 528 U.S. 62 (2000).

Retaliation

CBOCS West, Inc. v. Humphries, 553 U.S. 442 (2008) (section 1981).

Crawford v. Metropolitan Government of Nashville, 555 U.S. 271 (2009) (Title VII).

Jackson v. Birmingham Board of Education, 544 U.S. 167 (2005) (Title IX).

Pennsylvania State Police v. Suders, 542 U.S. 129 (2004) (sexual harassment case).

Univ. of Texas Southwestern Med. Ctr. v. Nassar, 133 S. Ct. 2517 (2013) (Title VII).

Continuing Violations

National Railroad Passenger Corporation v. Morgan, 536 U.S. 101 (2002).

Cat's Paw Doctrine

Staub v. Proctor Hosp., 131 S. Ct. 1186 (2011).

Section 1981

CBOCS West, Inc. v. Humphries, 553 U.S. 442 (2008) (retaliation case).

Domino's Pizza, Inc. v. McDonald, 546 U.S. 470 (2006).

Patterson v. McLean Credit Union, 491 U.S. 164 (1989).

Arbitration

(some are non-employment cases with implications for employment cases)

AT&T Mobility LLC v. Concepcion, 131 S. Ct. 1740 (2011).

Buckeye Check Cashing, Inc. v. Cardegna, 546 U.S. 440 (2006).

Circuit City Stores v. Adams, 532 U.S. 105 (2001).

EEOC v. Waffle House Inc., 534 U.S. 279 (2002).

Hall Street Associates, L.L.C. v. Mattel, Inc., 552 U.S. 576 (2008).

Preston v. Ferrer, 552 U.S. 346 (2008) (and preemption).

Southland Corp. v. Keating, 465 U.S. 1 (1984).

Vaden v. Discover Bank, 129 S.Ct. 1262 (2009) (and procedure).

Procedural Issues

Arbaugh v. Y & H Corp., 546 U.S. 500 (2006).

Federal Express Corp. v. Holowecki, 552 U.S. 389 (2008).

EXERCISE

Create the same type of chart for relevant statutes.[54] Complete the chart below (or whatever portion of the chart is assigned by your professor), and describe how you found the relevant information. If a statute covers more than employment issues, provide the citation to the relevant employment law portion of the statute. If you believe statutes are missing from the chart, add them and explain their relevance to employment discrimination law.

Statute	Statutory Citation	Citation to Relevant Administrative Regulations, if Any
Civil Rights Act of 1991		
Fair Labor Standards Act		
Age Discrimination in Employment Act of 1967		
Section 1983		

---

[54] Note that some of these "Acts" actually just amended an earlier act rather than being a separate act themselves. Where you discover this is the case, note it in your chart.

Statute	Statutory Citation	Citation to Relevant Administrative Regulations, if Any
Section 1981		
Americans with Disabilities Act of 1990		
Americans with Disabilities Amendments Act		
Sections 501 and 505 of the Rehabilitation Act of 1973		
Genetic Information Nondiscrimination Act of 2008		
Equal Pay Act of 1963		
Title VII of the Civil Rights Act of 1964		
Family and Medical Leave Act		
Pregnancy Discrimination Act		
Civil Service Reform Act of 1968		

FINAL RESEARCH EXERCISES

For these research questions, perform the following tasks: First, identify the best place to begin your research (government website, treatise, general internet search, etc.) Be specific. If you think a specific website will be relevant, list it. Second, try to find the answer three ways: (1) using the method you initially thought would be simplest and most effective; (2) using only government websites and treatises (unless that was the way you chose initially); and (3) using only terms searching on Westlaw, Lexis, or Loislaw (unless that was the way you chose initially). Describe your research process (including search terms) in each source. Third, explain your answer to the research question and what you learned about the most effective way to research the particular problem you're working on.

1) Our client recently lost a jury trial in a sexual harassment and retaliation case brought under Title VII and the California Fair Employment Practices & Housing Act, Cal. Gov't Code §§ 12900-12996 (West 2009), after one of its long-time supervisors sexually harassed a new employee of the company. When the new employee complained, she was fired. (Of course, our client still maintains the employee was fired for legitimate reasons, though a jury decided otherwise.) Our client is now filing for bankruptcy (unrelated to the sexual harassment lawsuit). In the Eighth Circuit, is a monetary judgment against an employer for the sexual harassment of one of its supervisors a dischargeable debt in bankruptcy? Do other circuits agree? If not, what are conflicting opinions?

2) Do employers in California have to post a notice to employees regarding sexual harassment laws? If so, what information must that notice contain?

3) Are punitive damages available as a remedy for violation of prohibitions on sexual harassment under the Texas Commission on Human Rights Act?

4) We represent the city of Dallas. One of the employees at the City Manager's office has filed a complaint alleging race discrimination in Dallas State Court under the Texas Commission on Human Rights Act. Please research the following two questions:

    a) Was the employee required to first file an administrative complaint with the Texas Commission on Human Rights? In other words, is there an exhaustion requirement under Texas state law?

    b) Is the city of Dallas considered an "employer" under the Act?

5) Our client is an individual who wants to hire us to represent her in a sex discrimination lawsuit. She has already filed a sex discrimination complaint in California state court against her former employer, SuperMart, a large discount food chain with over 500 full-time employees, though she wrote it herself. (She went to law school for a year before leaving to take a job at SuperMart, and she thought she could handle the lawsuit on her own. She has since decided otherwise.) She would like us to represent her and to amend her complaint to add a claim for religious discrimination. I'm pretty sure that California law requires a discrimination plaintiff to exhaust administrative remedies before filing suit. Is this right? If so, are there any exceptions to the exhaustion requirement?

6) Under California law, does a church employing 15 employees qualify as an "employer" in a national origin discrimination case? A sexual harassment case?

7) Under California law, when (if ever) is an employer liable for an employee's same-sex sexual harassment of a co-worker?

DRAFTING IN THE EMPLOYMENT DISCRIMINATION CONTEXT AND COUNSELING CLIENTS

Lawyers who practice labor and employment law are often referred to more generally as litigators, and it is undoubtedly true that employment discrimination cases can and do end up in court. However, most lawyers who practice employment law spend far more time drafting documents and policies or counseling clients than they do arguing in court. Part III, therefore, provides a basic introduction to key skills that are often overlooked when educating new employment lawyers. Chapters 9 through 13 focus primarily on drafting issues, including learning key contract concepts, identifying the basic components of a contract, working with typical boilerplate provisions, addressing language issues in drafting, and choosing and using legal forms as a basis for creating new drafted documents. Chapter 14 essentially brings the entire text together, asking students to draft specific types of policies or documents in the employment discrimination context and to provide client counseling and advice regarding how to change policies to comply with a change in the law; how to draft new policies to avoid litigation; and how to educate clients or assigning attorneys regarding the law in a given area. When answering questions, it may help to go back and review the material on presenting research results from the preceding sections of this book.

BASIC CONTRACT CONCEPTS

Although most employment is at-will, some employees have employment contracts. Moreover, even in the case of at-will employment, employers may have certain policies they expect employees to follow or agreements employees must sign (like confidentiality agreements or covenants not to compete). As such, it is important to understand at least the basic contract concepts and the language used to express those concepts. In fact, it may be even more important in the case of an at-will employment relationship to understand these concepts in order to avoid *inadvertently* creating a right or duty your client did not want created.

This chapter represents only a very brief overview of these contract concepts. For students who would like a much more thorough discussion of contract concepts, one of the best student books on the subject is Tina Stark's book, *Drafting Contracts: How and Why Lawyers Do What they Do* (Wolters Kluwer Law & Business 2007). Other references are available throughout the book. The following discussion briefly covers key contract concepts, including representations, warranties, covenants, rights, conditions, discretionary authority, and declarations.

I. REPRESENTATIONS AND WARRANTIES

Representations and warranties are both promises of sorts, though they are not identical. A representation is "a statement of fact, as of a moment in time, intended to induce reliance."[1] A warranty is "a promise by the maker of a statement that the statement is true."[2]

---

[1] Tina L. Stark, *Drafting Contracts: How and Why Lawyers Do What They Do* 12 (2007) (citing *Harold Cohn & Co. v. Harco Int'l, LLC*, 804 A.2d 218 (Conn. Ct. App. 2002)).
[2] *Id.* (citing *CBS Inc. v. Ziff-Davis Publ'g Co.*, 553 N.E.2d 997 (N.Y. 1990)).

In practice, representations and warranties almost always come together ("Employer represents and warrants as follows . . ."). This common coupling has led some commentators to suggest that one or the other term is essentially superfluous and should be avoided.[3] In our opinion, however, the better view is that most contracts should retain both representations and warranties, as the distinction between the two is not merely academic or theoretical.[4] For example, only a misrepresentation can serve as a basis for restitution or punitive damages; however, if a plaintiff cannot show proof of scienter, the plaintiff will only have a claim for breach of warranty.[5]

Representations and warranties should always be written in the present tense, as they are statements of fact made as of a particular moment in time.

■ EXAMPLES

Employee represents and warrants that he is licensed by the state of Texas to practice law.

Employer represents and warrants that it is fully authorized to enter into this Employment Agreement and that entering into this Employment Agreement will not violate any other agreement to which either the Employer or the Executive is a party.

> ■ **PRACTICE NOTE:** Importantly, because representations and warranties are statements made as of a specific moment in time, they do not carry forward into the future unless you specifically provide that the representations and warranties continue to remain true at future points in time. This is often accomplished with a condition:
>
> *Throughout Employee's employment with Law Firm, L.L.P., Employee must remain a member in good standing of the Texas State Bar.*

II. COVENANTS AND RIGHTS

Covenants and rights, like representations and warranties, are closely related to each other. A covenant is "a promise to do or not do something" which "creates a duty to perform."[6] Covenants thus comprise the "meat" of the contract,

---

[3] *See, e.g.*, Kenneth A. Adams, *A Lesson in Drafting Contracts: What's up with "Representations and Warranties"?*, Bus. L. Today, Nov.-Dec. 2005, at 8 (advising lawyers to "represent" in all instances).
[4] *See, e.g.*, Tina L. Stark, *Nonbinding Opinion: Another View on Reps and Warranties*, Bus. L. Today, Jan.-Feb. 2006, at 8 (noting that representations and warranties are, in fact different, and making a forceful case for retaining both representations and warranties in most contracts).
[5] *Id.; see also* Tina L. Stark, *Drafting Contracts: How and Why Lawyers Do What They Do* 16 (2007).
[6] Tina L. Stark, *Drafting Contracts: How and Why Lawyers Do What They Do* 20 (2007).

its essential terms.[7] A right is the opposite of a covenant—it "entitles a party to the other party's performance."[8] In general, the operative effect of rights and covenants is the same; if there is a duty, there must also be a corresponding right. However, it is probably better to phrase contract obligations as covenants rather than rights.

■ **EXAMPLES**

Covenant: *Employer shall pay Employee monthly, with payment on the first day of each month.*

Right: *Employee is entitled to payment monthly, with payment on the first day of each month.*

Although these two statements express the same underlying concept, the first sentence is better because it avoids ambiguity. Most importantly, it places the emphasis on the actor undertaking the obligation.[9]

■ **PRACTICE NOTE:** Express a covenant using the word "shall."[10] Express a right using the words "has a right to" or "is entitled to." A more in-depth discussion of the precise use of "shall" appears later in this section.

III. CONDITIONS

A condition is "a state of facts that must exist before a party is obligated to perform."[11] More technically, it represents "[a]n operative fact or event, one on which the existence of some particular legal relation depends."[12] Regardless of phrasing, the idea is simply this: if a particular contract term is made to depend on the occurrence or non-occurrence of a given, uncertain future event, the (non-) occurrence of that event is a condition.[13]

---

[7] For a less exalted view of covenants, see *Corbin on Contracts* § 30.12 (rev. ed. 1999) ("The word 'covenant' has come to be not much more than a synonym of 'promise'. . . .").
[8] Tina L. Stark, *Drafting Contracts: How and Why Lawyers Do What They Do* 10 (2007).
[9] *See id*. at 24.
[10] Some people prefer to use the words "must" or "agree(s) to" when drafting covenants. For consistency in interpretation, we believe it is best to use "shall" for covenants. If you are asked to use a different word to express covenants, at least make sure you use the same word consistently throughout your documents.
[11] *Id*. at 25.
[12] *Corbin on Contracts* § 30.6.
[13] Many treatises include pages and pages on various types of conditions, including conditions precedent, conditions subsequent, and the like. A deep discussion of these distinctions is largely academic and, at any rate, is beyond the scope of this book.

> ■ **PRACTICE NOTE:** Express a condition using the word(s) "must," "subject to," "provided that," or "conditioned on/upon." For example:
>
> *Throughout Employee's employment with Law Firm, L.L.P., Employee must remain a member in good standing of the Texas State Bar.*
>
> *Employee's continued employment with Law Firm, L.L.P. is subject to Employee's remaining a member in good standing of the Texas State Bar.*
>
> Another way to clearly signal to a court later interpreting an Employment Agreement that the parties intended to draft a condition is to use an "if/then" statement. For example:
>
> *If Employee remains a member in good standing of the Texas State Bar, then Law Firm, L.L.P. will continue to employ Employee, subject to the termination provisions set out in Article 3.*

IV. DISCRETIONARY AUTHORITY

Discretionary authority, also referred to as a "privilege," is a "choice or permission to act."[14] It gives its holder the option, but not the requirement, to act or refrain from acting in a particular way. Like an obligation, a privilege may also be subject to a condition.[15]

> ■ **PRACTICE NOTE:** Express discretionary authority using the word "may." For example:
>
> *Either party may terminate the Employment Agreement at any time, subject only to the provisions set out in Section II.B.*
>
> *If Employee is not in good standing with the Texas State Bar, Law Firm, L.L.P. may terminate Employee's employment without notice.*

V. DECLARATIONS

A declaration is simply a "statement of fact as to which the parties agree."[16] It differs from a representation or warranty in that neither party has stated the fact to induce the other to act, and no rights or remedies are associated with it.[17]

---

[14] Tina L. Stark, *Drafting Contracts: How and Why Lawyers Do What They Do* 29 (2007).
[15] *Id.* at 31.
[16] *Id.*
[17] *Id.*

A definition, for instance, is a classic example of a declaration. Like an obligation or a right, a declaration may also be subject to a condition.[18]

Many boilerplate provisions (discussed below) are also declarations. For example, a governing law provision is simply a declaration regarding what state's law will govern interpretation of the rights and obligations of the parties to the contract:

The laws of Delaware govern all matters arising under or related to this Employment Agreement, including statutory discrimination claims.

---

[18] *Id.* at 32.

CHAPTER 10

BASIC COMPONENTS OF A CONTRACT

I. SUMMARY OF BASIC COMPONENTS OF A CONTRACT

Different sources suggest varying approaches to the main components/provisions in a standard contract. The essential substance is, of course, quite similar, but sources differ in how they order, categorize, and define the working parts of the contract. The following table summarizes the layout suggested in three well-respected texts on drafting.

STARK, DRAFTING CONTRACTS[19]	FAJANS, FALK & SHAPO, WRITING FOR LAW PRACTICE[20]	RAY & COX, BEYOND THE BASICS[21]
- Preamble - Recitals - Words of agreement - Definitions - Action sections - Other substantive business provisions - Endgame provisions - General provisions - Signature lines	- Heading and introductory paragraph - Recitals - Definitions - Terms/body of contract - Housekeeping provisions - Signatures	- Initial clauses (recitals, definitions, statement of consideration) - Duties of the parties - Remedies - Assignability - Miscellaneous clauses to help the contract work (severability, integration) - Ending clauses (signatures, dates)

---

[19] *Id.* at 37.
[20] Elizabeth Fajans, Mary R. Falk & Helene S. Shapo, *Writing for Law Practice* 468-73 (2004).
[21] Mary Barnard Ray & Barbara J. Cox, *Beyond the Basics: A Text for Advanced Legal Writing* 99-100 (2d ed. 2003).

All of these organizational schemes are acceptable. We do not endorse one organizational scheme over another. Rather, in this chapter and the next one, we have simply attempted to address key provisions and boilerplate with particular relevance to employment contracts.

II. RECITALS OR BACKGROUND

The recitals explain the background behind the contract and the parties' reasons for entering into it; they "tell 'the story of the deal.' "[22] The recitals generally set out (explicitly or implicitly) why the contract includes or omits a particular term, and are often relied upon in the event a court is called on to interpret the document.[23] However, because recitals are not enforceable, they should not be promissory, and they should not include representations or warranties.[24]

In the traditional language of contracts, recitals are typically incomplete sentences that begin with "Whereas." For example:

> *Whereas Employer is desirous of employing Employee, and whereas Employee is desirous of accepting such employment, upon the terms and conditions set forth herein.*

III. STATEMENT OF CONSIDERATION OR WORDS OF AGREEMENT

Increasingly, however, drafters may opt to phrase recitals in language more closely resembling ordinary English.[25] In this case, while the substance remains the same, the recitals take the form of complete sentences and drop the "Whereas."[26]

Language confirming the consideration for the contract generally appears at the conclusion of the recitals.[27] Here are two examples of a traditional ***statement of consideration***:

---

[22] Elizabeth Fajans, Mary R. Falk & Helene S. Shapo, *Writing for Law Practice* 469 (2004) (quoting Sidney G. Saltz, *Drafting Made Easy*, Prob. & Prop., May-June 2001, at 32, 32).
[23] *Id.*
[24] *Id.* at 469-70.
[25] *See* Tina L. Stark, *Drafting Contracts: How and Why Lawyers Do What They Do* 50 (2007)
[26] Some recitals are written in such archaic language that mere deletion of the "whereas" will not be enough to simplify and modernize the recital. Consider the following recital excerpted from the Executive Employment Agreement between Richard B. Cheney and Halliburton Company:

WITNESSETH:

WHEREAS, Employer is desirous of employing Employee pursuant to the terms and conditions and for the consideration set forth in this Agreement, and Employee is desirous of entering the employ of Employer pursuant to such terms and conditions and for such consideration.

Executive Employment Agreement between Richard B. Cheney and Halliburton Company, http://contracts. corporate.findlaw.com/compensation/employment/2082.html (last accessed June 20, 2012).
[27] Elizabeth Fajans, Mary R. Falk & Helene S. Shapo, *Writing for Law Practice* 470 (2004).

NOW, THEREFORE, for and in consideration of the mutual promises, covenants, and obligations contained herein, Employer and Employee agree as follows:[28]

NOW, THEREFORE, in consideration of the representations, warranties, covenants, and agreements hereinafter contained in this Employment Agreement, the receipt and sufficiency of which are hereby acknowledged, recognized, and accepted, both the Employer and Employee agree to be legally bound to the following provisions:

Here, too, the modern trend is toward simplicity and brevity.[29] In keeping with these ideals, the statement of consideration (also known as the words of agreement) can be succinctly rephrased:

Accordingly, the parties agree as follows:

IV. DEFINITIONS

Almost every contract requires at least a few defined terms. However, the same effect can be accomplished in several different ways. Some drafters include a definition section up front, following the recitals and statement of consideration. Others place the definitions closer to the end, after the main substance of the agreement. A third option is to add definitions as the concepts logically arise, in either a separate sentence or a parenthetical aside. A final option is to have a separate definition section and some in-text definitions that are also cross-referenced in the definition section. Each of these options can be employed effectively; which to choose is generally "a matter of style."[30] However, many drafters prefer a separate definitions section to "in context" definitions, as it is much easier to print out the definitions and keep them as a reference as one reads a contract than to find embedded definitions. Thus, unless you are writing a very short contract, a separate definitions section is probably preferable.

---

[28] Executive Employment Agreement between Richard B. Cheney and Halliburton Company, http://contracts.corporate.findlaw.com/compensation/employment/2082.html (last accessed June 20, 2012).
[29] Tina L. Stark, *Drafting Contracts: How and Why Lawyers Do What They Do* 50 (2007).
[30] Peter Siviglia, *Exercises in Commercial Transactions* 96 (1995).

TYPICAL BOILERPLATE PROVISIONS

Although this text generally deals solely with employment discrimination, it is important to understand at least basic boilerplate provisions appearing in most contracts, as those provisions often have a profound effect on the parties. For example, a boilerplate provision specifying which state's law will govern the employment arrangement may very well determine whether the employee has additional rights not afforded under federal law. A contract governed by Texas law would not, for example, protect an employee from discrimination on the basis of sexual orientation, whereas a contract governed by New York law would.

The following list includes a brief discussion of some common boilerplate provisions appearing in contracts.

I. GOVERNING LAW

Contracts often contain a clause specifying which jurisdiction's law will govern the agreement. In fact, many contracts do not need such a provision (for instance, a contract between two parties located in the same jurisdiction to be performed in the same jurisdiction).[31] If a governing law clause is to be included, the contract must have some reasonable relationship to the state whose law is invoked.[32] The clause reads something like the following:

This Employment Agreement is governed by the laws of the state of Georgia.

---

[31] *Id.* at 86.
[32] *Id.*

II. ARBITRATION

Mandatory arbitration clauses are discussed in much greater detail below. Importantly, if an employment contract contains an arbitration clause, special care must be taken to preserve other provisions of the agreement which may provide for injunctive relief regarding confidentiality, competition, or similar matters.[33] This can be accomplished by including a clause like the following:

The agreement to arbitrate contained in this Agreement does not prevent the aggrieved party from seeking injunctive or other equitable relief in a court of law, provided that the aggrieved party's complaint relates to an alleged grievance explicitly enumerated in Section ____ of this Agreement.

III. INDEMNITY

An indemnity is simply a promise by one party to pay certain costs, expenses, or obligations incurred by another party. In an employment contract, this sort of provision often takes the form of an indemnification by the employer against particular obligations of the employee. States often require employers to indemnify employees in certain situations. For example, section 2802(a) of the California Labor Code provides that "[a]n employer shall indemnify his or her employee for all necessary expenditures or losses incurred by the employee in direct consequence of the discharge of his or her duties, or of his or her obedience to the directions of the employer, even though unlawful, unless the employee, at the time of obeying the directions, believed them to be unlawful." Here is a sample indemnity clause in a California employment contract:

Employer shall indemnify Employee for all necessary expenditures or losses incurred by Employee in direct consequence of the discharge of Employee's duties. To the extent required by applicable law, Employer shall pay any expenses, judgments, fines, or penalties resulting from any claim or litigation filed against Employee for actions Employee took while discharging Employee's duties for Employer.

In executive employment agreements, the indemnification provision may be quite long and complex. It may, in fact, take the form of its own agreement. For example, the Executive Employment Agreement between Richard B. Cheney and Halliburton included a separate indemnification agreement that was over five pages long.[34]

---

[33] Peter Siviglia, *Exercises in Commercial Transactions* 87 (1995).
[34] *See* Exhibit A to the Executive Employment Agreement between Richard B. Cheney and Halliburton Company, http://contracts.corporate.findlaw.com/compensation/employment/2082.html (last accessed June 20, 2012).

IV. SEVERABILITY

Severability clauses are designed to avoid frustration of an entire contract in the event that one of its provisions is held unenforceable. They typically appear in contracts where one party with a powerful bargaining position includes harsh terms that may be unenforceable.[35] Such provisions are often included in employment contracts because of provisions regarding competition and equitable remedies.[36] A severability clause might read as follows:

If any provision of this Employment Agreement is held invalid or unenforceable for any reason, the remainder of this Employment Agreement will remain fully in effect.

V. TERMINATION

Provisions regarding termination of an Employment Agreement require special care: some rights and obligations should survive the termination of the agreement and must be handled appropriately to avoid later arguments that the rights died with the contract. For example, an employer expects non-competition agreements to continue after termination of employment. An employer would also want confidentiality agreements to survive termination of an employee's employment with the company; otherwise, an employer's trade secrets and proprietary information could be at risk. One solution is to add a termination clause ("The provisions of this section survive termination of the employment."); the danger with this one-size-fits-all solution is that every such section must then have an equivalent clause lest a court draw a negative implication based on its absence.[37] The best solution probably is, however, to specifically state the provisions of the contract that the parties expect to survive termination. This should be accomplished with clear, precise language, a task discussed in Chapter 12.

---

[35] Peter Siviglia, *Exercises in Commercial Transactions* 95 (1995).
[36] *Id.*
[37] *Id.*

CHAPTER

12

LANGUAGE ISSUES
IN DRAFTING

I. DRAFTING IN PLAIN ENGLISH AND AVOIDING AMBIGUITY

Lawyers are not known for their clear, concise prose. In fact, as Joseph Kimble correctly recognized in his book, *Lifting the Fog of Legalese*,

> Although lawyers write for a living, most legal writing is bad and has been for centuries; . . . most lawyers prefer other writers' prose to be plainer, simpler, shorter, clearer, but they also strongly resist changing their own style (that's the great disconnect); every possible rationalization for traditional legal writing has been discredited and the costs of our bad writing and funny talk—the time and money wasted and the public disrespect—are incalculable . . . [The] traditional style . . . [is] a stew of all the worst faults of formal and official prose, seasoned with the peculiar expressions and mannerisms that lawyers perpetuate . . . [I]n its effort to be precise and exhaustive, [legal writing often] becomes excessively detailed and too often sinks into redundancy, ambiguity, and error . . . The result is legalese—a form of prose so jumbled, dense, verbose, and overloaded that it confuses most everyday readers and even many lawyers.[38]

In recent years, however, there has been a movement to make legal writing more coherent. For example, both states and the federal government have passed legislation requiring documents like consumer contracts and IRS guidance to be drafted in plain English. And Supreme Court Justices have spoken out regarding the need for lawyers to hone their writing skills.[39] Chief Justice John G. Roberts, Jr.

---

[38] Joseph Kimble, *Lifting the Fog of Legalese: Essays on Plain Language* xi-xii (Carolina Academic Press 2006).
[39] *See, e.g.*, Interviews of United States Supreme Court Justices John G. Roberts, Jr., John Paul Stevens, Antonin Scalia, Anthony M. Kennedy, Clarence Thomas, Ruth Bader Ginsburg, Stephen G. Breyer, and Samuel A. Alito, Jr., conducted by Bryan A. Garner and published in 13 Scribes J. Leg. Writing (2010).

specifically noted that "[l]anguage is the central tool of our trade . . . if we're not fastidious . . . with language, it dilutes the effectiveness and clarity of the law."[40]

Realize, however, that there is a very real distinction between unnecessary jargon, legalese, and Latin phrases on the one hand and terms of art on the other hand. As Justice Antonin Scalia and Bryan A. Garner noted in their book *Making Your Case: The Art of Persuading Judges*, "jargon . . . mean[s] the words and phrases used almost exclusively by lawyers in place of plain-English words and phrases that express the same thought. Jargon adds nothing but a phony air of expertise."[41] Likewise, most Latin phrases are unnecessary. If a Latin phrase has an English equivalent, use it. Only retain Latin phrases that don't have corresponding English phrases.[42]

On the other hand, lawyers must sometimes use terms of art. In the beginning, it is very difficult for a novice legal writer to discern the difference between unnecessary jargon and necessary terms of art. When in doubt, look up a term before deleting it. Make sure it doesn't have specialized meaning in the legal context.

A complete primer on plain language drafting is beyond the scope of this book. However, the following pages provide a good foundation. No lawyer wants to have a judge or other attorney note that the lawyer's writing is so bad that "it's almost like hacking through a jungle with a machete to try to get to the point."[43] In this section, we will discuss the following tools for developing a clear, concise, and precise legal writing style: (1) replacing unnecessary phrases with shorter synonyms; (2) replacing unnecessarily complex words with simpler synonyms; (3) identifying and deleting unnecessary doublets or triplets; (4) using sentence structure to craft cleaner, clearer sentences; (5) avoiding unnecessary nominalizations; (6) editing out unnecessary use of the passive voice; (7) avoiding elegant variation; and (8) avoiding misplaced modifiers. There are few exercises in this section, as you will have to incorporate all of these concepts into the specific drafting exercises later in Part IV.

A. REPLACE UNNECESSARY PHRASES WITH SHORTER SYNONYMS

Lawyers often use bloated phrases to say things that they could have said using one, simple word. Here are some examples of unnecessary phrases and their plain English equivalents:[44]

---

[40] *Id.* at 5 (interview of Chief Justice John G. Roberts, Jr. by Bryan A. Garner).
[41] Antonin Scalia & Bryan A. Garner, *Making Your Case: The Art of Persuading Judges* 113-14 (Thomson/West 2008).
[42] *See id.*
[43] *Id.* at 5 (interview of Chief Justice John G. Roberts, Jr. by Bryan A. Garner).
[44] The material in this section on drafting in plain English and avoiding ambiguity draws from a number of sources, including original material provided by the authors of this textbook as well as reference material from many other highly-respected scholars in the field. In compiling this material, we looked to the following additional resources: Eugene Volokh, UCLA Law School, *Eschew, Evade, and/or Eradicate Legalese*, http://www2.law.ucla.edu/volokh/legalese.htm (last accessed December 30, 2012); Tina Stark, *Drafting Contracts: How and Why Lawyers Do What They Do* 199-263 (Wolters Kluwer Law & Business 2007) (citing Reed Dickerson, *The Fundamentals of Legal Drafting* (2d ed., Little, Brown & Co. 1986)); 13 Scribes Journal of Legal Writing (2010) (Interviews of United States Supreme Court Justices by Bryan A. Garner); Richard Wydick, *Plain English for Lawyers* (5th ed., Carolina Acad. Press 2005); Joe Kimble, *Lifting the Fog of Legalese: Essays on Plain Language* (Carolina Acad. Press 2006).

Unnecessary Phrase	Plain English Equivalent
accord respect to, give respect to, pay respect to	respect
as a consequence of	because of
at the present time	presently (or, even better, now)
at this point in time	now (or a specific date, if that specific date is relevant)
at that point in time	then (or a specific date, if that specific date is relevant)
because of the fact that, due to the fact that, in light of the fact that, in view of the fact that	because
circumstances under which, circumstances in which	when, where
concerning the matter of	about
consensus of opinion, consensus of opinions	consensus, agreement
despite the fact that, notwithstanding the fact that	despite, though, although
for the duration of	during
for the purpose of doing	to do
for the purpose of saying	to say
has a negative impact, has a negative effect	hurts, harms, damages
in a case in which, in a case under which	when, where
in accordance with	by, under
in order to	to
in reference to	about
in the course of	during
in the event that	if
is able to	can
is binding on	binds
it is clear that, it should be noted that, it is apparent that	Almost always omit entirely. These are throat-clearing introductions that say very little.
make an attempt to	attempt, try
on a number of occasions	sometimes, often, twice (if you know the exact number)
on the part of	by
on the assumption that, under the assumption that	assuming
on the subject of	about, concerning
point in time	time (or a specific time if you know it and it is relevant)

Unnecessary Phrase	Plain English Equivalent
prior to	before
referred to as	called
render assistance	help
the instant case, the instant contract	this case, the Agreement
the manner in which	how
to the effect that	that
until such time as	until
was aware	knew
with reference to, with regard to	about, regarding, concerning

B. REPLACE UNNECESSARILY COMPLEX WORDS WITH SIMPLER SYNONYMS

Never use a complex word when a simpler one will convey the same meaning. Here is just a small sampling of the types of words to look for (and replace) in your writing:

Look for ...	Replace with ...
afforded (when it means given)	given
ascertain	find out, discover
assist	help
cease	stop
commence	start, begin
endeavor	try
evince	show, demonstrate
facilitate	help
forthwith	immediately
herein, hereinafter, hereinbefore	Delete or, if necessary, replace with reference to specific page, section, or paragraph.
methodology	method
objective	goal
opined	stated (as in "stated an opinion")
possess	have
procure	get
said (when used as an adjective)	Replace "the said Agreement" with "the Agreement"
therein	Replace with specific reference to location ("in the Employment Agreement," "in Exhibit A to the Executive Employment Agreement," etc.).
utilize	use

C. IDENTIFY AND DELETE UNNECESSARY WORDS IN DOUBLETS AND TRIPLETS

Legal writing is full of doublets and triplets, lists of words that are often synonyms that could be replaced with one clear word. Here are a couple of common examples:

Give, devise, and bequeath (give is usually sufficient)

Indemnify and hold harmless (indemnify is acceptable)

Sometimes each word in a doublet or triplet has its own distinct legal meaning. In that case, you should not delete any of the words. However, doublets and triplets are always suspect. Examine them to make sure that every word serves a purpose.

EXERCISES

Here are a few examples of doublets and triplets from actual employment agreements. What words would you keep? What could you delete without changing the meaning of the phrase?

1) Each and every term, provision, or part of this Agreement is binding on the Employer and the Employee.

2) A change, modification, or waiver of any term, provision, or part of this Agreement must be made in writing and signed by both the Employer and the Employee.

3) Executive's bonus is due and payable by January 21, 2013.

4) The Parties to this Employment Agreement agree that any and all claims, controversies, disagreements, and disputes will be submitted to binding and mandatory arbitration.

D. USE SENTENCE STRUCTURE TO CRAFT CLEANER, CLEARER SENTENCES

Although authors have written entire books on grammar and sentence structure, three simple edits will make your writing clearer and more precise. First, once you have written a document, go back through and edit your sentences to get the subject, verb, and object close together. Readers almost always find it easier to follow a sentence where the subject of the sentence and the action that subject is performing appear close together in the sentence. Lawyers, however, often mistakenly separate the subject and verb by long prepositional phrases or other explanatory information. For example:

> *The Employer, in the event that an Employee has more than three unexcused absences from work in a given Calendar Year and the Employer has provided written warning after the first or second unexcused absence, may terminate the Employee.*

The subject of the sentence is "Employer." The verb is "may terminate." The object is "Employee." However, the drafter has obscured that connection by placing the limitations on the Employer's right to terminate in the middle of the sentence. To clarify, the drafter should move the limitations to the end of the sentence and use tabulation to show the relationship of the limitations to the main rule:

> *The Employer may terminate the Employee if*
>
> (a) *the Employee has more than three unexcused absences from work in a given Calendar Year; and*
>
> (b) *the Employer has provided the Employee with a written warning after the first or second unexcused absence.*

The preceding example also highlights the second way to significantly improve legal writing. When you have a list of common items (exceptions, conditions, requirements, etc.), place them in a tabulated list. Of course, you must make sure the list is grammatically parallel.

■ EXAMPLE

Incorrect:
At least five days prior to taking scheduled vacation time, the Employee shall provide the following documentation to his or her Supervisor:
(a) a list of all incomplete projects on which the Employee is working;
(b) a detailed plan for completing incomplete projects upon the Employee's return; and
(c) the Employee shall promise to meet all deadlines for incomplete projects.

Correct:
At least five days prior to taking scheduled vacation time, the Employee shall provide the following documentation to his or her Supervisor:
(a) a list of all incomplete projects on which the Employee is working;
(b) a detailed plan for completing incomplete projects upon the Employee's return; and
(c) a form certifying that the Employee's vacation time will not prevent Employee from meeting all scheduled deadlines for incomplete projects.

The third way to improve writing significantly is to identify long, unwieldy sentences, and break them into more than one sentence. A good rule of thumb is that you should examine any sentence that runs longer than three lines to determine whether the reader would find the provision easier to follow if you broke it up into smaller pieces. If so, break the sentence up into separate ideas. Place main points in front and exceptions in separate sentences. Omit unnecessary surplus words.

E. AVOID UNNECESSARY NOMINALIZATIONS

When we tell our students to avoid nominalizations, we often hear the question, "What is a nominalization?" It's a rather simple concept, really, though one even very bright students might not have been exposed to. A nominalization is simply a verb that the writer has changed into a noun. For example, the word "implication" is a nominalization of the verb "to imply."

So what's wrong with using a nominalization? Most importantly, using a nominalization often obscures both the subject of the sentence and the action in the sentence. That makes the writing more difficult for the reader to follow. Consider this example:

The implication is that she failed to adequately perform her job duties.

Isn't the point that a *specific* someone implied that the employee failed to adequately perform her job duties? It probably matters a lot *who* implied that she failed to adequately perform her job duties. If it was her supervisor, then she's in trouble. If it's a co-worker jealous of the employee's swift advancement, then the employee has nothing to worry about. Here are two possible interpretations of the sentence with the nominalization:

The employee's supervisor implied that the employee failed to adequately perform her job duties when the supervisor did not give the employee a year-end bonus.

The employee's co-workers were unhappy to hear that the employee got a bigger raise than the other employees. The co-workers left a note in the employee break room that implied that the employee failed to adequately perform her job duties.

Unless you want to obscure the actor in a sentence and water down the verb, learn to identify and eradicate nominalizations from your writing.

F. EDIT OUT UNNECESSARY USE OF THE PASSIVE VOICE

Some students have a very difficult time identifying the passive voice. A simple way to test whether the verb in a sentence is passive is to ask whether the subject of the sentence performed the action in the sentence. For example:

Ms. Smith was harassed by her supervisor.

In this example, the subject is "Ms. Smith." The verb is "harassed." Ask yourself, "Did Ms. Smith do the harassing?" If not, then you have a passive sentence. If you are a lawyer representing the victim, you would not want to obscure the actor. You would replace the passive framing with the following active sentence:

The supervisor sexually harassed Ms. Smith.

Of course, the passive voice is not always a bad thing. If you want to be intentionally vague about the actor in the sentence, the passive voice is a perfect tool. For example, if you represented the harasser in a case arising from the facts above, you would probably prefer a sentence like this:

Ms. Smith has alleged that she was harassed.

The second part of this sentence is deliberately written in the passive voice to obscure the actor. To obscure the actor even further, the writer has deleted entirely the object in the sentence: "supervisor."

G. AVOID ELEGANT VARIATION

Elegant variation is a simple concept. Basically, it means varying the words you use to describe things by using synonyms. Many disciplines actually encourage elegant variation, as repeating the same term can be seen as leading to dull, lifeless writing. For example, a poet would probably not write a poem about a scene that was "picturesque" and repeat the word "picturesque" every time the writer mentioned something about the scenery (the flowers were "picturesque," the sky was "picturesque," the view was "picturesque," etc.).

However, elegant variation rarely has a place in the law. Synonyms are words that are similar. Two words that are similar are not necessarily identical. When a lawyer or judge comes across a new term in a legal document, that lawyer or judge will assume that the writer intended to introduce a new concept. This is particularly true in contract drafting. Defined terms are generally capitalized, so if you refer to the "Employee" in most places but the "employee" in other places, the reader will assume that the "employee" is not the same employee as the "Employee" defined in the contract.

Likewise, a term like "best efforts" is not the same as "reasonable efforts," "customary effort," or "consistent with industry standard." When in doubt, do not vary your language to express the same concept.

H. EDIT TO CORRECT MISPLACED MODIFIERS

A modifier is simply a word that adds description or detail to another word. For example, consider the following sentence:

She drove the red car slowly.

The word "red" is an adjective that modifies the word "car." The word "slowly" is an adverb that modifies the word "drove." In a simple sentence like this one, it is unlikely that the reader will become confused regarding which word modifies each part of the sentence. However, lawyers' sentences are often much more complex. As a result, writers often inadvertently introduce misplaced modifiers into legal documents. Misplaced modifiers are a nightmare for interpretation and can lead to litigation. Usually, the easiest way to fix an ambiguity caused by a misplaced modifier is to move the modifier closer to the word or phrase to which it relates.

II. IDENTIFYING THE DIFFERENCE BETWEEN AMBIGUITY AND VAGUENESS

Some students (and attorneys) assume that ambiguity and vagueness are the same thing. Nothing could be further from the truth. Ambiguity is always bad; vagueness may be bad, but it may also be a perfectly acceptable strategy.

According to Tina Stark, "[a] word or phrase is vague if its meaning varies depending upon the context or if its parameters are not plainly delineated. For example, *reasonable* is vague. What is reasonable in one context may be wholly unreasonable in another."[45] Drafters often want to leave a term vague to allow for flexibility. Common vague references include things like "reasonable," "best efforts," and the like. Some drafters might want to define what these terms mean, but sometimes the only way to reach a negotiated agreement is to retain some vagueness in the agreement's terms. The decision to use a vague reference rather than something more precise depends upon the importance of the provision to your client, the need to get the deal done, and your client's level of risk aversion.

Ambiguity occurs when the way in which a drafter has written something could lead to two or more mutually exclusive interpretations. Thus, ambiguity is a nightmare for a client seeking predictability and for an attorney later defending an ambiguous term in a court of law. So, for example, consider the following provision in an employment agreement:

Employer and Employee agree to submit all disputes arising from the employment relationship to binding arbitration. Prior to submitting a dispute to binding arbitration, however, he agrees to use best efforts to resolve the dispute amicably through the company's mediation process.

The term "best efforts" is vague, but the parties may want that vagueness. However, the use of the term "he" is ambiguous. Does it refer to only the Employer? The Employee? Both? Only male employees? The term is certainly not vague, but its application is ambiguous.

---

[45] Tina Stark, *Drafting Contracts: How and Why Lawyers Do what they Do* 236 (emphasis in original).

EXERCISE

Rewrite the preceding clause to fix the ambiguity. If you identify any other ambiguities, list them, and edit to fix those ambiguities as well.

III. SPECIFIC WORDING ISSUES: SHALL vs. WILL

The word "shall" probably causes more problems for drafters than any other word. It is regularly used, but often used incorrectly. According to Bryan Garner's *Dictionary of Modern Legal Usage*, for example, "shall" has "as many as eight senses in drafted documents," at most one of which is correct.[46]

Modern attitudes toward "shall" divide along geographic lines. The so-called "ABC rule," most often advocated in Australia, Britain, and Canada, holds that "shall" is simply more trouble than it's worth, and directs drafters to avoid the word entirely.[47] The alternative "American rule" provides a less drastic solution. This school of thought would confine use of "shall" to a single, narrow correct usage: employ it to mean "has a duty to," and use it only to impose a duty on a capable actor.[48] So, for example:

In the event of a change in status, Employee shall provide notification and updated information to Employer within seven days.

One point on which both the ABC and American schools agree is that in the vast majority of its appearances in drafted documents, "shall" is used incorrectly. A full catalog of such errors would probably be impossible, and in any event very long, but following are three particularly common misuses:

Employee shall receive a salary of $36,000.00 per year, payable in equal installments on the first of each month.

While "shall" is properly used to express a mandatory term in a contract, it requires a capable actor for its subject. Here, the duty is actually being imposed on the *employer*, not the *employee*, so the sentence should be rephrased with Employer as its subject ("Employer shall pay. . . .").

This Agreement shall be governed by the law of the State of Michigan.

Here "shall" is wrongly used to declare a legal result, rather than to express a duty imposed on a capable party to the contract.

---

[46] Bryan A. Garner, *A Dictionary of Modern Legal Usage* 939 (2d ed. 1995).
[47] *Id.* at 940; *see also* Michèle M. Asprey, *Shall Must Go*, 3 Scribes J. Legal Writing 79 (1992).
[48] Bryan A. Garner, *A Dictionary of Modern Legal Usage* 940 (2d ed. 1995).

In the event either party elects to terminate the employment, Employee agrees to return to Employer any company property that he shall have in his possession at that time.

"Shall" should never be used in a conditional or relative clause.[49]

Compared with "shall," some believe that the use of "will" is simple. In contracts, you will probably see the word "will" used in one of two senses (though, as Bryan Garner warns, "[t]his word, like any other, ought to bear a consistent meaning within any drafted document"[50]). The first situation is one in which drafters use "will" to impose an obligation in a tone that seems less "bossy" than "shall" or "must."[51] For example, a contract may state that "Employee will notify Employer at least two weeks prior to taking scheduled vacation time." The drafter's intention is that an employee cannot take vacation time without letting the employer know at least two weeks in advance. This might make sense, as the employer might need to schedule a replacement for that time period. Although drafters often use this phrasing, it is not ideal. Precise drafters use "shall" to signify covenants and "must" to signify conditions. Thus, if the employer wants to condition the right to take vacation on the employee giving proper notice, the better phrasing would be "Employee must notify Employer at least two weeks prior to taking scheduled vacation time" (assuming that federal, state, and local law permit such a limitation on vacation time).

The second possibility is to use "will" merely to describe a future event or contingency. This second use is also dispreferred, however, because most contract terms should generally be worded in the present tense whenever possible.[52]

DRAFTING EXERCISES

Review the following contract provisions. For each sentence, note whether the drafter has used the word *shall* or *will* correctly. If not, explain what the drafter did wrong, and correct the sentence. Correct any language or punctuation that may cause interpretive problems or other ambiguities.

1) The Company's new sexual harassment policy shall take effect on March 12, 2013.

2) This Employee Handbook shall not be construed to alter the at-will employment status of Employee.

---

[49] The above examples are drawn from Joseph Kimble, *The Many Misuses of Shall*, 3 Scribes J. Legal Writing 61 (1992).

[50] Bryan A. Garner, *A Dictionary of Modern Legal Usage* 941 (2d ed. 1995).

[51] *Id.* ("[S]ome drafters consider *must* inappropriately bossy. The word may strike the wrong tone particularly when both parties to a contract are known quantities, such as two well-known corporations. . . . The word *will* is probably the best solution here.").

[52] *Id.* at 941-42.

3) Employer will not discriminate on the basis of race, gender, national origin, disability, or sexual orientation.

4) Employee shall arrive five minutes prior to the beginning of Employee's shift.

5) Employee uniforms shall be professionally dry-cleaned at least once a week.

6) Supervisors shall be notified of any material changes to Employee's personnel data, including changes to mailing addresses, telephone numbers, and names, ages, and number of dependents.

LOCATING, EVALUATING, AND USING FORMS

Lawyers very rarely draft a contract or a contract provision from scratch. Rather, they often start with a form and edit that form to meet the needs of a particular client or transaction. There are a number of good reasons to use forms. First, using a form from a prior deal saves time and money. Clients do not want to pay hundreds or thousands of dollars to their attorneys to recreate the wheel. Second, lawyers are quite risk averse, as are many corporate clients. A client would rather use a provision that has either never been challenged or has been challenged and found acceptable by courts than a provision drafted from scratch that may or may not stand up to a legal challenge.

Of course, there are numerous sources for forms, and not all forms are equal. The remainder of this section discusses how to locate good forms, evaluate their quality, and edit them to meet the business needs of a particular client.

I. SOURCES FOR FORMS

Whether you end up working for a law firm, a government agency, a company, or a public interest organization, the first place to look for forms is with your employer. If you have a supervising attorney, that attorney will likely be able to point you to forms that he or she prefers. A form recommended by a supervising attorney has a huge advantage over other forms you might use; the person reviewing your work has already placed a stamp of approval on at least the basic structure of the document from which you will work.

If the supervising attorney does not offer you a starting point, many employers keep internal document banks that you can search electronically. Some employers will even provide forms that have been annotated with supporting case law and explanations of various provisions. Again, these form banks are a very good starting point, as the quality of the forms is likely high, and you may be able to speak to the specific drafter if you have questions.

If your employer does not have forms available, you can find them in a variety of other places. For example, a number of specialized treatises and formbooks provide relevant forms and sample provisions. Formbooks range from general formbooks such as Am. Jur. Legal Forms 2d, to subject-specific formbooks such as Am. Jur. Pleading & Practice Forms - Civil Rights - Employment Discrimination. In addition, formbooks may also be jurisdiction-specific, like Bender's Federal Practice Forms or the Washington Practice Series. Finally, formbooks may be tailored to a particular type of document, such as Bender's Forms of Discovery. Even if you choose not to model your document on a form from a formbook, formbooks provide a good starting point for drafting unfamiliar documents in that they set out a general framework for documents and raise issues to be considered in drafting.

Likewise, trade associations may provide relevant forms. Forms may also be available in practice manuals and continuing legal education materials provided by private vendors and state bar associations. The websites of law firms and other special-interest organizations are another resource. Other internet resources for forms include: Findlaw, Lexis One, Washlaw, the 'Lectric Law Library, USA.gov, and the Practical Law Company.

Finally, courts provide another source for forms, as many courts have created forms for frequently used pleadings. Court-created forms can usually be found on the court's website. See, for example, the U.S. Courts website: www.uscourts.gov.

■ **PRACTICE NOTE:** Use of court forms may be optional or mandatory, depending on the form and the jurisdiction. Be sure to check local court rules regarding the use of forms, as failure to use a court-prepared form may be grounds for dismissal, default, or other sanctions.

Not all forms are created equal. One of the most difficult tasks for a new lawyer is to evaluate the quality of a form and to edit the form to reflect the needs of the current client. The next two sub-sections of this chapter discuss these crucial skills.

II. EVALUATING FORMS

When evaluating a form, the first question to consider is whether the source of the form is reliable. This list ranks the most common sources of forms for employment-related documents from most reliable to least reliable:

1. Internal employer-generated forms or mandatory forms from court websites;
2. Forms from employment law formbooks and jurisdiction-specific formbooks;
3. Forms from general formbooks;
4. Non-mandatory forms from court websites;
5. External practitioner-drafted sample documents used in real transactions; and
6. Forms from free non-court websites.

Internal employer-generated forms are generally considered most reliable for the reasons mentioned in the previous sub-section: the quality of the forms is likely high, as the forms have usually already undergone revisions to improve their quality and remain compliant with current law. In addition, these forms have been drafted with your employer's typical client in mind. For example, a form created by a firm that generally represents employers will be drafted to be as favorable for employers as possible without violating the relevant law.

Forms from formbooks are reliable depending on how closely tailored the forms are to your situation. The more general the form, the less likely it is that the form takes into account the law in the relevant area (such as employment discrimination law) or law from the relevant jurisdiction. As such, forms from employment law formbooks and jurisdiction-specific formbooks have a key advantage over general formbooks: they are tailored more specifically to the law and facts relevant to your client's situation.

Next, forms from court websites are generally reliable when the forms are being used for litigation in that court. However, the range of available court-created forms is limited to litigation documents. Moreover, the form documents that are available are often drafted very generally. For some examples, see the General Civil Litigation forms available from the Michigan Courts: www.courts.michigan.gov/administration/scao/forms/pages/search-for-a-form.aspx. As a result, these forms may provide a general framework for drafting, but you would need to significantly revise them to take your client's factual and legal situation into account and advocate for your client.

External practitioner-drafted documents used in real transactions can be a helpful resource because, like internal employer-generated forms, they have been drafted and vetted by attorneys and are often of high quality. Furthermore, databases with practitioner-drafted documents or clauses such as Bloomberg's Deal-Maker can be convenient because they are searchable using various criteria (such as type of document, industry, etc.). However, these databases provide limited information about the context in which the form was drafted, making it difficult to determine how that context differs from the context in which you are drafting. It may be unclear, for example, the reason for the inclusion of a particular provision or whether the document was the result of a one-sided negotiation or negotiation by relatively equal parties. Moreover, the documents found on DealMaker in particular are necessarily limited because they are gathered from publicly available documents filed with the Securities and Exchange Commission (SEC). By definition, this means that the database includes documents used only by companies of the size required to file documents with the SEC. If you are drafting a document on behalf of a non-public company, a smaller company, or an employee, the documents used by these large companies may not provide an appropriate starting point for your purposes.

Finally, freely available forms from non-court websites are of limited trustworthiness—you get what you pay for. In most instances, it is unclear whether these forms were drafted by practitioners, whether they were drafted for a particular jurisdiction, or when they were most recently updated.

The next question to consider is whether the form was created for the appropriate jurisdiction. A form drafted for another jurisdiction may include provisions unnecessary for your client's jurisdiction or may not include provisions that are necessary in your client's jurisdiction. Consequently, general forms or forms drafted for other jurisdictions require substantial review and revision to adapt them to the law in your client's jurisdiction.

The last question is how recently the form has been updated. Like forms from a different jurisdiction, forms that are not current often require time-consuming review to determine whether the provisions are in compliance with current law and how to update those provisions that are out-of-date.

III. REVISING AND EDITING FORMS

All forms must be tailored to meet your client's specific needs. By definition, forms contain standardized language that has not been drafted with the specific needs of your client in mind. As a result, revisions will be necessary to account for your client's factual and legal situation. Even internal employer-generated form documents will need to be examined carefully to ensure that the provisions are relevant and appropriate for your client, rather than the client for whom the form was originally drafted.

In addition, you should ensure that the form reflects constantly changing current law. This means that you should conduct independent research regarding the relevant legal standards, even if the form has been recently updated. A word of caution regarding formbooks: while the online versions of formbooks may appear to have been updated recently, this often means that some portion of the formbook has been recently updated, not the entire formbook. As a result, even those forms that appear to be up-to-date should be carefully reviewed for compliance with current law.

Finally, because forms are not necessarily well-written, they should be edited for clarity and concision. Ensure that the document is organized clearly, uses plain English, and does not contain ambiguity or legalese. Many drafters make the mistake of assuming that legalese is included because it has been tested in the courts, but generally this is not the case. Another word of caution: before removing what appears to be legalese, double check to make sure that it is not a term of art. For additional guidance on language issues in drafting, see the advice in the preceding chapter.

EXERCISES

1) Review the following forms. Provide a short paragraph explaining what form you believe is the most authoritative and why. If you need more information to make an informed decision, explain what information you think you need.

 ☐ Sexual and other Unlawful Harassment Policy: 24A West's Legal Forms, Employment § 3.42 (3d ed. 2012);
 ☐ Sexual Harassment Policy: Forms for Small Business Entities § 22:23 (2012);
 ☐ Sexual harassment policy – Sample form: 7 Emp. Discrim. Coord. Forms, Pleadings and Practice Aids § 6:13 (2012); and
 ☐ Sample Harassment Policy: State of Wisconsin Department of Workforce Development: Equal Rights Publication ERD-10449-P.

2) You have been asked to draft a settlement agreement and release to resolve a dispute between your client, a company located and incorporated in California, and a former employee who threatened to sue your client for discrimination. You located a settlement agreement and release form in 2 Employment Law Checklists and Forms § 26:10 (quoted below). Note that the form is not included in its entirety and has been edited for length.

 a) Research California law regarding settlement agreements and releases to determine what claims can be released as part of a settlement agreement. Based on your research, modify the form to be in compliance with this area of California law.

 b) Because the employee is over 40 the release must comply with the ADEA. Conduct research to determine how to modify the form to be in compliance with the ADEA, and make modifications as needed.

 c) Rephrase the form where necessary to make sure the agreement is written in plain English. Omit unnecessary redundancies. Do not make any substantive modifications other than those required by California law governing releases or the ADEA.

SETTLEMENT AGREEMENT AND RELEASE[53]

This Settlement Agreement and General Release is made and entered into by and between (hereinafter "Employee"), and the (hereinafter "the Company").

---

[53] "Sample Settlement Agreement and Release" taken from 2 Employment Law Checklists and Forms § 26:10.

Witnesseth

WHEREAS, Employee was employed by the Company from on or about _____ to _____; and

WHEREAS, Employee has filed an action in the United States District Court for the District of _____, Division _____ as Case No. _____, alleging that his discharge was discriminatorily based upon his age, breached contractual obligations, wrongfully interfered with his pension rights, and defamed him causing emotional distress, mental anguish, frustration, and humiliation; and

WHEREAS, Employee has filed a claim for unemployment compensation with the Bureau of Employment Services; and

WHEREAS, Employee and the Company desire to settle fully and finally all differences between them, including, but in no way limited to, those differences embodied in the aforementioned actions and claims;

NOW, THEREFORE, in consideration of the premises and mutual promises herein contained, it is agreed as follows:

. . .

SECOND: Employee represents and agrees that Employee's employment with the Company terminated on _____, that Employee will not be reemployed by the Company, and that Employee will not apply for or otherwise seek employment with the Company at any time.

THIRD: Employee agrees to dismiss with prejudice, with each party bearing its own costs, the action filed by Employee against the Company in Case No. currently pending in the United States District Court for the District of _____, _____ Division.

FOURTH: Employee agrees to withdraw with prejudice, with each party bearing its own costs, all claims for unemployment compensation filed by Employee against the Company with the Bureau of Employment Services Board of Review.

FIFTH: The Company agrees that when the steps set forth in Paragraphs THIRD and FOURTH above have been completed and documentation of such completion and the fully executed original of this Settlement Agreement and Release have been received by counsel of record for the Company, the Company will cause to be paid to Employee the gross amount of $ as full, final and complete settlement of the matters set forth herein with said amount to be paid as follows:

(a) $ in back pay less required legal deductions; and

(b) $ in full settlement of all fees and costs of any kind or nature and compensatory (other than back pay) and punitive damages; and

(c) Employee represents to the Company that the portion of the settlement amount which is back pay subject to withholding is $ and agrees to be solely responsible for any additional withholding amount deemed due by the Internal Revenue Service.

SIXTH: The Company agrees to place a memorandum in Employee's personnel file stating as follows:

In the event that the work performance or any related matter concerning the employment or discontinuation of employment of Employee is discussed with, or we receive an inquiry from, anyone outside the Company concerning Employee, such individual will be informed that the Company will release only beginning dates of employment, ending dates of employment, job or jobs held, and the letter of reference supplied to the Employee, and only that information will be released.

. . .

NINTH: Employee represents that Employee has not filed any other Claim or Claims (as defined in Paragraph ELEVENTH below) against the Company or other Releases (as defined in Paragraph ELEVENTH below) with the Equal Employment Opportunity Commission or the Civil Rights Commission other than those which have already been withdrawn by Employee (i.e., Defense Agency Complaint No.) or already terminated by the appropriate agency (i.e., EEOC Charge No.), or with any other local, state or federal agency or court other than the Claim presently before the Unemployment Compensation Board of Review (i.e., No. which is to be withdrawn with prejudice under Paragraph FOURTH above), that Employee will not so file at any time hereafter, and that if any such agency or court assumes jurisdiction of any Claim or Claims against the Company or other Releases on behalf of Employee, Employee will request such agency or court to withdraw from the matter, and will not participate, unless compelled by law to do so, in the agency or court processing of that matter.

TENTH: Employee represents and agrees that the terms and conditions of this Settlement Agreement and General Release shall be maintained completely confidential . . .

ELEVENTH: As a material inducement to the Company to enter into this Settlement Agreement and General Release, Employee hereby irrevocably and unconditionally releases, acquits, and forever discharges the Company and each of the Company's owners, stockholders, predecessors, successors, assigns, agents, directors, officers, employees, representatives, attorneys, divisions, subsidiaries, affiliates (and agents, directors, officers, employees, representatives and attorneys of such divisions, subsidiaries and affiliates), the heirs, executors, and administrators of such of the foregoing as are natural persons, and all persons acting by, through, under or in concert with any of the foregoing (collectively "Company Releases"), or any of them, from any and all charges, complaints, claims, liabilities, obligations, promises, agreements, controversies, damages, actions, causes of action, suits, rights, demands, costs, losses, debts and expenses (including attorney's fees and costs actually incurred), of any nature whatsoever, known or unknown ("Claim" or "Claims"), which Employee now has, owns, or holds, or claims to have, own, or hold, or which Employee at any time heretofore had, owned, or held, or claimed to have, own, or hold, or which Employee at any time hereafter may have, own, or hold, or claim to have, own, or hold, against each or any of the Company Releases, other than for a breach of this Settlement Agreement and General Release.

TWELFTH: As a material inducement to the Employee to enter into this Settlement Agreement and General Release, the Company hereby irrevocably and unconditionally releases, acquits, and forever discharges Employee and his heirs, administrators, representatives, executors, successors, and assigns, and all persons acting by, through, under or in concert with any of the foregoing (collectively "Employee Releases"), or any of them, from any and all charges, complaints, claims, liabilities, obligations, promises, agreements, controversies, damages, actions, causes of action, suits, rights, demands, costs, losses, debts and expenses (including attorney's fees and costs actually incurred), of any nature whatsoever, known or unknown ("Claim" or "Claims"), which the Company now has, owns, or holds, or claims to have, own, or hold, or which the Company at any time heretofore had, owned, or held, or claimed to have, own, or hold, or which the company at any time hereafter may have, own, or hold, or claim to have own, or hold, against each or any of the Employee Releases, other than for a breach of this Settlement Agreement and General Release.

THIRTEENTH: For the purpose of implementing a full and complete release and discharge of the Company and Employee Releases, the Company and Employee expressly acknowledge that this Settlement Agreement and General Release is intended to include in its effect, without limitation, all Claims which the Company or Employee does not know or suspect to exist in either's favor at the time of execution hereof, and that this Settlement Agreement and General Release contemplates the extinguishment of any such Claim or Claims, other than for a breach of this Settlement Agreement and General Release.

. . .

EIGHTEENTH: This Settlement Agreement and General Release is made and entered into in the State of _____, and shall in all respects be interpreted, enforced and governed under the laws of said State. The language of all parts of this Settlement Agreement and General Release shall in all cases be construed as a whole, according to its fair meaning, and not strictly for or against any of the parties.

NINETEENTH: Should any provision of this Settlement Agreement and General Release be declared or be determined by any court to be illegal or invalid, the validity of the remaining parts, terms or provisions shall not be affected thereby and said illegal or invalid part, term, or provisions shall be deemed not to be a part of this Settlement Agreement and General Release.

TWENTIETH: This Settlement Agreement and General Release sets forth the entire agreement between the parties, and fully supersedes any and all prior agreements or understandings between the parties hereto pertaining to the subject matter hereof.

TWENTY-FIRST: The Company and Employee represent and agree that all aspects of this Settlement Agreement and General Release have been thoroughly discussed with their respective legal counsel, that all provisions hereof have been carefully read and are fully understood, and that this Settlement Agreement and General Release is voluntarily entered into.

. . .

CHAPTER

14

COMMON CONTRACT PROVISIONS RELATED TO EMPLOYMENT DISCRIMINATION LAW

I. A NOTE ON EMPLOYEE HANDBOOKS

As discussed earlier in this text, most employees are at-will employees working without a written employment contract. However, even employers who do not provide written employment contracts for their employees may wish to provide written policies and procedures for employees to follow. Of course, employers could simply provide employees with a stack of individual policies. Most sophisticated employers, however, will collect policies and procedures in an employee handbook.

There are many reasons why an employer might want to provide employees with an employee handbook. First, a well-written employee handbook provides a single location for collecting clear and uniform standards for all employees. As you probably know by now, employment discrimination lawsuits often arise when an employer fails to treat all employees the same. Uniform treatment of employees helps reduce the risk of lawsuits alleging disparate treatment.

Another reason why an employer might want an employee handbook is that regular review of the policies in that handbook (by in-house counsel or other attorneys hired to represent the employer) ensures that the employer's policies remain compliant with existing law. Employment discrimination law is constantly changing, and policies must change with the law. An updated handbook may persuade a judge or jury that an employer was trying to comply with the law.

In fact, in certain situations, the existence of a policy can be used as part of an employer's official defense in civil litigation. As discussed below, the Supreme Court has issued guidance regarding how an employer can raise an affirmative defense to a claim of hostile environment sexual harassment. *See Burlington Indus., Inc. v. Ellerth*, 524 U.S. 742 (1998) and *Faragher v. City of Boca Raton*, 524 U.S. 775 (1998). A clear, well-drafted sexual harassment policy is a key aspect of that affirmative defense.

One final benefit to having an official employee handbook is that it helps ensure that the employer actually communicates policies to employees and that employees understand what is expected of them. It is not sufficient to have anti-harassment or anti-discrimination policies; employees must know those policies exist and how to report infractions to the employer. Employers often require new and existing employees to sign an acknowledgement of receipt and review of the employee handbook or any later revisions.

Of course, creating an employee handbook also has some risks. An out-of-date handbook that doesn't take into account changes in the law could be seen as evidence that the employer is not complying with current law. Employers must regularly review and update the handbook to ensure that policies comply with rapidly changing law in developing areas.

Second, although it should go without saying, once an employer has written policies in place, it must follow them. Failure to uniformly follow policies could be used by a plaintiff in civil litigation as evidence of disparate treatment.

Third, the handbook must be complete. Although employers are not required to have a handbook, some laws require a particular policy to be included in the employee handbook if an employer has one. And failure to include an anti-harassment policy forecloses an affirmative defense to harassment claims.

Finally, if not drafted appropriately, an employee handbook may be interpreted by the court as an employment contract. If a court finds that a handbook creates a contract, it will invalidate an employee's at-will employment status. Employers should take great care to include appropriate language to avoid this problem.

EXERCISE

Your client is an auto parts manufacturer in St. Paul, Minnesota. You are drafting an employee handbook for your client, and your client wants to make sure that the handbook does not alter the at-will status of its employees. Read the relevant parts of the following cases:

☐ *Feges v. Perkins Restaurants, Inc.*, 483 N.W.2d 701 (Minn. 1992)
☐ *Coursolle v. EMC Ins. Group, Inc.*, 794 N.W.2d 652 (Minn. Ct. App. 2011)

1) Draft an e-mail to the HR manager, Heidi Smith, explaining (1) what the test is for determining whether a provision in an employee handbook creates a contract; and (2) how to avoid such a determination.

2) Draft a suggested disclaimer to accompany the handbook.

The remainder of this section addresses various types of policies related to employment discrimination that could appear either as freestanding policies or as policies included in an employee handbook. The list of policies is not exclusive. For example, we have not included a discussion of progressive disciplinary policies, which are often used to show that an employer has treated all employees uniformly in the disciplinary process. However, we have included some of the most common policies employment discrimination lawyers may be asked to draft for employees. In drafting all exercises, make sure to incorporate what you learned in previous sections on plain English drafting and drafting to avoid ambiguity.

II. MANDATORY ARBITRATION AGREEMENTS

A. BASIC LEGAL PRINCIPLES

Mandatory arbitration is a form of alternative dispute resolution where the parties present arguments and evidence to an impartial third party who makes a decision that is binding on the parties.[54] Unlike mediation, mandatory arbitration is binding on the parties; unlike litigation, mandatory arbitration is generally informal and private. The exact process for arbitration depends on the forum and rules chosen by the parties. Although it is referred to as an "alternative" form of dispute resolution, use of mandatory arbitration and other alternative dispute resolution procedures is increasingly common.[55]

Mandatory arbitration agreements are governed by both federal and state law. First, the Federal Arbitration Act (FAA) governs arbitration agreements and preempts state arbitration laws for any agreement "involving commerce."[56] Pursuant to the FAA, where the parties have entered into an arbitration agreement, the court "shall . . . stay the trial of the action until such arbitration has been had in accordance with the terms of the agreement."[57] Moreover, where an arbitration agreement exists and one of the parties has refused to arbitrate, "the court shall make an order directing the parties to proceed to arbitration in accordance with

---

[54] Mary Dunnewold, *Alternative Dispute Resolution: What Every Law Student Should Know, Student Lawyer*, October 2009, Vol. 38, No. 2.

[55] As of 2000, one provider of alternative dispute resolution services estimated that "more than 500 employers and 5 million employees worldwide" used its arbitration programs. Am. Arbitration Ass'n, Proud Past, Bold Future: 75th Anniversary 2000 Annual Report, p. 30 available at www.adr.org/aaa/faces/s/about/annualreports.

[56] 9 U.S.C. § 2. Section 1's exemption for "contracts of employment of seamen, railroad employees, and any other class of workers engaged in foreign or interstate commerce" applies only to the employment contracts of "transportation workers." *Circuit City Stores v. Adams*, 32 U.S. 105 (2001).

[57] 9 U.S.C. § 3.

the terms of the agreement."[58] Second, because section 2 of the FAA provides that arbitration agreements are "valid, irrevocable and enforceable, save upon such grounds as exist under state law for the revocation of any contract," state contract law governs challenges to arbitration agreements.

■ **PRACTICE NOTE:** Attorneys are frequently asked to counsel clients on the implementation of mandatory arbitration agreements and to draft or revise mandatory arbitration agreements to be implemented by the employer. These issues often arise in the course of a review of employment policies prior to or following a merger or acquisition or during other routine reviews of employment policies and employment handbooks.

B. CONTEMPLATING KEY RULINGS AND PROVIDING CLIENT ADVICE

1. In *Alexander v. Gardner-Denver Co.*, the Supreme Court held that the completion of an arbitration hearing pursuant to an employer's collective bargaining agreement did not preclude an employee from pursuing a race discrimination claim in federal court under Title VII. 415 U.S. 36 (1974). The Court reasoned, "Title VII's purpose and procedures strongly suggest that an individual does not forfeit his private cause of action if he first pursues his grievance to final arbitration under the nondiscrimination clause of a collective-bargaining agreement." *Id.* at 49. In its subsequent decision in *Gilmer v. Interstate/Johnson Lane Corp.*, however, the Supreme Court held that a mandatory agreement to arbitrate a claim under the Age Discrimination in Employment Act (ADEA) was enforceable under the FAA, precluding the plaintiff from pursuing an ADEA claim in federal court. 500 U.S. 20 (1991); *see also EEOC v. Luce*, 345 F.3d 742 (9th Cir. 2003). Review the Supreme Court's reasoning in *Alexander* and *Gilmer* and determine how you would advise a client regarding the enforceability of a mandatory arbitration agreement that includes employment discrimination claims.

2. In *AT&T Mobility LLC v. Concepcion*, the Court held that class action arbitration waivers in consumer contracts are enforceable under the FAA. 131 S. Ct. 1740 (2011). Based on the reasoning in this case, how would you advise a client that has asked whether a mandatory agreement to arbitrate employment-related class-action claims is enforceable under the FAA? Further, what impact does this case have on the EEOC's role in pursuing employment-related class action claims on behalf of employees? What advice would you provide to the client regarding whether employment-related class-action claims should be included in a mandatory arbitration agreement?

---

[58] 9 U.S.C § 4.

3. One argument used by employees to challenge the enforceability of a mandatory arbitration agreement is a lack of consideration for an agreement. For example, in *EEOC v. Luce, Forward, Hamilton & Scripps*, the Ninth Circuit held that there is sufficient consideration for an agreement where pre-employment agreements to arbitrate are signed prior to employment, i.e. in exchange for employment.[59] Other cases addressing this issue include: *Tinder v. Pinkerton Sec.*, 305 F.3d 725, 734-35 (7th Cir. 2002), *Seawright v. Am. Gen. Fin. Servs.*, 507 F.3d 967, 972 (6th Cir. 2007), *Hardin v. First Cash Fin. Services, Inc.*, 465 F.3d 470, 478 (10th Cir. 2006), and *Floss v. Ryan's Family Steak Houses, Inc.*, 211 F.3d 306, 315 (6th Cir. 2000). Based on your review of these cases, explain to your client how to ensure that a court would find sufficient consideration for a mandatory arbitration agreement implemented during an employee's employment.

4. Another common basis for challenging a mandatory arbitration agreement is a lack of procedural or substantive fairness (unconscionability). Examine the D.C Circuit's reasoning in *Cole v. Burns International Security Services*, 105 F.3d 1465 (D.C. Cir. 1997), to determine what criteria courts frequently assess to determine whether an agreement is unconscionable. Based on these criteria (which vary by jurisdiction), how would you draft the following provisions in a mandatory arbitration agreement to ensure that the agreement is enforceable: (1) the procedure for selecting an arbitrator; (2) the cost to the employee of the arbitration; (3) the method for delivery of the arbitrator's decision; (4) whether and how the arbitrator's decision may be subject to judicial review; and (5) the types of recovery permitted?

5. Employers must provide sufficient notice to employees of mandatory arbitration agreements. Your client has informed you that it intends to introduce a mandatory arbitration agreement as part of its employee handbook or manual. After reviewing the reasoning in *Campbell v. General Dynamics Government Systems Corp.*, 407 F.3d 546, 555 (1st Cir. 2005) and *Gibson v. Neighborhood Health Clinics, Inc.*, 121 F.3d 1126, 1130 (7th Cir. 1997), summarize how you would advise the client about how to implement the agreement to provide sufficient notice to employees. Also, draft any provisions that should be included along with the arbitration agreement to show sufficient notice to the employee.

DRAFTING EXERCISES

1) Our client, Super Pet Stuff, has asked us to review various employment-related documents for accuracy, readability, and compliance with current California law. I want you to help me rework the mandatory arbitration agreement Super Pet Stuff makes its employees sign as a condition of employment. It was last revised in January of 2000.

---

[59] *See e.g. EEOC v. Luce, Forward, Hamilton & Scripps*, 345 F.3d 742, 754 (9th Cir. 2003).

The California Supreme Court has placed strict limitations on binding arbitration agreements. Such binding agreements to arbitrate disputes must meet certain criteria, or they will be deemed unconscionable (and thus unenforceable). The first key decision in this area came out of the California Supreme Court in 2000, and there are probably several other important cases on the issue decided since then.

Review California Supreme Court cases from 2000 to the present to determine the standards for enforcing a mandatory arbitration agreement in an employment contract or handbook. Then, please review and revise the current language of the Super Pet Stuff arbitration agreement (attached). In doing so, please do the following:

1) Draft terms as favorable to Super Pet Stuff as you can make them without violating current California law governing enforceability of binding arbitration agreements; and

2) Rephrase where necessary to make sure the agreement is written in plain English. Omit unnecessary redundancies.

DISPUTE RESOLUTION

Employee and Employer and its affiliated companies, businesses, subsidiaries, and entities agree that any and all controversies, claims, disagreements, or legal disputes or conflicts arising from, out of, or in any way relating to this Employment Agreement or to a breach or alleged breach or violation or alleged violation of this Employment Agreement, including, but not limited to, any and all disputes concerning the termination, ending, or cancellation of this Employment Agreement by Employer, shall be settled by final and binding arbitration in accordance with the Commercial Arbitration Rules of the American Arbitration Association (the "Association"). The judgment upon any award rendered by the arbitrator regarding said controversies, claims, disagreements, or legal disputes or conflicts mentioned herein may be entered in any court of competent jurisdiction unless otherwise provided herein. Employee and Employer further agree that, at Employer's sole and complete discretion, any and all claims by Employer arising out of Employee's breach or threatened breach or dissolution of this Employment Agreement may be submitted to judicial proceedings rather than arbitration and Employer shall have the right to seek injunctive relief as well as damages in a competent court of law.

Any demand for arbitration filed by the Employee must be filed with the American Arbitration Association in California and must be served on the Employer within forty-five (45) days of the alleged wrongful act. Any claim, controversy, dispute or legal disagreement arising from an alleged wrongful act about which Employee fails to demand arbitration shall be deemed waived if the Employee fails to bring such claim within the aforementioned forty-five (45) days of said dispute or wrongful act.

There shall be one arbitrator who shall be appointed by the employer in the following manner: the Employer shall furnish a list of ten (10) potential arbitrators. The Employee may remove up to three (3) names from the list. The Employer shall then choose the arbitrator from the remaining list of names. Each party shall pay the fees of that party's own attorney, and the expenses for that party's witnesses as well as all other expenses connected with the presentation of the party's case. All other costs of arbitration, including the costs of any record or transcript of the arbitration proceeding, all administrative fees, the fee of the arbitrator, and all other fees, costs, expenses, and/or expenditures shall in all respects and with no exceptions whatsoever be borne by the Employee. The arbitrator shall not extend, modify, change, alter, increase, diminish, or suspend any of the terms of this Employment Agreement or modify or change or disregard the reasonable standards of business performance established in good faith by Employer. The decision of the arbitrator within the scope of this submission (as provided by this Paragraph) shall be mandatory, final, and binding on all parties, and accordingly, the parties to this agreement agree and concur that any right to judicial action in this matter subject to arbitration hereunder is expressly waived (unless otherwise provided by applicable law or provisions in this Paragraph), except the right to judicial action to compel arbitration or to enforce the arbitration award or as provided in this Paragraph, or except in the event arbitration is unavailable to the parties for any reason. The parties agree that there shall be no judicial review of the arbitrator's decision. The parties may, however, petition the arbitrator to reconsider the decision within fifteen (15) days of the date the written arbitration judgment is issued. Any costs associated with a petition to reconsider shall be borne by the party seeking the motion to reconsider. If the rules of the Association differ from this Paragraph, the provisions of this Paragraph shall control.

In the event that Employee prevails in a claim, controversy, disagreement, or legal dispute submitted to arbitration, Employee shall be entitled to compensatory damages (to be set by the arbitrator) not exceeding those that would have been available had the claim, controversy, disagreement, or legal dispute been resolved in a competent court of law. Employee shall under no circumstances and in no situation be entitled to or receive punitive damages or attorney's fees. In the event that the arbitrator orders reinstatement of a terminated or fired Employee, the Employer may, in its sole discretion, choose to pay compensatory damages (set by the arbitrator) rather than to rehire said terminated or fired Employee. These compensatory damages shall not exceed those that would have been available had the claim, controversy, disagreement, or legal dispute been resolved in a competent court of law.

2) You now represent an individual, Hank Blum, who has been offered a position as a Human Resources Manager for Super Pet Stuff. Mr. Blum has been asked to sign the mandatory arbitration agreement above as a condition of employment, and he would like you to review the agreement and suggest changes. Revise the agreement above to include terms as favorable to Mr. Blum as you can make them without violating current California law governing enforceability of binding arbitration agreements.

III. SEXUAL HARASSMENT POLICIES

A. BASIC LEGAL PRINCIPLES

The language of Title VII does not specifically mention sexual harassment. The general prohibition in Title VII provides that "[i]t shall be an unlawful employment practice for an employer . . . to fail or refuse to hire or to discharge any individual, or otherwise to discriminate against any individual with respect to his compensation, terms, conditions, or privileges of employment, because of such individual's . . . sex."[60] Nevertheless, the United States Supreme Court has explicitly held that sexual harassment is prohibited by Title VII under the general prohibition on sex discrimination.[61] Importantly, the Supreme Court also recognized that an employee can establish sexual harassment has occurred even in the absence of specific "tangible" or "economic" harm.[62] Thus, in addition to what is traditionally referred to as quid pro quo sexual harassment,[63] the court in *Meritor* recognized that sexually harassing conduct that creates a "hostile" or "abusive" working environment also violates Title VII.[64]

B. CONTEMPLATING KEY RULINGS AND PROVIDING CLIENT ADVICE

1. In *Meritor*, the employer argued that the "sex-related conduct was 'voluntary,' in the sense that the complainant was not forced to participate against her will."[65] The court noted that this was not a defense to a sexual harassment claim. Rather, the court noted that "[t]he gravamen of any sexual harassment claim is that the alleged sexual advances were 'unwelcome.'"[66] Review the relevant discussion in *Meritor*. Come to class prepared to explain to a mock employer-client what the legal distinction is between "voluntary" and "unwelcome."

2. In *Meritor*, the court began to explain the distinction between standards of liability for hostile environment harassment and harassment that results in a tangible employment action of some sort. Explain that distinction, and list any questions you still have on that issue after *Meritor*.

3. The court in *Meritor* noted that hostile environment sexual harassment must be "severe and pervasive" to be actionable. What guidance does the court give regarding what that means? Would you feel comfortable giving a client advice based solely on the *Meritor* court's discussion of what "severe and pervasive" harassment is? If not, what questions

---

[60] 42 U.S.C. § 2000e-2 (2012).
[61] *Meritor Sav. Bank FSB v. Vinson*, 477 U.S. 57, 64-65 (1986) (recognizing that the EEOC regulations had prohibited sexual harassment since 1980).
[62] *Id.* at 64.
[63] Quid pro quo sexual harassment occurs when an employer either conditions tangible employment benefits on an employee's submission to unwelcome sexual conduct or takes a tangible employment action against an employee based on that employee's rejection of unwelcome sexual advances. 29 C.F.R. § 1604.11(a).
[64] *Id.* at 67-68.
[65] *Id.* at 68.
[66] *Id.*

do you have after *Meritor*? Read *Harris v. Forklift Systems, Inc.*, 510 U.S. 17 (1993). Does *Harris* answer some of the questions you identified regarding the scope of what constitutes "severe and pervasive" harassment?

4. In *Oncale v. Sundowner Offshore Services, Inc.*, 523 U.S. 75, 79 (1998), the Supreme Court clarified that Title VII does not prohibit a claim of sexual harassment "merely because the plaintiff and the defendant (or the person charged with acting on behalf of the defendant) are of the same sex." Importantly, the court recognized that "harassing conduct need not be motivated by sexual desire to support an inference of discrimination on the basis of sex." *Id.* at 80. Review the court's opinion in *Oncale*. In light of the discussion in *Oncale*, what advice might you give a client about the specific language one might use in a comprehensive sexual harassment policy?

5. In a set of Supreme Court opinions decided twelve years after *Meritor*, the court issued clearer guidance regarding the need for an appropriate sexual harassment policy. It did so by specifically explaining the affirmative defense available to employers in limited situations in hostile environment sexual harassment cases. *See Burlington Indus., Inc. v. Ellerth*, 524 U.S. 742 (1998) and *Faragher v. City of Boca Raton*, 524 U.S. 775 (1998). Review these cases and be prepared to discuss how they change the relevant legal landscape in the area of sexual harassment policies.

6. Various sources provide checklists for creating effective policies. For example, consider the following checklist for creating an effective sexual harassment policy, found in the *HR Series Fair Employment Practices*, 2 Fair Employment Practices § 16:8:

POLICY CONTENTS

- The company's policy clearly defines sexual harassment and gives examples of actions that are considered harassment.
- The company's policy prohibits a sexually charged atmosphere, including sexual joking, lewd pictures, or any actions that tend to make employees of one gender "sex objects."
- The company's policy states emphatically that sexual harassment will not be tolerated and that immediate discipline, up to and including discharge, will be imposed on any employee found guilty of sexual harassment.
- The company's policy includes a procedure for progressive discipline of employees found guilty of sexual harassment.
- The company's policy includes a clear and effective procedure for reporting sexual harassment and employees have been informed that reporting incidents of sexual harassment is their responsibility.
- The company's policy includes alternative avenues for reporting sexual harassment in the event an employee's supervisor is the harasser.

POLICY IMPLEMENTATION

- The company's sexual harassment policy is communicated to all employees.
- Routine training sessions on sexual harassment and company policy are held for supervisors, managers, and employees.
- Sexual harassment investigations are as confidential as possible.
- Sexual harassment complainants are protected from retaliation for filing complaints.
- Investigations of sexual harassment complaints are as prompt and thorough as possible and include interviews with both parties as well as anyone who might have information concerning the alleged harassment.
- Sexual harassment investigations are conducted by a disinterested, objective party, generally someone from the human resources department.
- The results of sexual harassment investigations are reported to the complainant and the alleged harasser. The only other individuals given results of sexual harassment investigations are those with a need to know.

CORRECTING SEXUAL HARASSMENT

- The company imposes progressive discipline, ranging from counseling to discharge, for acts of sexual harassment.[67]

These types of checklists are a good starting point, but you should still make sure they are based on current law. Look up any EEOC guidance on effective sexual harassment policies. Also, conduct research to determine whether the United States Supreme Court has issued any guidance regarding sexual harassment claims since its decisions in 1998. Be prepared to discuss whether you think the above checklist adequately covers the necessary issues and, if not, what you would change or add to the checklist.

■ **PRACTICE NOTE:** As the checklist above indicates, it is not enough for an employer to draft a policy that complies with the law. The employer must also follow that policy. Courts have found policies deficient as written, but courts have also found employers liable for failing to fully and correctly implement an otherwise lawful policy.[68]

---

7. The Supreme Court recently resolved a circuit split regarding who constitutes a supervisor for purposes of Title VII hostile work environment claims. *See Vance v. Ball State Univ.*, 133 S. Ct. 2434 (2013). Review the Supreme Court's decision, and be prepared to explain how the Court's

---

[67] Checklist quoted from HR Series Fair Employment Practices, 2 Fair Employment Practices § 16:8.
[68] *See, e.g., Corp. Counsel's Guide to Legal Aspects of Employee Handbooks & Policies* § 3:8 (last updated Sept. 2011)("Considerations in drafting harassment policies—What makes a policy ineffective?").

holding will affect employment discrimination claims from the perspective of both employee and employer.

DRAFTING EXERCISES

1) Read the Tenth Circuit's decision in *Wilson v. Tulsa Junior College*, 164 F.3d 534 (10th Cir. 1998), a case in which the court found the college's sexual harassment deficient for a number of reasons. In light of the court's opinion in *Wilson*, draft a sexual harassment policy for the college that you believe would remedy the deficiencies noted by the court.

2) Given the risk of being sued for sexual harassment, some companies have banned office relationships entirely. Others have experimented with something colloquially referred to as a "love contract." These contracts are written agreements between co-workers in which the dating co-workers acknowledge that they are engaged in a consensual relationship. Employment lawyers disagree regarding whether such contracts are helpful or even advisable. Read the opposing viewpoints expressed in The *Costco Connections* newsletter published in February 2009. [69] Assume your client, a large retail grocery chain called Big Box Store, Inc., saw this article and has asked you to provide advice regarding whether it should (1) ban office relationships; (2) require dating co-workers to sign a "love contract"; or (3) rely on the company's existing sexual harassment policy as sufficient to deal with office romances that go sour. Draft a letter to your client explaining your advice. Also draft a possible form "love contract" that your client's employees could sign if the client decides to go that route.

IV. NON-DISCRIMINATION POLICIES

A. BASIC LEGAL PRINCIPLES

Title VII prohibits discrimination in employment against an employee or applicant because of race, color, religion, sex (including pregnancy), or national origin.[70] In addition, the ADEA prohibits discrimination based on age,[71] while the ADA prohibits discrimination based on disability.[72] Each statute also prohibits

---

[69] http://www.ngelaw.com/files/Publication/d722d24a-63c7-457c-aae2-46803ae0679a/Presentation/Publication Attachment/6847ea88-13f1-4c2d-94fd-b7fd8806b490/Costco.Connections.Ritter.Feb.2009.pdf
[70] 42 U.S.C. § 2000e-2(1), (2); *see also* 42 U.S.C. § 1981 (prohibiting race discrimination in all aspects of contractual relationships).
[71] 29 U.S.C. § 623(a); *see also* Older Workers Benefit Protection Act of 1990, 29 U.S.C. § 626(f) (requiring "knowing and voluntary" waivers of age discrimination claims); 29 C.F.R. § 1625.22 (setting out rules governing waivers of age discrimination claims under section 626(f)).
[72] 42 U.S.C. § 12112(a).

retaliation against an employee or applicant who has opposed an unlawful employment practice.[73]

■ **PRACTICE NOTE:** Most states also prohibit discrimination on the basis of race, color, religion, sex, or national origin. Moreover, while federal law does not prohibit discrimination on the basis of sexual orientation, many state and local laws do.

Employees may claim discrimination based on disparate treatment or disparate impact. Disparate treatment occurs when an employer intentionally treats employees differently because of their protected status. For example, disparate treatment exists when an employer refuses to promote women to supervisory positions while promoting men to the same positions. In contrast, disparate impact does not require an unlawful motive, and occurs when a facially neutral policy or practice nonetheless adversely impacts employees in a protected class.[74] For example, in *Lewis v. City of Chicago*, African-American applicants for firefighter positions alleged that the written examination administered to applicants resulted in a disproportionate number of non-African-American applicants being selected for positions.[75] Finally, an employee may allege discrimination based on a failure to accommodate his or her disability or religion.[76]

■ **PRACTICE NOTE:** Public sector employees may base discrimination claims on the religious freedom clause of the First Amendment, the due process clause of the Fifth Amendment, or the privileges and immunities, due process, or equal protection clause of the Fourteenth Amendment.

B. CONTEMPLATING KEY RULINGS AND PROVIDING CLIENT ADVICE

1. A plaintiff may attempt to show disparate treatment using direct evidence, "meaning evidence that proves discrimination 'without the need for inference or presumption.'"[77] In most cases, however, the plaintiff

---

[73] 29 U.S.C. § 623(d); 42 U.S.C. § 12203; 42 U.S.C. § 2000e-3(a); *see also Univ. of Tex. Sw. Med. Ctr. v. Nassar*, 133 S. Ct. 2517 (2013) (holding that employees must establish "but for" causation for retaliation claims under Title VII); *CBOCS West, Inc. v. Humphries*, 128 S. Ct. 1951 (2008) (holding that section 1981 encompasses retaliation claims).
[74] *Int'l Bhd. of Teamsters v. United States*, 431 U.S. 324 (1977); *McDonald v. Santa Fe Trail Transp. Corp.*, 427 U.S. 273 (1976).
[75] *Lewis v. City of Chicago*, 130 S. Ct. 2191, 2195-96 (2010).
[76] 42 U.S.C. § 12112(b)(5); 42 U.S.C. § 200e(j); 29 C.F.R. § 1605.2.
[77] *Troupe v. May Dept. Stores Co.*, 20 F.3d 734, 736 (7th Cir. 1994).

does not have direct evidence of discrimination. Instead, the plaintiff may show disparate treatment by inference. In *McDonnell Douglas Corp. v. Green*, the Supreme Court set out the burden-shifting test used to establish disparate treatment using the indirect method. First, the plaintiff must establish a prima facie case of discrimination by showing that (1) he or she belongs to a protected class; (2) he or she was meeting the employer's legitimate expectations; (3) he or she suffered an adverse employment action; and (4) his or her employer treated similarly situated employees outside his or her classification more favorably.[78] This "creates a presumption that the employer unlawfully discriminated against the employee."[79] Some courts, such as the Tenth Circuit, have modified this test for cases involving reverse discrimination. Review the relevant reasoning in *Notari v. Denver Water Department*, 971 F.2d 585 (10th Cir. 1992), and be prepared to explain the prima facie test set out for cases of reverse discrimination, along with the court's justification for the variation. In addition, determine whether the viability of this test was affected by the Supreme Court's decision in *Oncale v. Sundowner Offshore Services, Inc.*, 523 U.S. 75 (1998).

2. Once the plaintiff has established a prima facie case of discrimination, the burden then "shift[s] to the employer to articulate some legitimate, nondiscriminatory reason for" its actions.[80] The Court clarified this requirement in *St. Mary's Honor Center v. Hicks*, 509 U.S. 502 (1993). Review *St. Mary's*, and come to class prepared to explain how an employer can meet this burden and the effect that meeting the burden has on the ultimate question of whether the employer discriminated against the employee.

3. Finally, the plaintiff must have the opportunity to show "that [the employer's] stated reason . . . was in fact pretext" for discrimination.[81] In *Texas Department of Community Affairs v. Burdine*, 450 U.S. 248 (1981), the Supreme Court held that "[t]his burden now merges with the ultimate burden of persuading the court that she has been the victim of intentional discrimination. She may succeed in this either directly by persuading the court that a discriminatory reason more likely motivated the employer or indirectly by showing that the employer's proffered explanation is unworthy of credence."[82] Following *Burdine*, some courts held that a plaintiff's prima facie case of discrimination combined with evidence of pretext is sufficient to show discrimination.[83] Others held that the plaintiff was required to show evidence of discriminatory

---

[78] *McDonnell Douglas Corp. v. Green*, 411 U.S. 792, 802 (1973).
[79] *Id.*
[80] *McDonnell Douglas*, 411 U.S. at 802.
[81] *Id.* at 804.
[82] *Texas Dept. of Cmty. Affairs*, 450 U.S. at 256.
[83] *See e.g. Kline v. TVA*, 128 F.3d 337 (6th Cir. 1997); *Combs v. Plantation Patterns*, 106 F.3d 1519 (11th Cir. 1997); *Sheridan v. E.I. DuPont de Nemours & Co.*, 100 F.3d 1061 (3d Cir. 1996); *Anderson v. Baxter Healthcare Corp.*, 13 F.3d 1120 (7th Cir. 1994); *Gaworski v. ITT Commercial Fin. Corp.*, 17 F.3d 1104 (8th Cir. 1994); *Wash. v. Garrett*, 10 F.3d 1421 (9th Cir. 1993).

intent in addition to pretext.[84] The Supreme Court addressed this dispute in *Reeves v. Sanderson Plumbing Products, Inc.*, 530 U.S. 133 (2000). Examine the Court's decision in *Reeves*, and be prepared to explain (1) how the Supreme Court resolved this question; and (2) what questions remain unresolved following this decision.

4. In *Price Waterhouse v. Hopkins*, 490 U.S. 228 (1989), the Supreme Court concluded that when an employer makes a decision for both non-discriminatory and discriminatory reasons (i.e. a "mixed motive"), the employer could "avoid a finding of liability . . . by proving that it would have made the same decision even if it had not allowed [the employee's protected status] to play a role."[85] The Court was divided over when the employer would be required to show that it would have made the same decision even absent the discriminatory reason: when the plaintiff showed that the protected status was a "motivating part" of the employment decision, a "substantial factor" in the employment decision, or when the plaintiff showed by direct evidence that the protected status was a substantial factor in the employment decision.[86] Congress responded to *Price Waterhouse* by amending Title VII to state that "an unlawful employment practice is established when the complaining party demonstrates that race, color, religion, sex, or national origin was a motivating factor for any employment practice, even though other factors also motivated the practice."[87] The Court subsequently reconsidered mixed motive cases in *Desert Palace, Inc. v. Costa*, 539 U.S. 90 (2003). Examine *Desert Palace* and prepare to explain how the Court's decision affected the burden of proof in mixed motive cases, particularly for employers defending against discrimination claims.

5. In *Ricci v. DeStefano*, 557 U.S. 557 (2009), the Supreme Court held that "before an employer can engage in intentional discrimination for the asserted purpose of avoiding or remedying an unintentional disparate impact, the employer must have a strong basis in evidence to believe it will be subject to disparate-impact liability if it fails to take the race-conscious, discriminatory action."[88] In light of this decision, what advice might you give an employer considering how to avoid liability for a policy or practice (such as administering a test to assess applicants' qualifications) that has a disparate impact?

6. Title VII makes it "an unlawful employment practice for an employer to discriminate against any of his employees . . . because he has opposed any practice made an unlawful employment practice by this subchapter, or because he has made a charge, testified, assisted, or participated in any manner in an investigation, proceeding, or hearing under this

---

[84] *See e.g. Aka v. Wash. Hosp. Ctr.*, 156 F.3d 1284 (D.C. Cir. 1998); *Fisher v. Vassar Coll.*, 114 F.3d 1332 (2d Cir. 1997); *Rhodes v. Guiberson Oil Tools*, 75 F.3d 989 (5th Cir. 1996); *Theard v. Glaxo, Inc.*, 47 F.3d 676 (4th Cir. 1995); *Woods v. Friction Materials, Inc.*, 30 F.3d 255 (1st Cir. 1994).
[85] *Price Waterhouse v. Hopkins*, 490 U.S. 228, 244 (1989).
[86] *Price Waterhouse*, 490 U.S. at 258-59, 276.
[87] 42 U.S.C. § 2000e–2(m).
[88] *Ricci v. DeStefano*, 557 U.S. 557, 585 (2009).

subchapter."[89] In *Crawford v. Metropolitan Government of Nashville & Davidson County*, 555 U.S. 271 (2009), the Supreme Court reasoned that "to oppose" means "to resist or antagonize . . . ; to contend against; to confront; resist; withstand." Using this definition, the Court held that Title VII's prohibition against retaliation extends to an employee who complains about harassment during an employer's internal investigation into allegations of sexual harassment by another employee.[90] What questions do you have about the scope of Title VII's anti-retaliation provision following *Crawford*? Review *Thompson v. North American Stainless, LP*, 131 S. Ct. 863 (2011). Does *Thompson* answer some of the questions you identified regarding the scope of the anti-retaliation provision?

7. To establish a retaliation claim under Title VII, the employee must show that "(1) he engaged in a statutorily protected activity; (2) he suffered a materially adverse action by his employer; and (3) a causal connection exists between the two."[91] In *Burlington Northern & Santa Fe Railway Co. v. White*, 548 U.S. 53 (2006), the Supreme Court held that to be materially adverse, an action need not affect the terms and conditions of employment; instead, an action is materially adverse when "it well might have 'dissuaded a reasonable worker from making or supporting a charge of discrimination.'"[92] Review the relevant discussion in *Burlington*, and come to class prepared to explain to an employer-client what the legal distinction is between "affecting the terms and conditions of employment" and "dissuading a reasonable worker from making or supporting a charge of discrimination."

8. Although Title VII does not define discrimination based on "national origin," the EEOC defines it "broadly as including, but not limited to, the denial of equal employment opportunity because of an individual's, or his or her ancestor's, place of origin; or because an individual has the physical, cultural or linguistic characteristics of a national origin group."[93] Based on this definition, decisions based on linguistic characteristics such as accents may be subject to claims of national origin discrimination. Compare the reasoning in *Carino v. University of Oklahoma Board of Regents*, 750 F.2d 815 (10th Cir. 1984), with *Fragante v. City & County of Honolulu*, 888 F.2d 591 (9th Cir. 1989), to determine when it is appropriate to make employment decisions based on accent. In light of these cases, what advice would you give a client about making employment decisions based on an applicant's or employee's accent?

9. The Fifth Circuit recently issued a decision on the issue of whether Title VII prohibits employers from discriminating against women because of breastfeeding. *EEOC v. Houston Funding II, Ltd.*, 717 F.3d 425 (5th

---

[89] 42 U.S.C. § 2000e–3(a).
[90] *Crawford v. Metropolitan Government of Nashville & Davidson County*, 555 U.S. 271, 276 (2009).
[91] *Stephens v. Erickson*, 569 F.3d 779, 786 (7th Cir. 2009). If an employee wishes to establish retaliation using the indirect method of proof, the first two elements remain the same, "but instead of proving a direct causal link, the plaintiff must show that he was performing his job satisfactorily and that he was treated less favorably than a similarly situated employee who did not complain of discrimination." *Id.* at 786-87.
[92] *Burlington N. & Santa Fe Ry. Co. v. White*, 548 U.S. 53, 64, 68 (2006).
[93] 29 C.F.R. § 1606.1.

Cir. 2013). The EEOC had argued that discrimination based on breast-feeding is (1) sex discrimination because lactation is a singularly female trait and (2) discrimination based on "pregnancy, childbirth, or related conditions." Review the EEOC's brief (available at 2012 WL 1971020) and Houston Funding's brief (available at 2012 WL 2330404). Also review the Fifth Circuit's opinion in the case and any cases from other jurisdictions addressing the same or analogous issues. (You will need to complete independent research to find these cases.) Once you have done so, complete the following exercises:

- In light of the Fifth Circuit's reasoning in *Houston Funding*; the briefs filed in that case; and any opinions from other jurisdictions on the issue, how would you advise a corporate client in a jurisdiction that has not yet addressed the issue? Provide reasoning based on various courts' treatment of both of the EEOC's arguments.

- In light of the Fifth Circuit's decision in *Houston Funding*, what advice would you give Houston Funding about the parameters of a policy on breastfeeding or pumping in the workplace? If your professor asks you to do so, draft that policy.

- What other avenues might the EEOC or other agencies have for establishing rights for lactating women in the workplace? Research possible avenues of relief under the statutory or constitutional schemes listed below. In a memo format to an attorney at the relevant government agenc(ies), outline the possible arguments in favor of rights for lactating women under these laws, and summarize the pros and cons of using those legal avenues for relief. In doing so, you may want to summarize any existing decisions on the issue under (1) the Pregnancy Discrimination Act (rather than Title VII generally); (2) the Family Medical Leave Act; and (3) the U.S. Constitution (right to privacy arguments).

10. Section 2000e(j) of Title VII requires employers to accommodate employees' sincerely held religious beliefs unless the accommodation would cause an undue hardship. Your client, an Illinois hospital, has requested advice regarding a nurse in the Labor and Delivery Unit's request that she be allowed to trade assignments with other nurses as needed so that she could avoid assisting with abortions. The nurse's faith prohibits her from "directly or indirectly [participating] in ending a life." The hospital is unable to fulfill this request because there are not enough staff members willing to trade with her. However, the hospital could allow the nurse to transfer to a vacant nursing position in a different unit. Based on your review of the relevant portion of *Porter v. City of Chicago*, 700 F.3d 944 (7th Cir. 2012), does this solution comply with Title VII? Why or why not? If the hospital offers to transfer the nurse and she refuses the offer, what other options are available to the hospital?

11. Employees subject to racial discrimination may opt to pursue claims under both Title VII and Section 1981. While Title VII and Section 1981 have some similarities, there are also significant differences. For example, while Title VII applies to employers of 15 or more employees, Section

1981 applies to employers of any size. Review the language of Title VII and Section 1981 and conduct research to determine the other key differences. Be prepared to explain these differences to an employee-client.

DRAFTING EXERCISES

1) To establish a prima facie case of disability discrimination, an employee must prove that he or she is "disabled" within the meaning of the ADA. An individual is "disabled" if he or she suffers from a "physical or mental impairment that substantially limits one or more of [the employee's] major life activities."[94] In *Sutton v. United Airlines*, 119 S. Ct. 2139 (1999), the Supreme Court held that "if a person is taking measures to correct for, or mitigate, a physical or mental impairment, the effects of those measures—both positive and negative—must be taken into account when judging whether that person is 'substantially limited' in a major life activity and thus 'disabled' under the Act."[95] In response to *Sutton* and other decisions which Congress viewed as impermissibly narrowing the broad scope of the ADA, Congress enacted the ADA Amendments Act of 2008.[96] As amended, the ADA now provides that "[t]he determination of whether an impairment substantially limits a major life activity shall be made without regard to the ameliorative effects of mitigating measures such as . . . medication, medical supplies, equipment, or appliances."[97] In light of this change, draft a new policy for an employer-client on accommodating its employees' disabilities.

2) The Older Workers Benefit Protection Act (OWBPA) states: "An individual may not waive any right or claim under [the ADEA] unless the waiver is knowing and voluntary. . . . [A] waiver may not be considered knowing and voluntary unless at a minimum" it satisfies the requirements enumerated in 29 U.S.C. § 626(f)(1). Review the requirements of Section 626(f)(1), along with the reasoning in *Oubre v. Entergy Operations, Inc.*, 522 U.S. 422 (1998) and *Burlison v. McDonald's Corp.*, 455 F.3d 1242 (11th Cir. 2006). Based on this review, draft language for a release that complies with the OWBPA's requirements.

3) An employee wishing to challenge an employment practice under Title VII must first file a charge with the EEOC within either 180 or 300 days "after the alleged unlawful employment practice occurred."[98] If the employee does not file a timely EEOC charge, the employee is barred from pursuing litigation based on that employment practice.[99] The Supreme Court, in *National Railroad Passenger Corporation v. Morgan*, 536 U.S. 101, 114 (2002), interpreted this rule as applying to any "discrete act" of discrimination. In

---

[94] 42 U.S.C. § 12102(2)(A).

[95] *Sutton v. United Air Lines, Inc.*, 527 U.S. 471, 482 (1999).

[96] ADA Amendments Act of 2008, PL 110-325, Sep. 25, 2008, 122 Stat 3553.

[97] 42 U.S.C. § 12102(4).

[98] 42 U.S.C. § 2000e-5(1).

[99] 42 U.S.C. § 2000e–5(f)(1).

Ledbetter v. Goodyear Tire & Rubber Co., Inc., 550 U.S. 618 (2007), the employee claimed that she was subjected to sex discrimination when supervisors gave her poor evaluations because of her sex; as a result, her pay throughout her employment was not increased as much as it would have been if she had been evaluated fairly. The Supreme Court, however, agreed with the employer that the employee's pay discrimination claim was time barred because no pay decisions were made during the 180 day period preceding the employee's EEOC charge. The Court reasoned that "[t]he EEOC charging period is triggered when a discrete unlawful practice takes place. A new violation does not occur, and a new charging period does not commence, upon the occurrence of subsequent nondiscriminatory acts that entail adverse effects resulting from the past discrimination. But of course, if an employer engages in a series of acts each of which is intentionally discriminatory, then a fresh violation takes place when each act is committed."[100] In response, Congress enacted, and President Obama signed, the Lilly Ledbetter Fair Pay Act of 2009, Pub. L. No. 111-2, 125 Stat. 5. Review *Ledbetter* and the subsequent Act. Based on your review, draft an email to an employer-client explaining the impact of the Act on Title VII pay discrimination claims.

V. LEAVE POLICIES

A. BASIC LEGAL PRINCIPLES

Various federal, state, and local laws impose leave requirements on employers. Most significantly, both the FMLA[101] and the ADA[102] require covered employers to grant medical and other leave to eligible employees. In addition, many employers are required to provide leave for other reasons such as jury duty, voting, and military service.

The FMLA entitles employees to twelve weeks of leave during a 12-month period for:

- the birth of a child and to care for the newborn child within one year of birth;
- the placement with the employee of a child for adoption or foster care to care for the newly placed child within one year of placement;
- the care of an employee's spouse, child, or parent who has a serious health condition
- a serious health condition that makes the employee unable to perform the essential functions of his or her job; or[103]
- a "qualifying exigency . . . arising out of the fact that the spouse, or a son, daughter, or parent of the employee is on covered active duty (or has been notified of an impending call or order to covered active duty) in the Armed Forces."

---

[100] *Ledbetter v. Goodyear Tire & Rubber Co., Inc.*, 550 U.S. 618, 621-22, 628 (2007).
[101] 29 U.S.C. § 2601 (2012).
[102] 29 U.S.C. § 12102 (2012).
[103] 29 U.S.C. § 2612(a)(1).

The FMLA also entitles employees to 26 weeks of military caregiver leave during a 12-month period to care for a servicemember with a serious injury or illness if the servicemember is the employee's spouse, parent, child, or next of kin.[104] In addition to providing the FMLA leave itself, the employer must maintain the employee's group health benefits[105] and restore the employee to the same or an equivalent position at the end of the leave.[106] Finally, the FMLA prohibits employers from "interfering with, restraining, or denying the exercise of, or the attempt to exercise, any FMLA right" and from "discriminating or retaliating against an employee or prospective employee for having exercised or attempted to exercise any FMLA right."[107]

■ **PRACTICE NOTE:** While many states have adopted leave statutes similar to the FMLA, you should be aware that state statutes may apply more broadly than the FMLA. For example, while the FMLA applies to employers with fifty or more employees, some state leave laws apply to smaller employers. Similarly, some state leave laws have expanded the definition of family to cover other family members, such as domestic partners and in-laws.

Under the ADA, an employer is required to make a reasonable accommodation to the known disability of a qualified applicant or employee if it would not impose an "undue hardship" on the operation of the employer's business.[108] This reasonable accommodation may include a medical leave.[109] Failure to provide a reasonable accommodation (such as a leave) in the absence of an undue hardship constitutes unlawful discrimination.[110]

In some instances, an employee may have a "serious health condition" under the FMLA that also qualifies as a "disability" under the ADA. However, not all serious health conditions qualify as disabilities. A "disability" is "a physical or mental impairment that substantially limits one or more major life activities of [an] individual,"[111] while a "serious health condition" means "an illness, injury, impairment, or physical or mental condition that involves [] inpatient care in a hospital, hospice, or residential medical care facility; or [] continuing treatment by a health care provider."[112] For example, while cancer or a stroke would qualify as serious health conditions and disabilities, pregnancy or a broken leg are serious health conditions but (usually) not disabilities.[113]

---

[104] 29 U.S.C. § 2612(a)(3).
[105] 29 U.S.C. § 2614(c).
[106] 29 U.S.C. § 2614(a).
[107] 29 U.S.C. § 2615(a).
[108] 29 U.S.C. § 12112(b)(5).
[109] 29 U.S.C. § 12111(9)(B). A reasonable accommodation may include "job restructuring, part-time or modified work schedules . . . and other similar accommodations for individuals with disabilities." *Id.*
[110] 29 U.S.C. § 12112(b)(5). See also the Rehabilitation Act, 29 U.S.C. § 791, which prohibits federal agencies, programs receiving federal assistance, and federal contractors from discriminating on the basis of disability.
[111] 29 U.S.C. § 12102(1).
[112] 29 U.S.C. § 2611(11); *see also* 29 C.F.R. § 825.113.
[113] http://www.eeoc.gov/policy/docs/fmlaada.html.

> ■ **PRACTICE NOTE:** The FMLA applies to employers with 50 or more
> employees, while the ADA applies to employers with 15 or more employees.
> As a result, only employers with 50 or more employees should be concerned
> about the overlap between the FMLA and ADA.

Finally, federal and state law require employers to provide leave for employees performing civic duties such as jury duty, voting, and military service. For example, under the Uniformed Services Employment and Reemployment Rights Act (USERRA),[114] employers must provide leave to servicemembers[115] and reemploy returning servicemembers in the same job (or closest approximation) that they would have attained had they not been absent for military service, "plus the additional seniority and rights and benefits that [the employee] would have attained if . . . continuously employed.[116]

B. CONTEMPLATING KEY RULINGS AND REGULATIONS AND PROVIDING CLIENT ADVICE

1. As noted above, a "serious health condition" is "an illness, injury, impairment, or physical or mental condition that involves [] inpatient care in a hospital, hospice, or residential medical care facility; or [] continuing treatment by a health care provider."[117] The regulations further define "inpatient care" as "an overnight stay in a hospital, hospice, or residential medical care facility . . . or any subsequent treatment in connection with such inpatient care."[118] In addition, section 825.115 of the regulations defines "continuing treatment." Based on these definitions, would the following constitute a serious health condition requiring continuing treatment? Identify the relevant sub-section of section 825.115 for each.
   a. High blood pressure, which was not diagnosed until after several absences from work for doctors' appointments within a 30-day period, but which required only daily medication and yearly doctor visits following diagnosis;
   b. Migraines that were initially diagnosed by a physician over the phone and which are treated by over-the-counter pain medication along with biannual physician visits;
   c. Upper respiratory tract infection, where the employee was out of work for two days, was diagnosed during a doctor's appointment on the second day and also received two prescriptions, and returned to work the day after the doctor's appointment;

---

[114] 38 U.S.C. § 4301 (2012).
[115] 38 U.S.C. § 4316(b)(1).
[116] 38 U.S.C. § 4316(a). Note that some states require such leave to be paid, while others do not. *Compare* Cal. Elec. Code § 14000 (requiring employers to allow employees up to two hours of paid voting leave); Cons. Laws of New York § 3-110 (same) *and* 10 ILCS § 5/7-42 (requiring employers to provide time off for voting); Wis. Stat. Ann § 6.76 (same).
[117] 29 U.S.C. § 2611(11); *see also* 29 C.F.R. § 825.113.
[118] 29 C.F.R. § 825.114.

    d. Herniated disc, treated by a chiropractor who recommended two days off of work and one week of light duty;

    e. Depression, where the employee visited a physician twice to complain about depression and other health issues;

    f. Systemic lupus, diagnosed prior to the start of employment and where symptoms flare followed by a period of remission.

2. To establish a prima facie case of retaliation under the FMLA, "a plaintiff must show that: (1) she availed herself of a protected right; (2) she suffered an adverse employment decision; and (3) there is a causal connection between the protected activity and the adverse employment decision."[119] Your client, a paper supply company, plans to terminate one of its sales managers, and has contacted you for advice regarding the legal risks based on the following facts:

   - The sales manager has been with the company for four years, and returned four weeks ago from an FMLA leave for the birth of his daughter.

   - The sales manager's supervisor raised concerns about the sales manager's performance approximately five weeks ago.

   - According to the supervisor, the sales manager began having performance problems approximately six months prior to taking FMLA leave, including failing to achieve sales quotas and to properly train his sales staff. Up until that time, he had not had any performance problems.

   - In the past five years, when other sales managers have had similar problems, some have been terminated immediately while another was placed on probation before ultimately being terminated. One manager who was terminated had been with the company for three years and had previously had performance problems, while the other had been with the company for six months, but had not previously had performance problems. Another manager was placed on six months of probation before being terminated; she had been with the company for six years and had performance problems during the first year of her employment.

   "To establish the causal connection element, 'a plaintiff need only show 'that the protected activity and the adverse action were not wholly unrelated,' . . . [meaning] that the decision maker was aware of the protected conduct at the time of the adverse employment action."[120] Based on these facts and the reasoning in *Brungart v. BellSouth Telecommunications, Inc.,* **231 F.3d 791, 799 (11th Cir. 2000), would a court likely find that the sales manager could establish a prima facie case of FMLA retaliation?**

3. To qualify as a disability, a physical or mental impairment must substantially limit a major life activity. According to the ADA regulations, [p]hysical or mental impairment means: (1) Any physiological disorder, or condition, cosmetic disfigurement, or anatomical loss affecting one or more of the following body systems: neurological, musculoskeletal,

---

[119] *Earl v. Mervyns, Inc.,* 207 F.3d 1361, 1367 (11th Cir. 2000).
[120] *Brungart v. BellSouth Telecomm., Inc.,* 231 F.3d 791, 799 (11th Cir. 2000) (internal citations omitted).

special sense organs, respiratory (including speech organs), cardiovascular, reproductive, digestive, genito–urinary, hemic and lymphatic, skin, and endocrine; or (2) Any mental or psychological disorder, such as mental retardation, organic brain syndrome, emotional or mental illness, and specific learning disabilities.[121] In addition,

> [m]ajor life activities include, but are not limited to: (i) Caring for oneself, performing manual tasks, seeing, hearing, eating, sleeping, walking, standing, sitting, reaching, lifting, bending, speaking, breathing, learning, reading, concentrating, thinking, communicating, interacting with others, and working; and (ii) The operation of a major bodily function, including functions of the immune system, special sense organs and skin; normal cell growth; and digestive, genitourinary, bowel, bladder, neurological, brain, respiratory, circulatory, cardiovascular, endocrine, hemic, lymphatic, musculoskeletal, and reproductive functions. The operation of a major bodily function includes the operation of an individual organ within a body system.[122]

In addition to these definitions, examine the definition of "substantially limits" in section 1630.2(j). Based on these definitions, would the following conditions qualify as disabilities, i.e. physical or mental impairments that substantially limit a major life activity?

   a. High blood pressure that causes fatigue, difficulty breathing, and occasional vision problems;

   b. Migraines that cause pounding pain, accompanied by loss of appetite and dizziness;

   c. Respiratory tract infection that causes wheezing and a dry cough for two days followed by a cough accompanied by yellow mucus and streaks of blood for several days;

   d. Herniated disc that causes intermittent numbness in one leg beginning behind the knee and extending to the foot;

   e. Depression that causes overeating, fatigue, and excessive sleeping;

   f. Systemic lupus that causes flaky red spots on the arms, hands, and face, joint pain, and mild fatigue.

4. An employee who intends to take FMLA leave must provide notice to his or her employer. If the leave is foreseeable, the employee must provide at least 30 days' notice. If the leave is not foreseeable, the employee must provide notice as soon as is practicable.[123] Accordingly, "[a] claim under the FMLA cannot succeed unless the plaintiff can show that he gave his employer adequate and timely notice of his need for leave, and an employer has the right to request supporting information from the employee."[124]

---

[121] 29 C.F.R. § 1630.2(h).
[122] 29 C.F.R. § 1630.2(i).
[123] 29 U.S.C. § 2612(e)(1).
[124] *Woods v. DaimlerChrysler Corp.*, 409 F.3d 984, 991 (8th Cir. 2005).

A client has contacted you for advice about terminating an employee. Despite exhausting her sick and vacation days, an employee called in sick four times last week. In an email to the employee's supervisor two weeks ago, the employee mentioned that her husband was suffering from chronic depression. The employee did not mention her husband or his illness when she called in sick. Read *Greenwell v. State Farm Mutual Automobile Insurance Co.*, 486 F.3d 840 (5th Cir. 2007), and determine whether the employee has provided sufficient notice of a need for FMLA leave.

DRAFTING EXERCISES

1) The FMLA permits employees to take "leave intermittently or on a reduced leave schedule." "Intermittent leave is FMLA leave taken in separate blocks of time due to a single qualifying reason. A reduced leave schedule is a leave schedule that reduces an employee's usual number of working hours per workweek, or hours per workday. A reduced leave schedule is a change in the employee's schedule for a period of time, normally from full-time to part-time."[125]

An employee has requested intermittent FMLA leave to permit her to receive chemotherapy as part of her treatment for a serious medical condition, leukemia. Her employer has an FMLA leave policy, but it does not include any provision governing intermittent leave. Review the regulations governing intermittent leave, 29 C.F.R. §§ 825.202-206, and draft a policy that will govern this situation and future requests for intermittent leave, including for when intermittent leave is requested following the birth or placement of a child.

2) An employee is currently on FMLA leave because of his own serious health condition, type 1 diabetes. The FMLA leave will expire prior to the conclusion of the employee's treatment; as a result, the employee has requested that your client accommodate the disability caused by his diabetes by providing additional leave. The employer would prefer not to extend the employee's leave but is willing to consider other options to reasonably accommodate the employee's disability.

Locate and review the relevant FMLA regulations, 29 C.F.R. § 825.100 *et seq.*, and ADA regulations, 29 C.F.R. § 1630.1 *et seq.* Using the regulations as a guide, draft a letter to the employer explaining the options that could be presented to the employee.

3. Your client has received a letter from an attorney representing a former employee. The letter states:

> My client was a dedicated marketing manager for Hanna's Coffee Company for ten years, ending with her resignation last month. . . .

---

[125] 29 C.F.R. § 825.202(a).

As you know, the treatment for Ms. Lin's breast cancer, a disability under the ADA, required extensive treatment, including chemotherapy and radiation. Ms. Lin requested that Hanna's accommodate her disability, including by: (a) permitting her to work flexible hours; (b) allowing her time off as needed; and (c) adjusting the review process to permit Ms. Lin to pursue her promotion following the completion of her treatment. When Ms. Lin spoke with her supervisor, Ms. Bradenton, Ms. Bradenton advised her that Hanna's was happy to honor these requests, and that her review would be delayed until next year. . . .

Instead, Ms. Bradenton embarked on a campaign of harassment of and cruelty toward Ms. Lin, forcing Ms. Lin to resign. Among other things, Ms. Bradenton publicly accused Ms. Lin of working fewer hours than were previously agreed and of flouting her breast cancer diagnosis to leave work and "skip" work. Ms. Bradenton repeated these false accusations multiple times in front of the upper management team and Ms. Lin's marketing team. On at least three occasions, these accusations were made in front of Ms. Lin. Each time, after attempting to defend herself, Ms. Lin had to leave work for the day because the stress associated with Ms. Bradenton's harassment campaign exacerbated the side effects of her breast cancer treatment. . . .

When Ms. Lin complained to Ms. Bradenton's superior, Mr. Howe, he told her that there must be a misunderstanding and that she needed to "get a thicker skin." Two weeks later and despite Hanna's promise to delay her review until next year, Ms. Lin was summoned for her review, where Ms. Bradenton informed Ms. Lin that she would not be receiving the promotion that she had been working toward. . . .

These actions made it impossible for Ms. Lin to continue working for Hanna's. Ms. Bradenton's harassment made Ms. Lin miserable on a daily basis. Moreover, the denial of Ms. Lin's long-awaited promotion led her to conclude that she had no future at Hanna's.

The letter concludes with the allegation that Ms. Lin was constructively discharged in violation of the ADA, and indicates that the employee plans to file an EEOC charge followed by a lawsuit unless your client is willing to offer a satisfactory settlement.

Another associate is examining whether Hanna's could be found to have failed to reasonably accommodate Ms. Lin's disability, which would support a constructive discharge claim. You have been asked to research whether Hanna's created a hostile work environment, which could also be used to support a constructive discharge claim. Your research indicates that, in the Seventh Circuit (where your client is located), a plaintiff can establish constructive discharge by showing "that the employer made the working conditions so intolerable as to force a reasonable person to [resign]."[126] Moreover, there must be proof of aggravating factors constituting a severe pattern of discriminatory intent.[127] You have located two favorable cases: *Miranda v. Wisconsin Power & Light Co.,* 91 F.3d 1011 (7th Cir. 1996) and *Pellack v. Thorek Hospital & Medical Center,* 9 F. Supp. 2d 984 (N.D. Ill. 1998). Using the reasoning from these cases, outline an argument (in favor of your client) that the third element of a prima facie case of disability discrimination is not met. In addition, evaluate the strength of this argument and whether the client should consider offering a settlement to avoid litigation.

VI. GROOMING POLICIES AND DRESS CODES

A. BASIC LEGAL PRINCIPLES

Employers typically implement dress codes and grooming policies to ensure that employees maintain a professional appearance while at work and while conducting business on their employers' behalf. While employers have a right to establish such policies, this right is limited by federal, state, and local anti-discrimination laws. Accordingly, policies may not discriminate on the basis of immutable characteristics (such as race or gender), disabilities,[128] or religious beliefs.[129]

B. CONTEMPLATING KEY RULINGS AND PROVIDING CLIENT ADVICE

1. An employee may challenge a policy under Title VII when the policy is stated neutrally but nevertheless has a disproportionate impact on a protected class, i.e. a disparate impact.[130] For example, policies requiring male employees to be clean-shaven have been challenged as having an impermissible disparate impact on black men who suffer from a skin condition that is treatable only by refraining from shaving.[131] This skin condition is relatively uncommon among white men but affects a significant number of black men.[132] In *Bradley v. Pizzaco of Nebraska, Inc.,* 7 F.3d 795 (8th Cir. 1993), the Eighth Circuit found an employer's no-beard policy discriminatory because it had a disparate impact on black men. Moreover, a customer preference for clean-shaven deliverymen did not constitute a sufficient business justification.[133]

   Your client, a national restaurant chain, wishes to implement a no facial hair policy for its cooks and servers; its stated business justification

---

[126] *E.E.O.C. v. Sears, Roebuck & Co.,* 233 F.3d 432, 440 (7th Cir. 2000); *see also Miranda v. Wisconsin Power & Light Company,* 91 F.3d 1011, 1016–17 (7th Cir. 1996).

[127] *E.E.O.C. v. Sears, Roebuck & Co.,* 233 F.3d 432, 440-41 (7th Cir. 2000).

[128] *See e.g. Sawinski v. Bill Currie Ford, Inc.,* 881 F. Supp. 1571 (M.D. Fla. 1995).

[129] Though not within the scope of this section, note that dress codes and grooming policies may also be challenged on constitutional grounds. *See e.g. Goldman v. Weinberger,* 475 U.S. 503 (1986) (finding that air force regulation prohibiting wearing of yarmulke while on duty was not prohibited by the First Amendment).

[130] Griggs v. Duke Power Co., 401 U.S. 424 (1971).

[131] *See e.g. Bradley v. Pizzaco of Nebraska, Inc.,* 7 F.3d 795 (8th Cir. 1993).

[132] *Bradley,* 7 F.3d at 796.

[133] *Bradley,* 7 F.3d at 798-99.

is that this policy would ensure sanitary conditions in the restaurant. Based on the reasoning in *Bradley* and in *Fitzpatrick v. City of Atlanta*, 2 F.3d 1112 (11th Cir. 1993), if this policy were challenged because of a disparate impact on black men with a skin condition, would this be a sufficient business justification for the policy?

2. Despite Title VII's prohibition on treating an employee differently on the basis of gender,[134] not all grooming policies that differentiate on the basis of gender are impermissible. Policies with distinctions on the basis of gender are impermissible when the policy differentiates on the basis of immutable characteristics or a fundamental right. In *Willingham v. Macon Telegraph Publishing Co.*, 507 F.2d 1084 (5th Cir. 1975), the employer's grooming policy did not allow men to have long hair but did allow women to do so.[135] The Fifth Circuit Court of Appeals upheld the district court's grant of summary judgment for the employer, reasoning that "a hiring policy that distinguishes on [a] ground [other than an immutable characteristic or fundamental right], such as grooming codes or length of hair, is related more closely to the employer's choice of how to run his business than to equality of employment opportunity."[136]

Based on this reasoning and the reasoning in *Carroll v. Talman Federal Saving & Loan Association of Chicago*, 604 F.2d 1028 (7th Cir. 1979), how would you advise your client, a national restaurant chain, that wishes to implement a policy: (a) requiring male servers only to wear suits; (b) prohibiting female servers from wearing skirts; (c) requiring female servers to wear makeup; (d) prohibiting male servers from wearing jewelry other than watches; or (e) prohibiting female servers from wearing heels?

3. When an employer's dress code or grooming policy conflicts with an employee's religious beliefs or practices, the employee may ask for an exception to the policy as a reasonable accommodation. An employer's failure to provide a reasonable accommodation constitutes religious discrimination unless the accommodation would be an undue hardship to the employer.[137] An accommodation constitutes an undue hardship if it would impose more than a *de minimis* cost.[138] One court found undue hardship where an employee requested a modification to a dress code and grooming policy to allow her to wear facial piercings. The court found that the requested accommodation would adversely affect the "neat, clean and professional image" that the employer aimed to cultivate.[139] In contrast, another court denied summary judgment for an employer that claimed that modifying its dress code and grooming policy to allow visible religious tattoos would be inconsistent with its goal of having a family-oriented and kid-friendly image.[140]

---

[134] *McDonnell Douglas Corp. v. Green*, 411 U.S. 792 (1973).
[135] *Willingham v. Macon Tel. Pub. Co.*, 507 F.2d 1084, 1087 (5th Cir. 1975).
[136] *Willingham*, 507 F.2d at 1091.
[137] EEOC Compliance Manual, 12-IV(C)(4)(a), "Dress and Grooming Standards" (available at www.eeoc.gov/laws/guidance/compliance.cfm).
[138] *Trans World Airlines, Inc. v. Hardison*, 432 U.S. 63, 84 (1977).
[139] *Cloutier v. Costco Wholesale Corp.*, 390 F.3d 126 (1st Cir. 2004).
[140] *EEOC v. Red Robin Gourmet Burgers, Inc.*, 2005 WL 2090677 (W.D. Wash. Aug. 29, 2005).

Your client is a public university. A faculty assistant has requested an accommodation to the dress code policy prohibiting jewelry to allow her to wear a necklace with a large cross. Your client is concerned that this would cause the university to appear to endorse her religious views. Based on the reasoning in the preceding cases, would allowing her to wear the necklace constitute an undue hardship to the university? Would it be an undue hardship to accommodate the faculty assistant if she had visible religious tattoos?

EXERCISES

1) Your client, an apartment-finding company, currently has the following grooming policy:

GROOMING POLICY

The company wishes to ensure that its employees convey a professional and businesslike image. This image is important to the company's success because it contributes to the company's reputation as a leader in the field. It is essential for the company's customers to view it as reliable, thorough, and expert. Because appearance is a major element of the company's image, employees are required to abide by the following grooming rules:

a) Employees must maintain good personal hygiene.

b) Hair must be neat and clean. Extreme styles (such as mohawks and dreadlocks) and unnatural colors are prohibited.

c) Facial hair is prohibited.

d) Tattoos must not be visible.

e) Visible piercings (other than a maximum of two earrings per ear) are prohibited.

f) Jewelry should be worn only in moderation.

g) Cosmetics should be applied in moderation and should appear natural.

Employees who fail to comply with this policy will be sent home and may be subject to further discipline as determined by the company.

One of the client's employees has objected to the policy, arguing that his Christian religious beliefs require his religious tattoos and jewelry to be visible. In response, your client has decided that it would like to change the policy. Revise the grooming policy so that it maintains the company's professional image while also accommodating this employee's concerns. In addition, make any other modifications to the policy that you think would help the company avoid future claims of discrimination.

2) Your client, a department store, has an employee who has recently begun sex reassignment therapy as part of the process of transitioning from male

to female. The employee has also begun to wear feminine clothing to work. Because the store's dress code policy includes gender-specific guidelines, the store is unsure about whether and how to enforce the dress code. The client has asked you to provide advice regarding whether enforcing the policy to require the employee to wear masculine clothing would constitute a violation of Title VII. Read the Seventh Circuit's decision in *Ulane v. Eastern Airlines, Inc.*, 742 F.2d 1081(7th Cir. 1984) and the District Court for the District of Columbia's decision in *Schroer v. Billington*, 424 F. Supp. 2d 203, 213 (D.D.C. 2006), and draft an email to the client explaining your advice. Also, assuming that the client decides to modify its dress code policy, draft a gender-neutral dress code for retail associates that would help the client maintain its professional image.

VII. GOVERNMENT CONTRACTOR AFFIRMATIVE ACTION PLANS

A. BASIC LEGAL PRINCIPLES

An affirmative action plan is an effort by an employer to increase employment opportunities for groups that have historically faced obstacles to equal employment opportunity in the workplace. Employers may be required to adopt affirmative action plans or may adopt them voluntarily. First, an employer may be required to adopt an affirmative action plan if it is a federal contractor or subcontractor or if it is required to do so by a court order. Executive Order 11246,[141] Section 503 of the Rehabilitation Act,[142] and Section 402 of the Vietnam Era Veterans' Readjustment Assistance Act of 1972[143] (VEVRAA) require government contractors and subcontractors to take affirmative action to ensure that applicants are employed "without regard to their race, creed, color, sex, [] national origin,"[144] disability,[145] or Vietnam veteran or disabled veteran status.[146] These requirements are enforced by the DOL's Office of Federal Contract Compliance Programs (OFCCP).[147] (Many state and local laws impose similar requirements for state and local government contractors.) Second, Title VII gives courts discretion "to order such affirmative action as may be appropriate."[148] Accordingly, an employer may be required to adopt an affirmative action plan pursuant to a court order where egregious or persistent discrimination exists.[149] Finally, an employer may voluntarily adopt an affirmative action plan;[150] a voluntarily adopted plan is valid "if the policy is remedial and narrowly tailored to meet the

---

[141] Executive Order 11246 (1965), as amended by Executive Order 11375 (1967), Executive Order 11478 (1969), Executive Order 12086 (1978), Executive Order 12107 (1978), Executive Order 13279 (2002).
[142] 29 U.S.C. § 793.
[143] 38 U.S.C. § 4211.
[144] Executive Order 11246 § 202(1).
[145] 29 U.S.C. § 793.
[146] 38 U.S.C. § 4211.
[147] Executive Order 11246 § 201; 41 C.F.R. §§ 60-1 et seq.; see http://www.dol.gov/ofccp/aboutof.html.
[148] 42 U.S.C. § 2000e-5(g).
[149] *Local 28, Sheet Metal Workers' Int'l Ass'n v. EEOC*, 478 U.S. 421, 482 (1986).
[150] *Johnson v. Transp. Agency*, 480 U.S. 616, 627-33 (1987).

goal of remedying the effects of past discrimination."[151] This section focuses on the most common affirmative action plans: those required of federal contractors and subcontractors.

B. CONTEMPLATING KEY REGULATIONS AND PROVIDING CLIENT ADVICE

Your firm's client, Securiguards, is a security services company that is preparing to enter into a contract with the federal government to supply security guards to provide extra security for federal buildings during the 2016 Olympics in Chicago, Illinois. Securiguards is headquartered in Chicago (75 employees) and also does business in Buffalo, New York (25 employees) and Detroit, Michigan (40 employees). Under the proposed contract, Securiguards will receive $40,000 in installments prior to the Olympics and an additional $40,000 after the completion of the Olympics.

You believe that Securiguards must implement an affirmative action plan because it qualifies as a government contractor pursuant to Executive Order 11246 and 41 C.F.R. § 60-2.1, which sets out when non-construction contractors must establish affirmative action plans for women and minorities.[152] Your supervising attorney has asked you to help determine how to advise Securiguards regarding how to implement the affirmative action plan.

1. Review section 60-2.1 and determine (a) whether Securiguards must adopt a written or unwritten affirmative action plan; (b) how many plans Securiguards must develop; and (c) when Securiguards must adopt its plan(s).
2. Each affirmative action program pursuant to Executive Order 11246 must include quantitative analyses to determine whether women and minorities are "being employed at a rate to be expected given their availability in the relevant labor pool," along with the specific practical steps designed to address [] underutilization."[153] Analyze 41 C.F.R. §§ 60-2.10 – 2.16 to determine the types of quantitative analyses that must be included in the plan, along with the components for each type of quantitative analysis. In addition, review 41 C.F.R. §§ 60-2.10 and 60-2.17 to determine what non-quantitative components are required in an affirmative action plan.

You believe that Securiguards may also qualify as a government contractor pursuant to VEVRAA and/or the Rehabilitation Act; if so, Securiguards must

---

[151] *Humphries v. Pulaski Cnty. Special Sch. Dist.*, 580 F.3d 688, 695 (8th Cir. 2009). "A policy may be considered remedial if the employer has identified a 'manifest imbalance' in the work force. A policy may be shown to be remedial through evidence that it was implemented 'in adherence to a court order, whether entered by consent or after litigation. But a policy may not 'unnecessarily trammel' the rights of non-minorities, and it must be 'intended to attain a balance, not to maintain one.'" *Id.* at 695-96 (internal citations omitted).
[152] Note the separate sections of the regulations applicable to construction contractors, found at 41 C.F.R. §§ 60-4.1 *et seq.*
[153] 41 C.F.R. § 60–2.10(a)(1).

implement anaffirmative action plan(s) covering veterans, disabled veterans, and individuals with disabilities.

1. Review 41 C.F.R. §§ 60-250.40 and 60-300.40 and determine (a) whether Securiguards must adopt a plan under VEVRAA. If so, determine (b) whether the affirmative action plan pursuant to VEVRAA must be separate from any other affirmative action plan(s); and (c) when Securiguards must adopt the plan(s) pursuant to VEVRAA.

2. Identify the requirements for an affirmative action plan pursuant to VEVRAA (set out in 41 C.F.R. §§ 60-250.44 and 60-300.44) and compare them to the requirements for an affirmative action plan pursuant to Executive Order 11246.

3. Review 41 C.F.R. § 60-741.40 and determine (a) whether Securiguards must adopt a plan under the Rehabilitation Act. If so, determine (b) whether the affirmative action plan pursuant to the Rehabilitation Act must be separate from any other affirmative action plan(s); and (c) when Securiguards must adopt the plan(s) pursuant to the Rehabilitation Act.

4. Identify the requirements for an affirmative action plan pursuant to the Rehabilitation Act (set out in 41 C.F.R. § 60-741.44) and compare them to the requirements for an affirmative action plan pursuant to Executive Order 11246.

■ **PRACTICE NOTE:** Multiple secondary sources include model affirmative action plans that comply with Executive Order 11246, the Rehabilitation Act, and VEVRAA. While forms provide a useful starting point for drafting an affirmative action plan, they should be used only after ensuring that they are consistent with current law.

EXERCISES

1) Draft an email to Securiguards' human resources manager explaining why it must implement the affirmative action plan(s), along with a general explanation of what the affirmative action plan(s) must include.

2) Draft an email to Securiguards' human resources manager with a bulleted list that identifies the information necessary for you to draft the quantitative analysis portion of the affirmative action plan pursuant to Executive Order 11246.

INDEX